The Group of Twen

This work offers a concise examination of the purpose, function and practice of the Group of Twenty (G20) summit. Providing a comprehensive historical account of the G20 finance ministers and central bank governors process, the text then moves on to outline the conditions, events and debates that led to the formation of the permanent, expanded leaders-level forum. The historical span of the G20 Summit process is not long, but the global transformations that precipitated it are crucial when seeking to understand it.

Cooper and Thakur explore a variety of major debates, including:

- Governance by self-selected groups versus mandated multilateral organizations;
- The legitimacy of informal leadership;
- The issue of the G20's composition of both "solution" countries and "problem" countries;
- The role of the emerging powers; and
- New conceptions of North–South relationships.

This work offers a detailed examination of the ongoing shifts in economic power and the momentum toward global institutional reform, illustrating how the G20 has moved from a crisis committee to the premier global forum over this short but intense history, and mapping out its comparative advantages and key challenges ahead.

Andrew F. Cooper is Professor, Department of Political Science, and Director of the Centre for Studies on Rapid Global Change, University of Waterloo. Holding a DPhil from the University of Oxford, he was a Fulbright Research Chair in Public Diplomacy at the University of Southern California in 2009.

Ramesh Thakur is Professor of International Relations and Director of the Centre for Nuclear Non-proliferation and Disarmament at the Australian National University, and adjunct professor in the Institute of Ethics, Governance and Law at Griffith University.

Routledge Global Institutions Series
Edited by Thomas G. Weiss
The CUNY Graduate Center, New York, USA
and Rorden Wilkinson
University of Manchester, UK

About the series

The Global Institutions Series has two "streams." Those with blue covers offer comprehensive, accessible, and informative guides to the history, structure, and activities of key international organizations, and introductions to topics of key importance in contemporary global governance. Recognized experts use a similar structure to address the general purpose and rationale for specific organizations along with historical developments, membership, structure, decision-making procedures, key functions, and an annotated bibliography and guide to electronic sources. Those with red covers consist of research monographs and edited collections that advance knowledge about one aspect of global governance; they reflect a wide variety of intellectual orientations, theoretical persuasions, and methodological approaches. Together the two streams provide a coherent and complementary portrait of the problems, prospects, and possibilities confronting global institutions today.
The most recent related titles in the series include:

The Organisation for Economic Co-operation and Development (2009)
by Richard Woodward

Institutions of the Global South (2009)
by Jacqueline Anne Braveboy-Wagner

The European Union (2008)
by Clive Archer

The World Economic Forum (2007)
by Geoffrey Allen Pigman

The Group of 7/8 (2007)
by Hugo Dobson

The Group of Twenty (G20)

Andrew F. Cooper and Ramesh Thakur

Routledge
Taylor & Francis Group

LONDON AND NEW YORK

First published 2013
by Routledge
2 Park Square, Milton Park, Abingdon, Oxon OX14 4RN

Simultaneously published in the USA and Canada
by Routledge
711 Third Avenue, New York, NY 10017

Routledge is an imprint of the Taylor & Francis Group, an informa business

British Library Cataloguing in Publication Data
A catalogue record for this book is available from the British Library

Library of Congress Cataloging in Publication Data
Cooper, Andrew Fenton, 1950–
    The Group of Twenty (G20) / Andrew F. Cooper & Ramesh Thakur.
        p. cm. – (Routledge global institutions series; 73)
    Includes bibliographical references and index.
    1. Group of Twenty. 2. International economic relations. I. Thakur,
Ramesh Chandra, 1948- II. Title.
    HF1359.C693 2013
    337.1–dc23
                    2012028788

ISBN: 978-0-415-78088-9 (hbk)
ISBN: 978-0-415-78089-6 (pbk)
ISBN: 978-0-203-07123-6 (ebk)

Typeset in Times New Roman
by Taylor & Francis Books

MIX
Paper from
responsible sources
FSC
www.fsc.org FSC° C004839

Printed and bound in Great Britain by
TJ International Ltd, Padstow, Cornwall

Contents

Tables

Foreword

The Right Honourable Paul Martin
Former Prime Minister of Canada

This is a very good book; and so it should be, for its authors were both witnesses and participants in the evolution of the G20 from the beginning. That they have produced such an accessible overview despite their wealth of knowledge which so often renders unreadable efforts of this kind makes it even more important. What adds to its quality is that Cooper and Thakur do not hesitate to express their opinions, and while not all of the latter should go unchallenged those who would do so had better be well prepared.

The authors have collaborated on several inter-related projects dealing with the changes to multilateral global governance and the role of ideas in shaping the diplomatic landscape. Their joint efforts span the years from Thakur's leadership position at the United Nations University to Cooper's numerous writings; from being colleagues at the University of Waterloo to Thakur's new position at the Australian National University. As this book shows, they bring a formidable combination of complementary skills to telling the story of potentially one of the most critical innovations in the machinery of global governance.

Bringing a new institution into being is not easy—certainly not one seeking to represent not just the global powers but the regional economic powers as well. This was indeed true of the grouping of finance ministers and central bank governors that became known as the G20 finance ministers despite the fact that there were only 19 countries involved.

The first attempt was made during the Mexican Peso Crisis in the mid-1990s. However, it was only during the Asian debacle later in the decade when the countries at the root of the crisis made it clear to the G7 that they were not interested in the advice of a body so unrepresentative of their reality that the breakthrough occurred.

When years later, as prime minister I approached my counterparts to lay the groundwork for a Leaders' 20, I used the same logic and indeed

I continued to do so after leaving office. My argument was strengthened even more by the ever deepening integration of globalization and the consequent threat of contagion in all of its aspects. The need for a more effective crisis responder and a more prescient steering committee was evident, and I would point out that there was no need to reinvent the wheel—all they had to do was follow the precedent established by their own countries a decade earlier.

Eventually this argument prevailed. Unfortunately, as was the case with the finance ministers, it took a financial crisis to provide the impetus. Cooper and Thakur describe this well and I will not take up your time by commenting further.

What I will do here, however, is raise two points among the many that will determine whether the Leaders' G20 lives up to the hopes so many of us have for it. The first point responds in part to the issue the authors raise concerning the relationship between the G20 and the world's great multilateral institutions. Or to put it more to the point: is there an issue of rivalry here? The answer is No!

Not only would that be the one thing that would affect the G20's legitimacy, but it goes against its very *raison d'être*. I say this because the G20's overriding priority must be the strengthening of the institutions created to make globalization work. This is true whether one is addressing the United Nations and climate change, the Multilateral Development Banks and development aid, or the International Monetary Fund and global economic stability. It is also true when the G20 seeks to create new specialized institutions to deal with specialized global needs, such as the Financial Stability Board.

The second point I would make speaks to an essential element underlying the G20 finance ministers' initial success in getting the G20 off the ground. In large part this was due to the emphasis on informality that paved the way for unscripted discussions allowing contentious issues to be dealt with head on.

I raise this because as the "G20 leaders" evolves, it is becoming increasingly clear that the omnipresent pressures for "photo ops" and massive national delegations are threatening the greater benefits of informality so necessary for a productive exchange of views.

I am not naïve in raising this. Leaders summits are not finance ministers summits—the need to feed the demand for instant response to whatever happens to be the flavor of the week and the tendency of some countries to judge their global status by the size of their delegations will not change.

The fact is the work that is done between summits has proven to be immensely productive. Indeed, the progress made between summits alone justifies the meetings at the top because the latter provides the catalyst for the former. Yet those few sessions when the leaders are alone by themselves, these are the meetings when the global interest is best given its due and whatever can be done to give the leaders space in this instance should be done.

In summary, Cooper and Thakur provide an impressive study of the context, the motivation, the choices, the main players, and the outcomes, and gaps vis-à-vis the G20. Their book is in overall terms a positive assessment concerning the centrality of the G20, although mindful of its incomplete status. The book demonstrates that ideas are important, as is diplomatic skill, as is the speed and scale of response. The lasting effect of the G20 will continue to be the subject of debates in both scholarly and first-hand accounts. The G20 was a project the time for which came amid the urgency first of the Asian crisis and then the global financial crisis of 2008. That being said, I share the view reinforced by the authors that those concerns must now be extended to the range of issues which provide globalization with its chapter headings.

Foreword by the series editors

The current volume is the seventy-third title in a dynamic series on global institutions. These books provide readers with definitive guides to the most visible aspects of what many of us know as "global governance." Remarkable as it may seem, there exist relatively few books that offer in-depth treatments of prominent global bodies, processes, and associated issues, much less an entire series of concise and complementary volumes. Those that do exist are either out of date, inaccessible to the non-specialist reader, or seek to develop a specialized understanding of particular aspects of an institution or process rather than offer an overall account of its functioning and situate it within the increasingly dense global institutional network. Similarly, existing books have often been written in highly technical language or have been crafted "in-house" and are notoriously self-serving and narrow.

The advent of electronic media has undoubtedly helped research and teaching by making data and primary documents of international organizations more widely available, but it has complicated matters as well. The growing reliance on the Internet and other electronic methods of finding information about key international organizations and processes has served, ironically, to limit the educational and analytical materials to which most readers have ready access—namely, books. Public relations documents, raw data, and loosely refereed websites do not make for intelligent analysis. Official publications compete with a vast amount of electronically available information, much of which is suspect because of its ideological or self-promoting slant. Paradoxically, a growing range of purportedly independent websites offering analyses of the activities of particular organizations has emerged, but one inadvertent consequence has been to frustrate access to basic, authoritative, readable, critical, and well-researched texts. The market for such has actually been reduced by the ready availability of varying quality electronic materials.

For those of us who teach, research, and operate in the area, such restricted access to information and analyses has been frustrating. We were delighted when Routledge saw the value of a series that bucks this trend and provides key reference points to the most significant global institutions and issues. They are betting that serious students and professionals will want serious analyses. We have assembled a first-rate team of authors to address that market. Our intention is to provide one-stop shopping for all readers—students (both undergraduate and postgraduate), negotiators, diplomats, practitioners from nongovernmental and intergovernmental organizations, and interested parties alike—seeking insights into the most prominent institutional aspects of global governance.

The Group of Twenty (G20)

We need not tell our readers that global governance has become a "messy" business. As we write this foreword, the 2012 gathering in Rio de Janeiro was characterized by hundreds of side agreements that do not require government financing or approval which may result in concrete improvements, however incremental. "The outcome reflects big power shifts around the world," is how *The New York Times* summarized the new global governance terrain. "These include a new assertiveness by developing nations in international forums and the growing capacity of grass-roots organizations and corporations to mold effective environmental action without the blessing of governments."[1]

The Group of Twenty is yet another indication of the phenomenon of multi-multilateralisms that characterize contemporary international relations. Originally developed as a forum for economic policy discussions that brought together the finance ministers from the 19 largest economies and the European Union (EU), since the global financial meltdown of 2008 the G20 has become *the* place for heads of state of the most powerful countries to gather. While other types of international institutional reform, for instance of the Security Council, have foundered, this new informal "institution" (it has no secretariat and is a moveable semi-annual feast) represents a profound change in the ways of doing business. Representing approximately two-thirds of the world's population, 90 percent of global gross domestic product (GDP), and 80 percent of world trade, it has eclipsed the G7/8 group of industrialized states as the primary governmental forum for debate on economic issues.

This shift reflects the changing constellation of economic and political power in the post-Cold War world. No longer solely dominated by the United States and Europe, global trade and finance are increasingly shaped by the developing world's emerging powers—China, India, Turkey, and Brazil—and other growing regional powers, including South Africa, Mexico, and Indonesia, all of which are members of the G20.

The G20 may grow in significance as it becomes involved in more policy areas. For example, at the June 2012 summit of heads of state and government in Los Cabos, Mexico, a meeting of heads of national security was held—the first of its kind for the forum. As the G20 becomes a more significant part of the network of institutions and rules that constitute global governance, it is even more important to understand how the forum operates and helps shape world politics. Will it be a threat or a complement to the United Nations and the Organisation for Economic Co-operation and Development? What will the smaller and middle powers on the outside do to ensure their interests? Will the G20 become institutionalized and stay the course, or become another photo op for heads of state?

We are fortunate that two such distinguished scholars—both with prodigious publications and real-world experience—as Andrew Cooper and Ramesh Thakur agreed to write this much-needed book on an increasingly important forum. Andy has written extensively about global governance and diplomacy and was a member of the Warwick Commission on Multilateral Trade; he has attended as an observer all of the meetings of the G20. In addition to having held prestigious academic chairs, Ramesh has been an Assistant Secretary-General of the United Nations and a commissioner and one of the principal authors of the 2001 report of the International Commission on Intervention and State Sovereignty, *The Responsibility to Protect*. They both bring to this book extensive knowledge and understanding of global governance and its institutions from the inside as well as from the much maligned academic ivory tower.

We are delighted to have this book in the series because it enriches the literature on global institutions and governance, and various related international economic policy matters. We wholeheartedly recommend it and, as always, welcome comments from our readers.

Thomas G. Weiss
The CUNY Graduate Center, New York, USA
Rorden Wilkinson
University of Manchester, UK
July 2012

Note

1 Simon Romero and John M. Broder, "Progress on the Sidelines as Rio Conference Ends," *The New York Times*, 24 June 2012.

Acknowledgments

We are grateful to Thomas G. Weiss and Rorden Wilkinson first for their patience and understanding of the circumstances that greatly delayed the completion of this book. When we initially agreed to undertake the task, both of us were located at the University of Waterloo. However, shortly afterward Ramesh Thakur ended up returning to the Australian National University in Canberra. Such a major move across continents and hemispheres caused severe disruption to the planned calendar and the completion of this book took a lot longer than we had anticipated. We are grateful also to Tom and Rorden, second, for their insightful and constructive comments on the first draft of the manuscript. The result is a much improved book.

We owe a considerable debt of gratitude to Prime Minister Paul Martin of Canada. As this book makes abundantly clear, he played a principal role as the finance minister of Canada in the formation of the G20 group of finance ministers and central bank governors after the Asian financial crisis of the 1990s. When he became prime minister, he became keenly interested in elevating that grouping to a leaders-level summit. He was the driving force in keeping alive that idea even after retiring from politics, and mentored and guided both of us over several years as we studied and evaluated the proposal, the form it might take, and the circumstances in which it might come into being. It is therefore a signal honor for us that he has written the Foreword to this book.

As the preceding paragraphs suggest, we have been colleagues for many years and have collaborated in several projects over the last two decades. Having co-edited four books together previously, it was relatively easy for us to shift gears and write a jointly authored book on a topic that both of us have examined closely for some time.

Abbreviations

3G	Global Governance Group
APEC	Asia-Pacific Economic Cooperation
ASEAN	Association of Southeast Asian Nations
AU	African Union
BASIC	Brazil, South Africa, India, and China
BRICs	Brazil, Russia, India, and China
BRICS	Brazil, Russia, India, China, and South Africa
BRICSAM	Brazil, Russia, India, China, South Africa, a representative of ASEAN (Indonesia), and Mexico
ECOWAS	Economic Community of West African States
EFSF	European Financial Stability Facility
EU	European Union
FAO	Food and Agriculture Organization
FSB	Financial Stability Board
G7/8	Group of 7 (8) industrialized countries (Canada, France, Germany, Italy, Japan, the United Kingdom, and the United States, plus Russia as the eighth)
G77	Group of 77 developing countries
GDP	gross domestic product
GFC	global financial crisis
HIV/AIDS	human immunodeficiency virus/acquired immune deficiency syndrome
IBSA	India, Brazil, and South Africa
ICC	International Criminal Court
IFAD	International Fund for Agricultural Development
IFIs	international financial institutions
IMF	International Monetary Fund
KIA	South Korea, Indonesia, and Australia
MEM	Major Emitters Meeting
NAFTA	North American Free Trade Area

NAM	Non-Aligned Movement
NEPAD	New Economic Partnership for Africa's Development
NGO	nongovernmental organization
O5	Outreach 5 (Brazil, China, India, Mexico, and South Africa)
OAS	Organization of American States
OECD	Organisation for Economic Co-operation and Development
P5	the five permanent members of the UN Security Council (China, France, Russia, the United Kingdom, and the United States)
RMB	renminbi (China's currency, also known as the yuan)
SARS	Severe Acute Respiratory Syndrome
UK	United Kingdom
UN	United Nations
UNFCCC	United Nations Framework Convention on Climate Change
UNSC	United Nations Security Council
UNSG	United Nations Secretary-General
WFP	World Food Programme
WHO	World Health Organization
WTO	World Trade Organization

Introduction

- Multilateralism under challenge
- The United Nations
- The G7/8 in the postwar architecture of global financial governance
- The BRICS in the post-Cold War architecture
- The G20
- Conclusion

Tom Weiss and Ramesh Thakur pose the puzzle of how the world is governed, even in the absence of world government, "to produce norms, codes of conduct, and regulatory, surveillance, and compliance instruments?"[1] The answer, they argue, is global governance. There has been a remarkable growth in the number and types of actors in global governance, including formal international and regional organizations, and informal institutions and arrangements; however, their legitimacy, effectiveness, and interoperability are under intense scrutiny. Jean-Pierre Lehmann highlights the intersection of two trends. First, the major institutions of global governance, from the United Nations (UN) system to the World Bank, International Monetary Fund (IMF), World Trade Organization (WTO), and UN Framework Convention on Climate Change (UNFCCC), "have not only lost momentum, but also legitimacy and credibility." Second, "this trust deficit exists most notably, and most destructively ... between North and South."[2] The South bears a historical grudge for having been subjugated by the North and, despite the profound transformation of financial and geopolitical relations between the two, the North remains firmly in control.[3] Even the Doha Round of trade talks, which was supposed to encapsulate a development agenda, collapsed at the WTO ministerial meeting in Cancún in 2003 because, "Instead of approaching the meeting in a spirit of reconciliation and collaboration, the United States and the European Union confronted the South with a spirit of mercantilist intransigence," which provoked "mistrust, recrimination and confrontation" that still persists.[4]

Many in developing countries believe that the IMF has been captured to serve the global financial and banking interests ahead of the needs of development and growth. The West's trajectory of development included protection of infant industries, farmer subsidies, and investment in the health and education of citizens, but when developing countries in financial distress have turned to the IMF for help, its assistance has typically been made conditional on "structural adjustment" policies that slash public spending, cut back public subsidies to health, education, and fertilizers, collect fees from the people in return for health and educational services, and prioritize loan repayments to international lenders and donors. Results have included a two-thirds fall in the number of women seeking advice on sexually transmitted diseases in Kenya, a two-thirds fall in the number of rural families sending children to school in Ghana, and a doubling of infant mortality rates in Zambia. According to a disillusioned Joseph Stiglitz, the IMF is not interested in development or what helps to get a country out of poverty. Rather, its primary motivation is to make sure that banks and financial institutions are paid their dues.[5] Activists allege that IMF policies were directly responsible for causing a famine in Malawi in 2002; the country recovered by asking the IMF to leave, rejecting its advice, and resuming fertilizer subsidy to the poor farmers.[6]

The global governance architecture is made up of:

- Formal global organizations such as the UN system, the World Bank, the IMF, the World Health Organization (WHO), and the WTO;[7]
- Formal regional and subregional organizations like the African Union (AU), the Economic Community of West African States (ECOWAS), the Commonwealth of Nations, the Organization of American States (OAS), and the Association of Southeast Asian Nations (ASEAN);
- Informal general-purpose institutions like the G8 and the G20, which "serve as consensus incubators and direction-setters, not direct action decision-makers";[8] and
- Informal but functionally specific and single problem-oriented institutions such as the Proliferation Security Initiative.

In this framework of multiple and complementary actors of global governance, the potential of the G20 lies in augmenting the formal forums of organized multilateralism with an informal institutional setting for the key players to engage each other directly, personally, and yet informally in prenegotiations to break some particularly obdurate global deadlocks. By definition, therefore, only the "too hard" baskets of problems will be placed before the G20 leaders, and this should condition expectations of what the forum can deliver. Even so, for this purpose the G20 is potentially "the best available venue because it brings together the systemically significant economies without the bureaucratic baggage of the United Nations and international financial institutions."[9]

This raises a prior question. For any given global impasse, leaving aside differences and clash of interests over the substance, to what extent do existing and alternative forums and mechanisms for conducting negotiations—the institutions of international governance—facilitate, impede, or obstruct the ability to strike deals through a process of bargaining and accommodation? No single forum can guarantee resolution of clashing interests, but an intimate yet representative group whose members get to know, understand, and trust one another is more likely to succeed than either the G8 or the UN.

The G20 is a new leaders-level grouping of the world's economic heavyweights or systemically important countries. As well as representing two-thirds of the world's total population, the G20 account for 80–90 percent of the world's gross product, trade, and economic growth and, importantly, 60 percent of the world's poor.[10] What is unique about the emerging global economic order is that, for the first time in history, countries from the global South are likely to be at the forefront of the multipolar economic system. This is because they will be the main drivers of global economic growth and therefore provide the chief stimulus to the global economy.

The G20 was set up in response to the widely shared sentiment that innovations in international governance were required to deal with the "broken paradigms and failing multilateral institutions," in the words of Brazil's President Lula da Silva.[11] The international institutions (the UN Security Council, the World Bank, the IMF, the WTO, etc.) "make decisions that affect us all but without our consent," with the result that "Global governance is a tyranny speaking the language of democracy."[12] Beyond representational legitimacy and performance effectiveness, another major attraction was the group's potential to bridge the North–South international divide.

The G20 at the leaders' level was brought into existence in 2008 by the exogenous shock to the international financial system. Its first call to action accordingly was to manage the international financial crisis. However, its intellectual lineage predates the financial crisis and includes exploratory assessments of problem-solving governance contributions to a range of economic, environmental, social, and security policy issues. In part the G20 responds to perceptions of substantive inadequacies in the existing multilateral institutions of global governance; in part it seeks to align international governance institutions to a shifting global order that is witnessing the rise and reemergence of significant heavyweight players from the global South; and in part the G20 represents the hope that it will be a superior problem-solving constellation, with a better mix of legitimacy and efficiency than existing forums, for managing new crises of the global commons and resolving accumulating global deadlocks.[13]

International Relations is shaped by the interplay of power and ideas. The G20 stands out as a unique international institution that reflects the changing interplay of power and ideas. It emerged out of a financial crisis not through the rupture of war. As such it is not simply a grouping of the winners, setting out the rules as part of a victor's peace.[14] The G20 marks a dramatic shift in the global power constellation with a recognition that an expanded cluster of countries mattered to global policy making. Existing institutions and nodes of global governance were not widely considered to be discharging their functions and meeting international demands and expectations. Conversely, a loosely structured and informal grouping of leaders with clout—only leaders, not ministers, but leaders of countries with clout—could make the required shifts in politically sensitive policy issues, set new normative principles, frameworks, and mechanisms; and provide the necessary thrust for the newly formed shared understandings, and the will to cooperate, to be carried forward into the formal intergovernmental machinery.[15] If diplomacy as usual is not working, dissatisfaction and impatience with the flawed international machinery can entrench resignation or encourage a search for creative alternatives.

Yet ambition does not mean complete novelty. The G20 built on the legacy and the incremental culture derived from the G20 Finance made up of finance ministers and central bank governors, in operation since the Asian shocks of the late 1990s. If it can be viewed as a concert of big nations, it was big enough in composition to contain countries from all the major regions of the globe. Nor did 20 represent an absolute limit of 20 countries. Originally created as an institution with 19 members plus the European Union (EU), the G20's organizational structure has remained porous. Each summit from Washington, DC, in November 2008 up to Los Cabos in June 2012 has had its own dynamics about who is in and who is out.

The structure of the book is as follows. The introduction locates the developing sentiment for G reform within the accumulating crisis of global governance and both organized and informal multilateral institutions, in particular the UN and the G7/8. Chapter 1 describes the growing misalignment between the shifting global order and the structure of the existing major nodes of global governance. The G7/8 in particular was increasingly challenged on both legitimacy and efficiency grounds and the momentum for reform grew irresistibly strong. The G20 at the leaders' level is a legacy of its predecessor for finance ministers and central bank governors—G20 Finance—which was set up in response to the Asian financial crisis of the late 1990s. This background is discussed in some detail in Chapter 2, showing how the legitimacy and effectiveness of the existing institutional structure were compromised by the way in which they handled the crisis. In Chapter 3 and Chapter 4 we note that although the G20 leaders' group came into being as a result of the global financial crisis (GFC), it could have been created just as easily by other exogenous shocks. Similarly, the structure and composition that actually emerged were not the only possible options; others were also canvassed. Chapter 5 reviews the central purpose of the G20, in particular the question of whether it should function as the premier global economic governance group or expand or shrink its agenda once the financial crisis is over. This also entails a discussion of its relationship with other institutions in the context of the ever-present tension between efficiency and legitimacy. In Chapter 6 we review the series of G20 leaders' summits from the inaugural one in 2008 to the eve of the first to be held in Latin America at Los Cabos, Mexico, in 2012. We argue also for the merits of the G20 transitioning from a crisis committee mitigating the harm of the GFC to a global steering committee for a wide range of international policy challenges. The concluding chapter returns to the theme of the G20 as a possible solution to the accumulating efficiency and legitimacy deficits of the existing architecture of global governance. In order to do so, however, it will have to function as the hub of networked consultative governance rather than follow a command-and-control club model of governance.

Multilateralism under challenge

The world is interdependent in areas as diverse as financial markets, infectious diseases, climate change, terrorism, nuclear peace and safety, product safety, food supply and water tables, fish stocks, and ecosystem resources. In addition to their potential for provoking interstate military conflicts, these are all drivers of human insecurity because of the threat they pose to individual lives and welfare.

Multilateralism refers to collective, cooperative action by states—when necessary, in concert with nonstate actors—to deal with common problems and challenges when these are best managed collaboratively at the international level.[16] Areas such as maintaining international peace and security, economic development and international trade, human rights, functional and technical cooperation, and the protection of the environment and sustainability of resources require joint action to reduce costs and bring order and regularity to international relations. Such problems cannot be addressed unilaterally with optimum effectiveness. This rationale persists because all states, as well as some nonstate actors, face mutual vulnerabilities and intensifying interdependence. They will benefit from and are thus required to support global public goods. Even the most powerful states cannot achieve security nor maintain prosperity and health as effectively acting unilaterally or in isolation. The international system rests, accordingly, on a network of treaties, regimes, international organizations, and shared practices that embody common expectations, reciprocity, and equivalence of benefits.

In a multipolar, interdependent, globalized, and networked world, multilateralism will continue to be a key aspect of international relations. Limitations do and always will exist.[17] Powerful states may work through or around multilateral institutions at their pleasure and selectively. Some issues may defy multilateral approaches. Changing normative expectations may cast doubt on the constitutive values of specific international institutions, but the theoretical rationale of institutionalism—that all states benefit from a world in which agreed rules and common norms bind the behavior of all actors—is broadly intact and indisputable.

All actors depend upon multilateralism and the underwriting of regularity and public goods in the international system. Yet multilateralism is under unprecedented challenge, from arms control to climate change, international criminal justice, and the use of military force overseas. If they are to remain viable, international organizations and the values of multilateralism embedded in them must be reconstituted in line with twenty-first century principles of governance and legitimacy.[18] Just as importantly, they must be capable of addressing contemporary challenges effectively.

The United Nations

The paradigmatic institution at the center of the multilateral system of global governance is the UN. It is the symbol and core of global governance but lacks the attributes of a world government. It plays a central role in the development of global governance through filling five gaps in all issue areas: knowledge (empirical and theoretical), normative, policy, institutional, and compliance (monitoring and enforcement).[19]

The UN opened up new horizons in 1945, but the steps taken since then have been small, hesitant, and limited. This is not to deny the organization's many real accomplishments: decolonization, elimination of apartheid, peacekeeping missions, behind-the-scenes peacemaking, the development and extension of the rule of law, human rights promotion, gender empowerment, assistance to refugees, collective action for such common problems as resource depletion and environmental degradation, and so on. The UN record shows a surprising capacity for institutional innovation, conceptual advances, policy adaptation, and organizational learning.[20] This can be shown with respect to peacekeeping and peace operations, human security and human rights, atrocity crimes and international criminal justice, sanctions and the use of force, etc. Its strength is that it is the only universal forum for global cooperation and management. As such, it must continue to play a central role in establishing a world order which strikes a balance between social justice and political realism. In the theatre of world politics, the UN has been center stage in preventing and managing conflicts, regulating armaments, championing human rights and international humanitarian law, liberating the colonized, providing economic and technical aid in the newly liberated countries, organizing elections, empowering women, educating children, feeding the hungry, sheltering the dispossessed and displaced, housing the refugees, tending to the sick, and coordinating disaster relief and assistance: all on a 24/7 basis.

Until World War I, for example, war was an accepted and normal part of the states system, with distinctive rules, norms, and etiquette. The only protection against aggression was countervailing power, which increased both the cost of victory and the risk of failure. Since 1945, the UN has spawned a corpus of laws to stigmatize aggression and create a robust norm against it. On the one hand, therefore, one could argue that, on balance, the world has been a better and less bloody place with the UN in being than would have been the case without the organization's existence.

On the other hand, UN accomplishments have lagged well behind the promise, demands, and expectations.[21] Set up as a many-splendored forum for realizing humanity's loftiest aspirations, it has often been reduced to a many-splintered organization mired in petty squabbles. The founders created the General Assembly as the forum of choice for discussing the world's problems, resolving disputes, and articulating global norms;[22] the Security Council for keeping the peace and enforcing the norms;[23] the specialized agencies to address transnational technical problems; and the office of the Secretary-General to run this vast machinery smoothly and efficiently.[24] In fact the General Assembly has become a forum for public recriminations more than public diplomacy, the Cold War against the "evil empire" was won by the United States and its allies, and countries that have moved from poverty to prosperity have done so by embracing market principles rather than relying on UN handouts. According to its critics, the UN has played a scarcely discernible role either in keeping the peace, promoting successful development, or defeating the worst enemies of freedom and human rights since the end of World War II. The responses to date to calls for UN action have been neither as prompt, effective, nor uniform as they need to become.

"As a pre-cold-war organisation operating in a post-cold-war world, the UN has struggled to be relevant and effective."[25] In failing to accommodate its structures, processes, and agendas to the transformations sweeping the world, the UN has risked atrophy and irrelevance. The very feature that gives the UN General Assembly its unique international legitimacy, universal membership, makes it an extremely inefficient body for making collective decisions. The failure to reform the Security Council has been equally corrosive of the UN's moral authority. It suffers from a quadruple legitimacy deficit: performance, representational, procedural, and accountability. Its performance legitimacy suffers from two strikes: an uneven and a selective record. It is unrepresentative from almost any point of view.[26] Its procedural legitimacy is suspect on grounds of lack of democratization and transparency in decision making, and it is not answerable to the General Assembly, the World Court, or the nations of the world. There is also a growing gap between legality and legitimacy with respect to sanctions, the use of force, nuclear nonproliferation and disarmament, and the selection of the Secretary-General, among others.[27] Without continual structural and procedural reforms, the legitimacy and performance deficits will accumulate and there will be an intensifying crisis of confidence in the world's system of organized multilateralism centered on the UN.

Yet, for all its shortcomings, there is little evidence to suggest that any other organization or institution could substitute for the UN's unique mantle of universal legitimacy. Amidst intensifying interdependence, its mandated role becomes especially important in managing globalization to maximize common benefits while mitigating unequally distributed harm. For many, globalization is both desirable and irreversible for having underwritten a rising standard of living and material prosperity throughout the world for several decades. For some, however, globalization is the soft underbelly of corporate imperialism that plunders and profiteers on the back of rampant consumerism that almost brought the world to its knees in 2008–12.[28] No other body can tackle these pathologies more effectively, with greater legitimacy, lesser transaction and compliance costs, and higher comfort levels for most countries as their organization, than the UN.

The G7/8 in the postwar architecture of global financial governance

The North–South divide finds expression in many different global governance forums. With respect to the WTO, for example, the Warwick Commission identified five sets of challenges: a gap between the growing liberalization and internationalization of the industrial countries' economies and waning popular support for open markets; the increasingly multipolar nature of the global trade system, which reduces the level of like-mindedness among the major players; the partial and transitional protectionist instincts of the big emerging market countries and the desire of the industrial countries to keep the evolving WTO trade rules from stalling as well as to broaden the trade agenda to environmental and human rights issues; confidential and opaque vs. open and transparent decision-making processes; and the tension between the global trading regime and preferential trading arrangements.[29] Thus four of the five challenges—the first being the sole exception—can be viewed through the North–South alternative prisms.

For present purposes, however, the paradigmatic institutions at the two ends of the global divide are the G8 and the BRICS (Brazil, Russia, India, China, and South Africa). To understand their antecedents, it is necessary to go back more than 100 years. The current international financial architecture has its historical roots in the Great Depression. Following World War I, the previously fluid, open, and international economy became divided and segregated under the combined pressures of nationalism, protectionism, and currency isolation. The malaise deepened with the Great Depression. During World War II, John Maynard Keynes—possibly the most famous economist of the last century, whose name became synonymous with an active government role in managing the economy—called for a meeting of world leaders to design a new system of global finance. The United Nations [sic] Monetary and Financial Conference was held at Bretton Woods, New Hampshire in June–July 1944. In attendance were over 700 delegates from 44 countries.

The conference addressed the problem of postwar recovery and the reconstruction of Europe, which could only come about with a massive injection of capital. In order to facilitate a free flow of capital and investment across borders, a system that enabled exchange of different national currencies was necessary. The postwar architecture of global financial

governance emerged from the New Hampshire meeting. At the heart of
what is known as the Bretton Woods system are the IMF and the World
Bank. The cross-border flow of money was progressively separated from
political control as government and finance were hived off into separate
spheres, while international banking went its own unregulated way.

The G8 has its antecedents in the first informal meeting of the
Group of Four finance ministers (of France, West Germany, the United
Kingdom, and the United States) in the White House in March 1973,
followed by the Japanese Finance Minister to form the G5 (or "Library
Group") to discuss the world's monetary system. Italy joined the group
at the first scheduled informal summit of leaders in Rambouillet (Paris)
in 1975, and Canada was added in 1976 at US behest in order to offset
the European preponderance, to make it the G7 of the world's richest
countries and biggest economies. It was expanded again in 1997 with
the controversial addition of Russia. From 2005, the eight extended invitations to Brazil, China, India, Mexico, and South Africa—the Outreach
Five or O5—to join them for part of the discussions in what by 2007
became known as the Heiligendamm process.

The G7 was set up originally to coordinate macroeconomic policy
(sound monetary policy, stable exchange rates, growth with low inflation),
to which were added liberalization of world trade, energy consumption,
relations with developing countries, debt relief, terrorism, and so on. It
also took on the tasks of policy coordination and crisis management on
political and security issues, with varying results. Among the G7/8
achievements must be ranked managing the end of the Cold War, particularly in Europe; creating a role for itself in conflict prevention; and
highlighting the issue of debt relief. It registered these positive results
"by highlighting an issue, reaching a collective agreement, and then
delegating to the relevant international organization"[30]—a very good
example being Kosovo in the late 1990s. On the other hand, it was unsuccessful in concluding the Uruguay Round of trade talks on schedule or
muting transatlantic divisions over East–West trade in the 1980s.

Hugo Dobson lists three sets of criticisms that have been leveled at
the G8: *low legitimacy* owing to its narrow base, lack of transparency,
aloofness from dissenters, lack of legal basis or criteria for membership,
and pretensions to manage the world's affairs; *overlap* with much of the
work of other international organizations; and *questionable effectiveness*
and value for money, with a persistent failure to close the gap between
promises and pledges made at summits, and follow-up action and delivery
when it came time to implement the commitments.[31]

The influential British columnist Timothy Garton Ash believes that
"The G8 is an anachronistic survival of the old, cold war west ... If the

G8 did not exist today, no one would dream of inventing it." Its core business was to manage the world economy and this can no longer be done without the equal participation of Brazil, China, and India. The G20 may not be working very well but nonetheless, "it is a grouping much more appropriate to the economic, political and cultural realities of the 21st century." Accordingly, it would be better to roll the G8 into the G20 and focus efforts "on making the G20 more serious and effective than it is now."[32]

The BRICS in the post-Cold War architecture

The G8 was always a narrow club of self-selected countries and, as such, never possessed either electoral or representative legitimacy. However, for some years at least it reflected economic and geopolitical weight. No longer. On the eve of the first BRIC (Brazil, Russia, India, and China) summit in Yekaterinburg, Russia in 2009, Brazil's president noted that the four countries, with only 15 percent of world gross domestic product (GDP), account for some 65 percent of world growth.[33] China's ambassador to India similarly noted on the eve of the fourth BRICS summit in New Delhi on 29 March 2012 that the contributions of the BRICS to world economic growth was significantly greater than their share of global GDP, trade, and even population. The five BRICS countries "account for 42 percent of the global population, make up 18 percent of the world GDP and 15 percent of the world total trade volume. Their contribution to the world economic growth rate has exceeded 50 percent."[34]

The BRICS are projected to match the original G7's share of global output sometime around 2040. Put another way, in 2025 the G8—the world's eight biggest economies—will most likely be, in descending order: the United States, China, India, Japan, Germany, the United Kingdom, France, and Russia.[35] In other words, over the past decade emerging markets have shifted from the margins to the center of global economic action. While their membership and role in the G20 gives them a global forum and voice, the most powerful bloc of their own, a sort of counterpart to the G7, is BRICS. Their growing economic self-confidence finds expression increasingly in political assertiveness as well.

With the future of the BRICs still very much in train, there was no hiding the declaratory message of global transition that underlies the groups' policy priorities and public declarations. The Yekaterinburg summit was hailed as an "historic event" by Russia's President Dmitry Medvedev, and was punctuated by its call for "The emerging and developing economies [to] have a greater voice and representation in international financial institutions."[36] Brazilian President Lula da Silva, the host of the April 2010 summit, upped the ante by stating that: "A new global economic geography has been born."[37]

What is more, other putative "rising" states were showing interest in joining the club. On a trip to China with 13 cabinet members and a delegation of 370 business people, President Jacob Zuma said South Africa wanted to be considered for memberships, advocating that its participation "would mean that an entire continent that has a population of over 1 billion people is represented."[38] Reports in 2010 suggested that the BRICs group was considering bringing in not only South Africa but Indonesia and Mexico.[39] In 2011 South Africa was formally welcomed into the group to make it into BRICS, but not, at least not yet, any other country.

The G20

Thus the present period is one of diminished and "messy multilateralism"[40] in which rising powers jostle for competitive advantage with established powers in global (UN, World Bank, IMF), regional, and ad hoc (G20) institutions. In this fluid and shifting global order, all sides engage in "forum shopping," picking and choosing forums to maximize influence and suit individual political agendas. The BRICS at once illustrate that trend, but also point to a potential world order that is more principled in the global norms, has stronger representation of emergent and developing countries, and is more evenly weighted in its decision-making powers. Issues of sovereignty, legitimacy, and governance are central to the ongoing and necessary conversation among the influential members of the global North and South. Of all the existing or prospective institutions, the G20 provides the best forum for such a dialogue. In a world in which all politics is stubbornly local but most big-ticket problems are global, the G20 is uniquely placed to bridge this global governance gap.

The G8 was a club of the like-minded, essentially transatlantic with Japan co-opted in. The G20 is more representative of the global diversity of power, wealth, and values. Lacking political like-mindedness, it will be animated more by pragmatism and problem-solving than by ideology and social cohesion. Consequently, as attention shifts from one agenda item to another, the G20 is likely to see "shifting coalitions of consensus"[41] form and re-form between the North and the South, across the Atlantic, between the Atlantic and the Indo-Pacific, between and among the BRICS, and so on.

The 20-strong group of 19 finance ministers from the leading industrial and developing economies plus the EU was an initiative launched jointly by Canada's Finance Minister Paul Martin and US Treasury Secretary Lawrence Summers in 1999 in the aftermath of the Asian financial crisis. The G20 finance ministers met each year from then on. The idea for a G20 forum of the leaders of the world's most important economies was first outlined by Martin at the World Economic Forum in Davos in January 2004, shortly after he became prime minister. He recognized that the global dynamic was changing and the emerging new powers of China, India, and Brazil had to be brought into the dialogue. However, after Martin's Liberal Party lost power, there was not much enthusiasm within the bureaucratic establishment for Canada moving from one of eight to one of 20 participants at a top table of global governance, and it was left to think tanks to study the desirability and feasibility of the idea.[42]

With the systemic crisis roiling the world, the G20 Finance was dramatically upgraded to a summit of leaders in November 2008. None of the existing political or economic institutions—the IMF, the G8 or G20 Finance—proved adequate to the task of coordinating the response to the global crisis. The IMF had shown more skill and determination at preaching to the developing countries what they should do than at persuading industrial countries to act together, while the developing countries' G20 on trade was prone to blame all ills on the developed countries and ask them for handouts rather than tackle the domestic governance gaps within its own membership.

The first and most dramatic impact of the 2008 banking and financial crisis on the governance architecture was to bring the worlds of politics, money, and banking more sharply together again. A dawning realization that the system to manage the modern world of banking, capital, and finance had to be redesigned accompanied short-term, emergency measures. The reality is that corporations, markets, and financial flows are all global, but the regulatory and surveillance systems are national or, in a few cases such as Europe, regional.

In other words, under the present, deficient system of global governance, "We get the global perils without global benefits."[43] At present, the perils are global, the risks are socialized internationally, but the benefits remain privatized and are far from global. This is why we need cross-border supervision of financial institutions; shared global standards for accounting and regulation; and international institutions to provide early-warning systems for the world economy. For example, Eric Helleiner has suggested that capital controls and commodity future markets regulation can play distinctive roles in small and exposed economies.[44] The first can be a counter-cyclical regulatory tool that dampens excessive foreign borrowing in good times and curbs sudden capital outflows in the bad times. The second could mute speculative excesses in futures trading that may have been partly responsible for the spike in food prices in 2008.

Transcending the G8 concert

In some of its characteristics the G20 is both a rival and a successor to the G8. Akin to this post-1975 institution it is a summit of leaders radiating out into a wider network. It makes claim to be a "steering committee" for the world. It is an unelected forum, where the bulk of the marginal majority is left out.[45] It has an awkward, uneasy relationship with the UN. It is an innovative form of multilateralism. Nonetheless, the flavor of the G20 remains distinctly plurilateral,[46] even elitist.

Unlike the UN and the Bretton Woods institutions,[47] or the G8, the G20 cannot be viewed as an institution that has been created in the image of the Anglo-American or Western European world. The United States was very much present at its creation. Nevertheless, for the United States, the art of championing the G20 cannot be equated with a moment of triumph akin to the establishment of the post-World War II order, or for that matter the notion of a new world order in the aftermath of the Cold War.[48] Rather, the G20 was brought "off the shelf" by the George W. Bush administration at a time of vulnerability and relative decline.[49] For the events that precipitated the advent of the G20 were very much "Made in America"—the rescue of AIG, the fall of Bear Stearns and Lehman Brothers, and the overall context of the collapse of the sub-prime bubble housing market with attendant shocks to Wall Street.[50]

Unlike the G7, the G20 cannot be seen either as an institution that was animated into life by the good ideas, skillful diplomacy, and big personalities mainly emanating from Europe. French President Nicolas Sarkozy and British Prime Minister Gordon Brown played a significant role in the creation of the G20. Their efforts, however, were not of the same order as those of France's President Valéry Giscard d'Estaing and Germany's Chancellor Helmut Schmidt in the mid-1970s. Furthermore, they did not act alone. On the contrary, the establishment of the G20 rests on many shoulders, above all on the legacy of G20 Finance with its own set of ideas, diplomacy, and personalities. On the original G20 Finance, along with the efforts of the United States and selected European countries (for example, Germany) there was a significant contribution by Canada, embodied in the ideas and determination of Paul Martin. In the narrative relating to the advent of the elevated G20 at the leaders level, supporting roles were played by many others. It was the moment that the BRICs acted as more or less a common grouping.[51]

What is more, selected middle powers reconfigured their diplomacy to take advantage of the opportunities provided by the G20. The most notable signs of this activity came from the so-called KIA countries (South Korea, Indonesia, and Australia).[52]

This different mix in ideational leadership in turn influenced the procedural outcomes. The preference of Europe was biased in 2008 toward a "G8 Plus" composition for the G20, a formula that had much in common with the concept and practice of outreach or consultation as practiced through the G8. This meant that instead of a G20 their preference would have been for a smaller G13 or G14 grouping with a select group of emerging countries (China, India, Brazil, Mexico, and South Africa with or without Egypt) being added to the core G8 club members. Adoption of such an option was given some viability by the institutionalization of the Heiligendamm process.[53]

This model ran into a host of problems. Having established the G20 Finance as a forum of equals, a return to a two-tier body was very difficult. A strong argument could be made that China, India, and Brazil were countries that really mattered. The outreach process itself had built up some unanticipated success, including a sense of group solidarity among the O5 of the emerging countries that were privileged through this process. Still, this smaller group option was overwhelmed by the "off-the-shelf" G20 approach. With the financial crisis revealing not only the extent of interdependence, but the importance of emerging countries as problem solvers (not just problems as in previous crises) there was no going back to a smaller group, with a legacy of asymmetry in status.

Reinforcing the momentum toward a G20 as opposed to a smaller group was the recognition that the inclusion of some additional countries contained benefits. For the United States, a G20 had some geopolitical side-benefits. It restricted the ability of Sarkozy to mobilize a campaign against Anglo-American capitalism. It also rewarded a number of US allies, including South Korea, Australia, Indonesia, Saudi Arabia, and (although this became more contested) Turkey. For countries such as Canada (at least in terms of Martin's calculation) it precluded the prospect of the G8 going smaller not bigger. The worst-case option was a G2, G3, or G4 that cut out the smaller G8 members.[54] Of course, for Australia, South Korea, Indonesia, and the other "non-outreach" countries, the G20 formula brought them inside the tent. It was no wonder then that the KIA countries campaigned hard for an embedded G20.

What most distinguished the G20 from its predecessors, therefore, is its scope. The best known historical concerts in the past were welded together by a common pursuit of rewards, most often the distribution of territory. This was a main feature of the concert of Europe after the

Napoleonic Wars,[55] the 1919 Paris Peace Settlement which brought together US President Woodrow Wilson, British Prime Minister Lloyd George, and their French and Italian counterparts, as well as the Big Three in the post-1945 Yalta and Potsdam arrangements (US President Franklin Roosevelt, British Prime Minister Winston Churchill, and Soviet leader and Communist Party Secretary Joseph Stalin).

Efficiency vs. legitimacy

The G20 stands out as the first authentically "high table" forum that is global in composition. Although continuing to be weighted heavily toward Europe in composition (albeit not in leadership), the G20 contained a greater diversity of membership. If the way remained open for an informal G2 to be established,[56] at least in formal terms the G20 was very different from the small numbers that are tightly associated with the traditional concert model. There was no big 3, 4, or 5 as in previous constellations at times of re-orderings after massive upheavals.

In principle, stretching the size of the G20 added to the credibility of the forum. For the first time a major body of global governance started on the premise of uniformity of membership rights and responsibilities. There was no veto power, weighted voting, nor shares. There was no assumption that the hosting function was to be monopolized by the traditional elite members. At least formally the United States was no different than a country such as Argentina, a country which—notwithstanding its status as a debtor nation and not a putative emerging power—maintained its place as a legacy from G20 Finance.

At the same time the size of the G20 made the forum difficult to manage. As a partial replica of the G8 no secretariat was established. The G20 stood or fell on whether or not leaders and their advisors could work together and make the commitments, big deals and concessions required not only to solve problems on an issue-specific basis but to maintain the momentum for the G20 as a pivotal and innovative forum of global governance.

These dual purposes could only be achieved, however, with a buy-in or even a sense of ownership of the forum right across the membership. This proposition was of a very different order than G20 Finance, simply because the stakes of either success or failure were raised. The precipitating crisis for the elevated G20 at the leaders' level was global in reach, not a geographically defined set of shocks with a fear of contagion as in the late 1990s. The central role of the leaders' summit also meant that the tolerance of political risk was ratcheted up. Finance ministers could toil away, if not in obscurity, then at least within a set of technical silos. Leaders had lots of operational advantages in being able to break down these silos. The cost came in terms of sensitivity to setbacks, whether perceived or real.

Under the stress of financial shocks, the risks appeared very worthwhile. China, India, and Brazil—along with all the rest of the invitees (including Spain and the Netherlands, countries that were not on the original invitation list) quickly signaled that they were on board. Furthermore, they showed solidarity not only with the global North but also with the G8 countries in quickly acceding to the mantra of stimulus. Individually China led the way with a massive 4 trillion RMB package just before the Washington summit. Collectively the promises made in Washington by the G20 countries as a group displayed a marked show of synchronization.

The test was whether or not these big emerging countries would hedge or defect from the G20 project over time. After all, they were not responsible for the financial shocks. As such they did not have the same requirement for either immediate financial rescue plans or for redoing macro-prudential regulations. Their concerns were tied to the exigencies of globalization, a process that had brought impressive growth in terms of GDP and foreign direct investment to the emerging countries (although with deepened internal inequalities). Commercial interdependence, not normative values, served as the glue that held the array of G20 countries together—punctuated by a lifeboat ethos that the world economy was on the brink of a disaster in late 2008. The question was whether this glue would outlast the crisis, with competitive not cooperative instincts reappearing as the drivers and motivators of interest definition and diplomatic behavior.

Conclusion

As the newest global institution, with a concert-like design and an ambitious agenda "to save the world," exaggerated fears and hopes can be loaded onto the G20. Some critics see it as a threat to the universalistic spirit of the UN; others fear it as a means by which new forms of discipline and punishment can be meted out to non-members. With these various forms of contestation in mind,[57] the full roster of this fault-finding will be discussed in more depth in the next chapter.

Equally, even the foremost champions of the G20 express increased anxiety about whether the forum can hold the course, allowing it to morph seamlessly from a crisis committee of the big and the rich into a steering committee for the world. As the recession drags on, through a number of unanticipated extra episodes (most notably the protracted euro crisis), it is much harder to maintain coordination within the forum. Instead of working together, as they did when the world economy took a synchronized dive in late 2008,[58] the members increasingly looked as though they wanted to take autonomous action.

Before looking more closely at the future of the G20, major questions about its origins and development must be addressed in some depth. A nuanced retrospective in this fashion is important as the off-the-shelf model for the G20 was not the only option available. Nor was there even a guarantee that the G20 could work even as a crisis committee, never mind as a more sustained project. After all, the record of concerts at the time of financial shocks is not a good one. The failure of the 1933 London Monetary and Economic Conference bears out this pessimistic outlook. So do the obstacles located in the way of making the Cancún Conference in October 1981 a one-off (and very polarized) event.

The organizational evolution of the G20 also needs elaboration. Derived from its claims of equality, one of the main strengths of the institution is assumed to be the pluralistic form of leadership. Such an evolution in turn is linked to the relative decline of the United States and a shift of power more generally from the North to the global South. Such a process, however, was not dramatic or immediate. Rather, in terms of decision making it took place over a two-year period. The mode of leadership featured from Washington, to London, and on to Pittsburgh was very different from what appeared later on in Toronto, Seoul, Cannes, and subsequently.

The G20 stands at the apex of innovative thinking and re-crafting of the institutional design of global governance. It remains, nevertheless, very much a work in progress. Brought into being through the rupture of a financial crisis, it is in many ways technical and remote from high politics. Viewed as a club of pivotal states, its importance is embellished by the way it has become networked through other institutions. It has revitalized the IMF, expanded the membership and the agenda of the Financial Stability Forum and transformed it into the Financial Stability Board (FSB). It has acted as a catalyst for some additional reforms, yet it also has been dragged into slower motion through its work via the Basel III process. Viewed as a rearrangement of the relationship between the old G8 and the rising BRICS or wider group encompassing BRICSAM (BRICS plus Mexico), and/or KIA, it has also revitalized the concept and role of a second tier beyond the high-profile rising states.

The need for an appreciation of the multifaceted nature of the G20 in terms of its context, contours and impact is a central theme of this book. If highly detailed, what jumps out in each of the chapters is the richness of the institutional design of the G20.

1 Rebalancing world order

- Changing global equations
- The unstoppable momentum of the G20 vs. the immovable resistance of the G8
- The logic of G reform
- The logic of policy coordination
- Debating the pros and cons
- Conclusion

This chapter builds on the Introduction in looking at the challenges and promises of innovation in global governance. We discussed in the Introduction how the G8 and the United Nations (UN) have functioned as the two paradigmatic institutions of global governance. Although the G8 has been perceived as more efficient than the UN, and the latter is often described as possessing a unique international legitimacy flowing from its universal membership, we also noted how each has suffered legitimacy and efficiency deficits. The twin crises intensified for both institutions with the growing misalignment of global structural reconfigurations—of economic weight, military power, and diplomatic clout—with the distribution of membership and decision-making authority in the institutions of global governance. Such considerations provided some considerable logic for institutional reform, especially in terms of policy coordination at the apex of the system. As this chapter details, however, logic came up against enormous obstacles, both with respect to a defense of the institutional status quo and the "devil in the details" about what G reform would look like in practice. Before the G20 came into being there had to be a complex debate about the rationale and exercise of reform.

Changing global equations

From 1000 AD to 1800 AD, Asia, Africa, and Latin America—today's developing world—accounted for 65–75 percent of global population and income. Europe rode to world dominance through the industrial revolution, innovations in transport and communications, and the ideology and practice of colonialism, during which the developing countries suffered dramatic relative losses. From 1870 to 1950, Asia's per capita income plummeted from one-half to one-10th of West European levels.[1] The developing countries, led by Asia, have been bouncing back in economic output, industrialization, and trade. The importance of Brazil, China, and India lies in their future economic potential that already has translated into present political clout.

The early nineteenth century saw the displacement of Asia by Britain as the dominant actor of the times; the early twentieth century, of Britain by the United States. The early twenty-first century may be witnessing the beginning of the end of US and Western influence and the re-emergence of China and India. As part of the shifting global order, US influence and prestige have fallen but it remains the most influential international and the only truly global actor; Japan continues its slow decline; Russia is marking time; Europe's reach is shorter than its grasp; India is starting to recapture world attention and interest; and the real winner is China with an ascendant economy, growing poise, and expanding soft power assets.

The United States has no peer as a military power but cannot impose Pax Americana. Instead of demonstrating unlimited US power, Iraq and Afghanistan brutally exposed the limits to US power to impose American will on local populations willing to fight back. Paul Kennedy's thesis of implosion caused by unavoidable overreach on the inexorable logic of imperial rise and fall may yet prove correct,[2] but not in the near term. Washington can still veto most international action and no major world problem can be settled by working against it. The United States is still the guarantor of the transatlantic, trans-Pacific, and trans-American security orders. All three regions are caught between the desire to keep the United States fully engaged in the region to underwrite stability and prosperity, and the search for a sharper and autonomous regional identity.

Within the larger paradox of global governance—of how the world is governed to demonstrate attributes of order, stability, and regularity even in the absence of world government—there is a second paradox of US power. For several decades, the United States has been experiencing a slow but steady erosion of relative primacy. At the same time, as UN Secretary-General Kofi Annan's High-level Panel had argued, growing interdependence has fostered the realization of mutual vulnerabilities and shared insecurities, and hence a shared responsibility.[3] The United States is expected by many to take the lead in managing the systemic and structural challenges, but to refrain from doing so unilaterally. For the exercise of power to be efficient and legitimate, decisions on using it must be shared. This produces what Graeme Herd calls "coalitional primacy" as a successor to the primacy of the unipolar moment.[4]

Beside the United States, the other major world repository of democratic legitimacy, wealth, and power is Europe.[5] Where the United States sends soldiers to impose an increasingly fraying Pax Americana, Europe sends inspectors to expand its soft power reach through standards, rules, and regulations. However, this is within the union an inadequate recompense for the lack of material power to shape world events. Europe is less than the sum of its parts. In the Middle East, for example, Europe is the ATM that dispenses 1 billion euros annually without any visible influence over the Israel–Palestine conflict. In 2010–12 the continent was swept by successive waves of Euro-pessimism as the debt crisis hit one country after another and both internal and international confidence in the eurozone was badly shaken. The crisis brutally exposed the tensions and contradictions of the single European project, in particular the folly of a single currency without full fiscal integration and political union.

The vitality and survival of international organizations depend on two factors: the capacity to change and adapt and the quality of their governance. The center of the multilateral order cannot hold if the power and influence embedded in international institutions is significantly misaligned with the distribution of power in the real world. A global financial, political, and moral rebalancing is currently underway. From 2000 to 2010, the share of global GDP of the world's three leading emerging economies—Brazil, China, and India—doubled and their share of world trade almost tripled. Their dynamism and optimism is in marked contrast to Euro-pessimism.

Table 1.1 shows the steadily rising share of world product and trade accounted for by the 11 non-G8 members of the G20. Between 1980 and 2008, while the G8 combined gross domestic product (GDP) grew by 470 percent, comprising 54.6 percent of world growth in GDP, that of the G11 grew by 722 percent, accounting for 21.8 percent of total world growth. With respect to trade over the same period, the G8 grew by 621 percent and the G11 by 1,387 percent, accounting for 37.8 and 21.6 percent shares of growth in world trade, respectively.[6] In other words, first, the G20 accounted for 76.4 percent of world economic output and 59.4 percent of world trade growth; and second, even though their share of growth is smaller, the G11 have strongly outpaced the G8 both in GDP and trade growth. Moreover, the imbalance of economic performance between the G8 and G11 has grown more marked in the last few years during the global financial crisis.

Reinforcing the core narrative and messages of Table 1.1, Table 1.2 shows the importance of China and India in leading and sustaining the

Table 1.1 Relative shares of world population, economic product and trade, G8 and G11

	1976		1997		2008	
	G8	G11	G8	G11	G8	G11
World population	17.17*	49.29*	14.34	50.11	13.10	49.42
World product	56.25*	17.36*	52.26	23.35	45.25	29.21
World trade	51.11	9.43	48.63	13.64	39.40	20.35

Notes:
G8: Canada, France, Germany (West Germany in 1976), Italy, Japan, Russia, UK, USA.
G11: Argentina, Australia, Brazil, China, India, Indonesia, Mexico, Saudi Arabia, South Africa, South Korea, Turkey.
The "20th" member is the European Union, International Monetary Fund (IMF) and World Bank.
*1980 is the earliest available year, where marked; world product is measured in gross domestic product (GDP) using purchasing power parity (PPP) dollars; world trade is measured in total mercantile trade.
Source: *World Economic Outlook October 2009: Sustaining the Recovery* (Washington, DC: IMF, 2009), www.imf.org/external/pubs/ft/weo/2009/02/pdf/text.pdf; World Trade Organization, "Time Series on International Trade," Statistics Database (Geneva: WTO), stat.wto.org/StatisticalProgram/WSDBStatProgramHome.aspx?Language=E.

world economy and then recovery. While the outlook for the advanced economies was assessed as "continuing, but weak and bumpy, expansion," with the possibility of the euro area and/or the United States falling back into recession, for emerging market economies "growth is expected to remain fairly robust."[7] Unlike previous decades, therefore, the new unity of the global South, led by such contemporary heavyweights as Brazil, China, India, and South Africa, is based on a position of strength, not weakness. The Doha "Development" Trade Round, begun in 2001, was meant to be completed in 2005 but has been stuck in a stalemate. It resulted in a new coalition of the global South led by the Big Three of Brazil, China, and India, the rising power and influence of which, interrogating the waning hegemonic ability of the status quo economic powers to write the rules of the game for everyone, has produced several false starts and as many false conclusions.

The unstoppable momentum of the G20 vs. the immovable resistance of the G8

Looking back at the emergence of a new forum at the leaders' level, there is an air of inevitability about it. The pressures for moving beyond the

Table 1.2 GDP growth for G8, Brazil, China, India, and Mexico, 2007–12

	2007	2008	2009	2010	Projections	
					2011	2012
World output	5.2	3	-0.7	5.1	4	4
Advanced economies	2.7	0.6	-3.7	3.1	1.6	1.9
Canada	2.5	0.4	-2.8	3.2	2.1	1.9
France	2.3	0.3	-2.6	1.4	1.7	1.4
Germany	2.5	1.2	-5.1	3.6	2.7	1.3
Italy	1.6	-1	-5.2	1.3	0.6	0.3
Japan	2.3	-0.7	-6.3	4	-0.5	2.3
Russia	8.1	5.6	-7.8	4	4.3	4.1
UK	2.6	0.7	-4.9	1.4	1.1	1.6
US	2.1	0.4	-3.5	3	1.5	1.8
Brazil	5.7	5.1	-0.6	7.5	3.8	3.6
China	13	9	9.2	10.3	9.5	9
India	9.4	7.3	6.8	10.1	7.8	7.5
Mexico	3.3	1.3	-6.2	5.4	3.8	3.6

Sources: *World Economic Outlook October 2009: Sustaining the Recovery* (Washington, DC: IMF, 2009), 2, www.imf.org/external/pubs/ft/weo/2009/02/pdf/text.pdf; *World Economic Outlook September 2011: Slowing Growth, Rising Risks* (Washington, DC: IMF, 2011), 2, www.imf.org/external/pubs/ft/weo/2011/02/index.htm.

established G8 group, with the dual crisis of legitimacy and efficiency, mounted. The logic of bringing in emerging economic powers to the "high table" of international affairs seemed unassailable. Timothy Garton Ash put it forcefully in 2008: "The dangers of climate change, nuclear proliferation, disease, and poverty—not to mention the fragile state of globalized capitalism—demand a more credible and representative cast at the annual intergovernmental summit. As Asia rises, it is ever more absurd that the world's unofficial top table has a seat for Italy but not for China."[8]

Moreover, the means of bringing the new forum to life seemed available. Any initiative on UN Security Council (UNSC) reform had to run the gauntlet of a highly formalized and politicized process, with ample space for oppositional forces to mobilize and fight back.[9] Changes via the G8 took place in a very different format. As a self-elected forum, with no legal status, the G8 had considerable flexibility to do what it wanted. The original G5 could morph into a G7, and (under pressure especially from President Bill Clinton) the G7 could embrace Russia and become a G8.[10]

Intellectually, good arguments could be mustered and publicized via the efforts of a number of think tanks, and in Paul Martin, the project of G reform had an outstanding champion akin to Valéry Giscard d'Estaing and Helmut Schmidt, the leaders of France and Germany who had created the original G5.

Logic and ideas were necessary for G reform to take place. Yet, until there was the necessary shock in the system to induce change, the reform process remained stalled. A subsidiary problem was that the reformers themselves were divided on the detailed elements of G reform. Martin championed the notion of an L20 at the leaders' level, derived from his experience with G20 Finance from the 1997–98 Asian crisis and its mishandling by the International Monetary Fund (IMF). However, as previously noted, this format was not totally dominant. The alternative ideas of a G13 or G14 remained in play through to the time of the financial crisis.

Without a catalyst, however, the reform project could not overcome the formidable obstacles of embedded interests. The status quo remained more attractive to most of the G7/8 members than a leap into the unknown. The United States, under George W. Bush, was reluctant to share power unless there was a clear and present rationale for doing so. Reinforcing these instincts, there were concerns that such a revamped summit could be used to "gang up" on the United States. Smaller members of the G8 worried about a possible loss of status.

It is misleading to suggest also that the G20 attracted only enthusiasm from a normative perspective. While the idea of G reform continued to draw devotees, detractors focused on what they considered to be the flaws in the model. For some critics, G reform was marred because of the self-selected nature of any reformed forum. Although expansive, any G continued to have the same defects as the G8. For others, the problem was the explicit bias toward privileging the big members in the global system. Moreover, the G20 has the embedded characteristics of what Michael Zürn calls "executive" multilateralism.[11] The G20 is a classic expression of elite or top-down multilateralism (or more precisely plurilateralism); it is, after all, "reforming from the top."[12] The composition of the G20 around the old and new "bigs" is based on exclusionary principles and practices. Instead of precipitating a new form of expanded inclusion, therefore, an embedded form of institutional exclusion with distinctive privileges of membership is promoted, albeit with more legitimacy than that of the G8 process.

The logic of G reform

The logic of extended inclusion through the process of G reform adjoined to a variety of other rationales. In terms of membership, the whole premise of G reform is to go beyond the tightly defined limits of the

G8, based on an extension of the equality of membership. Operating on the basis of this principle is very different from the concept of "outreach" as advocated by the defenders of the concert in place. The eminent G8 watcher and former British diplomat Sir Nicholas Bayne recommended, for example, that leaders should maintain the practice, begun at Okinawa in 2000, of inviting a group of leaders from developing countries to meet them before the summit proper. He argued that the admission of new members to the G8 itself, however, should be approached with caution. The G8's great merit was the fact that "it is small and compact enough for the leaders to have a direct exchange around the table. This quality would be lost if extra members were added in the interest of making the G8 more widely representative."[13]

Another feature that adds weight to the progressive credentials of the G reform initiative is the global—and interregional—dimension. All of the other plurilateral initiatives have had an element of "we-ness" about them. In terms of concert plurilateralism, it is precisely the informality of the crucial top-down case—the G8—that produces the club-like atmosphere of the summit. Although tested by disagreements on a wide number of issues (most dramatically, of course, on the Iraq war) the glue that has held this forum together has been a shared mindset on basic rules and processes concerning "liberal democracy, individual liberty, and the rule of law."[14]

Even with bottom-up cases of new multilateralism, the bond among the actors has been a form of "like-mindedness." In addition to the amplified role of many established middle powers, including the Nordic countries, Canada, Australia, and New Zealand, an extended group of activist states became involved. Of these countries, the new, diplomatically active model citizen South Africa stands out. Taking a cue from the classic middle power copybook, it played a large role both on the landmines campaign and within the "Lifeline Nations," a group of states advocating an independent International Criminal Court (ICC) and independent prosecutor as opposed to an ICC under the control of the UNSC.[15]

Extending the G8 to a group of highly "unlike" states, therefore, is an idea that is both ambitious and risky. At an instrumental level the logic from a reformist (albeit not transformational) perspective is unassailable: to absorb rising powers such as China, India, Brazil, and others from the South into the longstanding club with all its informal rules, patterns of socialization, and voice and participation opportunities. This integrative motivation is tied in turn to the high level of anxiety about the future global order not only in the peripheral actors, but at the core of the global system. For from an institutional point of view, it is clear that if these emerging powers are not brought in and accommodated, they could concentrate their activities on other clubs like the BRICS (Brazil, Russia, India, China, South Africa) grouping, as we saw in the last chapter, and competitive activity with respect to rule making,[16] as the fourth BRICS summit in New Delhi in 2012 foreshadowed.

A third feature of G reform that lends it some credibility as an agent of change is its concern with legitimacy as well as effectiveness.[17] The greatest source of contestation (as well paradoxically as its strength in terms of club cohesion) was its self-selected (and un-elected) status. To China, India, as well as most other outsiders it was precisely this feature that marked the G8 as an illegitimate body, in contrast to the universal form of formal multilateralism via the UN system.

The G8 was meant to function as a body coordinating the practices of its own membership. This role was performed in a dualistic fashion: with a keen eye on both the one big G8 table and on the individual domestic tables back at home.[18] However, it has been a role that all members have had a stake in performing. In terms of managing the affairs of the rising powers, the G8 has little credibility. It could not simply dictate to others; it had to engage with the "upstarts" in the system. Thus with respect to the extra-UN sanctions imposed on Iran by the West, the day before the fourth BRICS summit in New Delhi, India's Commerce and Industry Minister Anand Sharma confirmed that "We respect UN resolutions." Similarly, China's Trade Minister insisted that China was "not obliged to follow any domestic laws and rules of any particular country."[19] The summit communiqué also signaled opposition to the US and European efforts to isolate Syria and Iran as preludes to regime change or war. It emphasized the importance of peaceful transition and diplomatic dialogue in "a Syrian-led inclusive process" that respects its independence, territorial integrity, and sovereignty.[20] "The situation concerning Iran cannot be allowed to escalate into conflict," the five leaders added.[21]

Given the growing willingness and capacity of the rest to challenge any consensus coming out of the G8, the way forward was to re-configure pivotal forums that enhanced both efficiency and legitimacy. As will be noted in the next chapter, G20 Finance composed of finance ministers and central bank governors provided a model in terms of effective problem solving. Triggered by the thinking and actions of key members of the Clinton administration—and finance ministers such as Canada's Paul Martin, Germany's Hans Eichel, and Britain's Gordon Brown in the North, and South Africa's Trevor Manuel from the South—G20 Finance was not only able to deliver some immediate tangible outcomes in terms of its core concerns of managing financial shocks and working toward crisis prevention. In addition, it was able to build momentum on a much wider agenda, most notably the action plan on terrorist financing with special attention to freezing terrorist assets and the implementation of an international strategy as a result of the 11 September 2001 tragedy.

Just as importantly, the process of G reform had to demonstrate that it could balance the efficiency agenda with some concern for equity. Again we should not exaggerate this tendency to seek a balance between the economic market and the social, but neither should we ignore the importance attached by the G20—and even more so the putative agenda of the L20[22]—to focus on the need to try to "shape" globalization in the interests of society.[23]

G reform offered in principle the prospect of extending this range of policy interests. Martin supported his argument for the L20 not on the basis of economic or strategic issues but on the need to deal collectively with social/health pandemics such as avian flu.[24] This shift allowed G reform, through the L20 model, to have some considerable advantages over rival forms of plurilateralism. From a top-down perspective, the G8 appeared to have passed its sell-by date. Klaus Schwab, for instance, dismissed the G8 as the guardians of the status quo, reflecting an outdated vision of the industrialized past.[25]

From a bottom-up perspective, L20 represented a signal that the status quo is too exclusionary—and that it needs to change. The main target of the global dissent movement is not national states but the neoliberal vision linked to corporate expansion over the realm of governance and the entrenchment of a homogenous "one size fits all" agenda. While the proposal for the creation of an extended summit of leaders may be viewed as part of a process of political globalization far removed from the ordinary concerns of individual citizens, "nothing could be further from the truth … By delegating authority to increase sovereignty, political globalization will overcome the democratic deficit and give governments the power to implement the policies their citizens demand."[26]

To put a positive hue on G20 via the L20 model is not to dismiss the normative criticisms. The G20—akin to the G8—operates fundamentally as a club of state representatives (albeit an enlarged one including members from the South and also representatives from the international financial institutions and the EU). Indeed, it is this club-like atmosphere that is the enticing feature for the champions of an extended G20 into a Leaders 20. As Martin concluded, the G20 avoids:

> … "us" versus "them" mentality that bedevils so many international meetings, and it has worked remarkably well—because peer pressure

is often a very effective way to force decisions. We believe a similar approach among leaders could help crack some of the toughest issues facing the world. We need to get the right mix of countries in the same room, talking without a set script.[27]

It is this aspect of the framework that fundamentally differentiates the L20 initiative from the bottom-up projects of new multilateralism, such as the landmines and the ICC.[28] All these initiatives operated as fluid networks, with only rudimentary formal institutionalism (as illustrated by the establishment in 1999 of the so-called Lysøen Group on human security). Links among like-minded actors, state and non-state, were honed and consolidated, whether through one central group (the International Campaign to Ban Landmines), or multiple partners (diverse groups such as Amnesty International, Human Rights Watch, and the Lawyers Committee for Human Rights on the ICC).

A related key question for the G20 concerns its shift from being an exclusive state-centric club. Anne-Marie Slaughter most notably expands the debate about an L20 summit not just as a contrast with the prevailing status quo but as the centerpiece of and conduit to a "network of networks."[29] An L20 in terms of this scenario would thus act as an informal hub or steering committee, with ideas and practices flowing both out from and into the L20, to and from other networks.

Such an approach is rife with questions, not the least being the formidable bureaucratic obstacles standing in the way of opening up the process to non-state actors. However, the model also contains considerable opportunities to move ahead of the curve in innovative thinking and design. As one of the authors of this book argued in 2004, cast in networking or brains trust terms, the attractions of an L20 are increased still further as it "would be a better forum for framing the issues, outlining choices, making decisions for setting, even anticipating, the agenda; for framing the rules, including for dispute settlement; for pledging and mobilizing resources; for implementing collective decisions; and for monitoring progress and [receiving] mid-term corrections and adjustments."[30]

The logic of policy coordination

The concerted logic of G8 reform places enormous responsibility on the heads of governments. Leaders must not only be willing and able to buy into the idea to get it off the ground. They must be willing and able to take on the level of commitment—with many attendant risks—to make the G20 summit proposal work. They must move ahead and deal with the selected issues that rise to the apex of this forum in a fashion that their ministers and officials cannot (whatever their own level of political acumen and technical skill). They must be able to see the way to recognize and jump over all the hurdles placed in front of "niche" initiatives both at their individual national level and at the collective group level.[31] They must be able to mobilize the requisite and often diverse follow-up at the bureaucratic level.

On top of vitality there is the need for an expanded G summit to provide some degree of coordination and oversight over issues that have moved onto their radar. Key to this notion is the wish to cut through the so-called silo effect at the institutional level, especially as "there is no other representative forum mandated to address ... inter-sectoral and inter-institutional issues."[32] Nonetheless, by devising this forum to be directed from the top down, it also plays to the strength of the proposal in that it allows leaders to adapt better to complexity, make choices, and cut through turf and distributional issues.

Debating the pros and cons

The generalized appeal of G reform prior to the financial crisis rested on two firm platforms. The first relates to the crisis of legitimacy facing the web of established institutions, especially, as noted in the last chapter, the G8 as the "club of the rich" but also the UN and the Bretton Woods institutions. The second source of attraction for G reform was due to the intrinsic appeal of its own institutional design. In terms of form, the transformation of G20 Finance to a summit for leaders brought back much of the original features of the G7. Instead of the carefully scripted communiqués as presented at recent G8 summits, the G20 could revert back to an informal and free-flowing format. In terms of scope of membership, a G20 along these lines offers a balance between the exclusivity of the G8 and the diffuseness associated with many other sites, ranging from the UN to the World Trade Organization (WTO). In terms of intensity, this mode of G20 governance balances a concentration on specific issue areas with a degree of representation wide enough to accommodate both legitimacy and delivery.

An emphasis on this generalized appeal of an upgraded G20 is not to overlook specific normative critiques and practical obstacles facing this model. An "end run" around existing institutions might open up some creative possibilities on a problem-solving basis but it might also have the effect of further delegitimizing the UN system. The question of the relationship of the G8 to the G20 as a summit for leaders remains unsettled. Can the former morph seamlessly into the latter? If so, will there be a "big bang" transformation or an incremental and staged process? What of the overhang between the established structure of the G20 as a meeting between finance ministers, central bank governors and representatives of the Bretton Woods institutions, to one featuring the engagement by heads of government? Finally, there is the sensitive question of the composition and configuration of this new G forum. As the profile and salience of the G20 is raised, so will the stakes attached to who is in and who is out.

The advocates of G reform were aware of this list of critiques and obstacles. However, they were not deterred in the pursuit of this model. For one thing, the need for such a breakthrough was simply too great. The G20 as a site for a summit of leaders represented a bold step that was badly needed to break the dysfunctional nature—and immobilization—found throughout the architecture of international governance. Indeed, without this initiative, there was an accentuated risk that anti-system or anti-globalization forces would be ascendant, filling the gap of legitimacy left by eroding alternative institutions.

Nor did the supporters of this option entertain much hope that other institutions could fill the necessary opportunity space themselves—thus negating their own prospects for becoming substitute catalysts for change by default. The prospects of reform of the UNSC—notwithstanding the rash of proposals—were played down. Although the image and functional effectiveness of the Bretton Woods institutions attracted strong debate and varying opinions, the embedded quality of the operational mode of these bodies was reinforced, especially in terms of their representativeness.

The essential intergovernmental nature of an upgraded G20 forum was a source of additional strength and support for the recommendation. Bottom-up "new" multilateralism has become an important ingredient in the architecture of international governance. The potential value of building inclusive devices for nongovernmental organizations (NGOs) as part of an ongoing process of dialogue, networking, and facility for governance increased the attractiveness of the model of G reform.[33] Nonetheless, a differentiation continued to be made between the role of NGOs for agenda-setting and ultimate decision-making by authorized governmental representatives. The fundamental attraction of G reform as a summit for leaders was that it offers a site to meet as a core network of governmental leaders, not an all-encompassing state-societal forum.

The key ingredient of "new" multilateralism for the revamping of the G8 was the opening up of this site to participation by a full complement of leaders from the South. With respect to motivation, this expansion was anticipated to be crucial for offsetting the attractions of other sites and strategies for some key leaders, such as a heightened orientation toward other Gs dominated by developing countries on an individual basis. Collectively, a central attraction of this move was to provide a focus on bridge-building between the leaders of the G8 and selected leaders from developing countries (a focus helped by the fact that individual countries were not picked off to join the G8 and hence away from groups dominated by the South). With respect to process, many advocates of G reform showcased the membership already established within G20 Finance as the best option to proceed with, albeit even some of them desired some flexibility of how this pattern of membership (heavy on regional hegemons) could be nuanced in the future.

The question of the relationship between the new G20 and the old G8 also was not firmly shut. To be sure, one strong line of reasoning supported the view that the best way forward was a merger between them. This scenario was viewed as consistent with the development of the G8 itself, not only through the addition of Canada, Italy, and Russia to the original members, but also the inclusion on a number of occasions of leaders from developing countries for a portion of the summit. Other arguments were made, however, that the transformation of the G20 should be done autonomously through a revamping of that institution from a meeting of finance ministers to leaders. The G8 and G20 would thus exist in parallel, just as the G7/8 had continued to do so. Whereas the merger argument was reinforced with references to the need for directness, grand design, and logistical concerns about a proliferation of meetings, the parallel model was predicated on the assumption that it was better to bend than break the existing institutional architecture.

Another scenario was directed at improving compliance with international rules and the pursuit of "best practices" by targeting the G20 as a summit of leaders addressing specific issue areas. Building on the notion that the credibility of the G reform process comes not from any extension of formal authority but as an expression of engagement by an extended set of leaders, the need before it was to gain success as a global problem-solver on a case-by-case basis. The most ambitious scenario with respect to the purpose of G reform was as a forum with extensive coordination and oversight responsibilities for global governance and the management of globalization. This objective is directed at enhancing the efficiency and legitimacy functions as well as strengthening accountability.

Both the symbolic optics and delivery application of such an approach hold some considerable appeal. The G20 initiative does not have the look of the "coalitions of the willing" put together on an ad hoc basis. Nor does it have diplomatic connotations associated with established institutions (an exclusive membership and/or veto power). The focus on networking—while privileging the interaction among leaders—permits spillover into a wide number of subsidiary and interconnected networks at both governmental and nongovernmental levels. Instead of requiring an elaborate "bricks and mortar" bureaucracy (or extensive secretariat), this model for an enhanced G20 remained lean, selective, and results driven. Government silos were broken down under the weight of top-down political pressures.

Conclusion

This chapter has provided the context for global governance innovation through the G20. To its advocates, the pattern of governance attached to G reform would defuse—although not completely eliminate—the criticisms facing the initiative. The potential of the initiative was not overblown in terms of its ability to deal with unlimited and intractable issues. Yet, by thinking out of the box, providing guidance at the apex of power and building on success, the prospect of G reform gaining traction had a catalytic effect on other institutions. While giving explicit pride of place procedurally to governmental representatives, this model contains an impetus for extending accountability in both its aims and results. Substantively, a new mode of summitry at the apex of the international institutional architecture had the capacity to fill a logical and necessary need in terms of filling governance gaps.

There was a two-step process in this reform process. As Chapter 2 will detail, the initial stage of reform was not at the leaders' level but at the level of finance ministers and governors of central banks. This more technical phase allowed a model that could eventually be built on for the breakthrough to the G20 at the leaders' level. If the two institutions had different actors and approaches, however, both were precipitated by major shocks to the system via financial crises. Whereas the G20 at the leaders' level was brought into being as a result of the global financial crisis of 2008, as elaborated upon in Chapter 2 the catalyst for the G20 Finance was the Asian financial crisis of 1997–98.

2 G20 Finance as prelude

- The Asian financial crisis of 1997–98
- The push for legitimacy without compromising efficiency
- Transcending or trapped in the legitimacy gap?
- Transcending a technical orientation
- The catalytic effect: turning the G20 into a leaders' summit
- Conclusion: from visionary policy innovation to reactive political opportunism

The G20 at the leaders' level did not emerge as a blank slate or tabula rasa. In many ways, it built on the experience of putting the original G20 Finance into place. As with the leaders' summit, the catalyst for the emergence of G20 Finance was a financial crisis. As with the creation of the leaders' summit in October 2008, the United States was willing to accept some forms of decisive leadership. If shaped as a top-down, club-oriented enterprise, the Clinton administration exhibited a strong degree of support for a form of multilateral problem solving. As with the post-2008 elevated G20 summit, the G20 Finance evolved from an institution with a crisis committee focus, acting as both an immediate shock absorber and an instrument designed to enhance crisis prevention in the future, to a forum with a more expansive agenda.

This chapter explores how the legitimacy and effectiveness of the established institutional structure—especially pertaining to the role of the International Monetary Fund (IMF)—were eroded by the Asian financial crisis. Core policy entrepreneurs from G7 countries, notably Paul Martin and Lawrence (Larry) Summers, moved to supplement the work of the IMF with new informal forums made up of key actors from a relatively small group of countries. Such a breakthrough, if done in an incremental fashion with a technical focus, provided the main building block for the G20 at the leaders' level when another formidable crisis hit in 2008.

To highlight these similarities is not to overdraw the parallels to an unwarranted degree. The shocks triggering G20 Finance became largely identified with a specific region, as witnessed by the common usage of the label, the Asian financial crisis. Even this label is misleading, as the crisis hit hardest a particular cluster of countries, namely Thailand, South Korea, Indonesia, and Malaysia.[1] The strong reaction at the global institutional level was generated not by the East Asian crisis per se but the fear of contagion. Notwithstanding these difference, however, one fundamental theme jumps out in this chapter as it does in later chapters: the firm connection between crises and institutional reform. When crises hit coordinated action becomes possible, using ideas and methods borrowed from previous periods of time.

The Asian financial crisis of 1997–98

The power of international capital and the symbiotic relationship between political authorities and market structures was vividly demonstrated across Asia in 1997–98. The defining characteristic of Asia-Pacific salience in world affairs until then had been economic dynamism. The Asian "tigers" grew thrice as fast as the average of the Organisation for Economic Co-operation and Development (OECD) economies in the 1980s–90s. In the quarter century between 1960 and 1995, the East Asian economies produced the fastest rise in incomes for the highest number of people in human history (see Table 2.1).

Table 2.1 The Asian miracle

	GDP per capita	GDP growth		
	(purchasing power parity dollars, 1995)	(annual average %)		
		1970–79	1980–89	1990–96
Hong Kong	23,900	9.2	7.5	5.0
Singapore	22,600	9.4	7.2	8.3
Taiwan	13,200	10.2	8.1	6.3
South Korea	11,900	9.3	8.0	7.7
Malaysia	10,400	8.0	5.7	8.8
Thailand	8,000	7.3	7.2	8.6
Indonesia	3,800	7.8	5.7	7.2
China	3,100	7.5	9.3	10.1
Industrial countries	19,400	3.4	2.6	2.0

Source: *The Economist*, 1 March 1997, 23.

The bubble burst with a currency crisis that began in Thailand. Its government was forced to abandon the peg of the baht to the US dollar on 2 July 1997 after a sustained attack on the local currency by international speculators. As market players responded to the herd instinct, the contagion spread quickly to Malaysia (August), Indonesia (September), Hong Kong (October), and South Korea (November). A brief ripple was felt even on Wall Street and in the major European finance and stock markets. By 21 January 1998, compared to their values on 31 December 1996, stock markets had tumbled to between one-half and one-fifth across the region. Indonesia was the worst affected: its rupiah fell to 21 percent and the stock market to 15 percent of their earlier values.

Attempts to halt the slide in currency values, stock market prices, and investor confidence—to stop the economic crisis from turning into a financial meltdown—were led by the IMF in partnership with the World Bank and the Asian Development Bank. They stepped in to help with the reform of the banking sector and capital markets and to provide better social safety nets. By the end of February 1998, the situation seemed to have stabilized in most countries, with the notable exception of Indonesia.

The international response to the Asian crisis highlighted deficiencies in the architecture of global economic management. The IMF prescriptions were questioned by Western analysts as well as Asian policy makers. They were contested on five fronts:

- For the "moral hazard" of interfering with market forces by absolving or rescuing international creditors from the consequences of bad investment decisions;
- For being excessively contractionary;
- For the rigid application of doctrinaire remedies developed in response to a different mix of policy failures in the entirely different context of Latin America;
- For eroding economic sovereignty; and
- For ignoring the social and political contexts and repercussions.

The IMF's macroeconomic policy conditions called for higher interest rates, low inflation targets ("price stability") despite the currency devaluation, cuts in government spending, and the termination or refusal of aid to troubled companies and banks. The net effect of such policies was deflationary. Companies and banks were killed under the weight of the tight fiscal and monetary policies. The conventional austerity measures deepened the self-fulfilling investor panic instead of easing it. They also turned what had been sound investment projects into problematic ones by feeding the cycle of self-sustaining decline in asset prices.

The IMF's prescription, of a squeeze on central bank credit and budget deficits, was based on the diagnosis of the ailment of government profligacy afflicting Latin America a decade earlier, the main symptoms of which were high budget deficits and public-sector debts.[2] Across East Asia in 1997, monetary policies were sound, budgets were in surplus, current account deficits ranged from 4 to 5 percent of gross domestic product (GDP) (except for Thailand at 8 percent), and savings rates were high. The main problems were private-, not public-sector debt; misallocated investment, not excessive consumption and inadequate saving; and a crisis of confidence amidst sound economic fundamentals. The requirement in Asia arguably was for counter-recessionary policies and selective aid to local financial institutions to minimize economic slowdown and restore confidence instead of aggravating its loss. A related lesson of the Asian crisis and the IMF response to it was the need for the Fund to acknowledge the reality of integrated financial markets. The IMF could no longer fly in experts to individual countries on a case-by-case basis; in a world of globalized capital markets, we need institutions of international economic management that can cope with multi-country crises.

The push for legitimacy without compromising efficiency

For some months the currency collapse across Asia outstripped the economic remedies prescribed by the IMF, which in turn eroded governmental and popular faith in the Fund. Many Asians concluded that the crisis had worsened because of, not despite, the bailout schemes for Thailand, Indonesia, and South Korea.[3] Paul Martin of Canada and Larry Summers of the United States took the lead in creating G20 Finance in recognition of the governance deficits as well as financial failures of the Asian crisis in the late 1990s.

By contrast, the 2008 crisis was perceived as a global phenomenon. Although a school of thought had developed that the big rising states and/ or emerging markets were decoupled from the reverse contagion (with the economic shocks spreading from the established industrial countries to the global South) the dominant scenario was considered to be the risk of a return to the great depression of the 1930s. This fear concentrated the minds of policy makers in China, India, Brazil, as well as the G8 countries—in other words those outside of the G8 but in G20 Finance.

Because of these differences in scope, from a critical perspective, the academic responses have been very different to the two episodes of institution building. Given the magnitude of the crisis in 2008, there was little in the way of a contrarian reaction about the intensity of the response. The main source of disagreement was the question of the G20 versus the United Nations as the forum of choice for ending the crisis and mitigating its harm. Only after the immediacy of the crisis began to wear off did the G20 come to be viewed by some observers more as a power grab by big countries from both the old and new members of the establishment.[4]

The reform process animated through G20 Finance was interpreted by its critics as a consolidation—not a loosening—of power by the G8 and by the ideology of neoliberalism more generally. Notwithstanding the signs that the G20 was operated through a culture of formal equality, and that the non-G8 members developed an enhanced comfort zone within this ambit, this forum was commonly portrayed as a process signifying, not a new mode of global governance, but a more concerted form of discipline emanating from the traditional core of the international system.[5]

What is most striking about the competing interpretations of the establishment of G20 Finance is the dichotomy between the emphasis of practitioners on efficiency and the accent placed by critics on legitimacy gaps. For the actual club insiders, the formation represented an extremely successful dynamic to solve a major collective action problem. Facing a crisis that had the potential to spread, the solution was not sought in the status quo. Priority was placed instead on looking to a fast and more inclusive initiative for global economic governance.

In journalistic accounts of the creation of G20 Finance, the theme that comes out is that imposed solutions were the wrong course of action. The right approach was to bring more countries around the table. The champion of this new model was Martin, the finance minister of Canada. However, when Martin called on Lawrence Summers, the Clinton nominee for treasury secretary, in April 1999, there was instant buy-in. In a classic variation of informal "back of the envelope" diplomacy, Martin and Summers put together a framework that constituted the basic ingredients of G20 Finance.

Such personalized efforts were required to break out of the status quo. As in the move toward the G20 as a leaders' summit, there was resistance among some European countries about diluting the influence of the G8. Akin to the reaction in almost every financial crisis, moreover, the voices of orthodoxy in state bureaucracies and banking sectors—the advocates and implementers of the "ultimatums" and "harsh fixes" that had been the hallmark of the initial response to the crisis in the late 1990s—had to be overcome.[6]

As a prelude with respect to the arrangement for the G20 at the leaders' level, the most obvious sign was the extensive composition of membership. In thinking about which countries were systemically important, China stood out in the minds of both Martin and Summers. Yet, instead of concentrating only on one country, the key element of the model was that there would be space for the emerging markets in a much more encompassing manner.

Adding to the debate about efficiency versus legitimacy was the top-down method by which Martin and Summers chose the membership. If the goal was a more inclusive form of governance, the means was patently club-like, with Martin and Summers writing up the list of who was in (and out) by themselves on a brown manila envelope in Summer's Washington office on 27 April 1999. As in almost any club endeavor, the rationale for choosing members was quite clearly a mix of instrumentalism and personal preference.

As acknowledged by Martin, a quantitative assessment of the candidates was part, but not the only part, of the process: "I felt very strongly that [the G20 had to be made up of] the regional powers," Martin states, and "Larry felt that [as well] and then he also had geopolitical concerns." However, these standard ingredients were not the only criteria in play: "I would love to say we sat down and ran the numbers on whose GDP was bigger, but we didn't."[7]

What is clear is that any sense of like-mindedness in national terms was not the driver for choice. In some cases, such as the choice of Indonesia over Thailand, the deciding factor was influence. The same is true with Saudi Arabia, although of course the Saudis were also close allies with the United States. However, other dimensions of club behavior may have played a part also, most obviously in the non-choice of Malaysia (which had imprisoned its finance minister, Anwar Ibrahim).[8] In other cases, it is unclear whether it was influence or personality that dictated the method of selection. Argentina, for example, was picked over Chile (despite the kudos given to the latter country for its impressive return to democracy and economic performance) largely because Argentina retained club credibility, even as it began to sink into crisis: a standing reinforced by the re-appointment of the Harvard-educated Domingo Cavallo as Argentina's minister of the economy in March 2001.[9]

While a unique variant, the G20 must be situated in a wider context of ripeness for institutional re-design. After all, there was an intense albeit awkward search for reform right across the spectrum of international forums. At the Asia-Pacific Economic Cooperation (APEC) leaders' meeting in Vancouver in November 1997, US President Bill Clinton orchestrated a tentative Group of Twenty-Two to try to deal with the evolving Asian financial crisis and the tools to strengthen the international financial architecture in response. As in the G20, this formulation centered on systemically important countries and was constructed in an informal style. Although the membership of this group continued to be loosely constructed, with Poland, Hong Kong, Malaysia, Singapore, and Thailand in addition to the eventual G20 group in attendance at the first meeting, plus Belgium, the Netherlands, Sweden, and Switzerland at the second, an important follow-up meeting was held at the Willard Hotel (imparting the name, the Willard Group) and again in April 1998 as the contagion effect of the crisis began to hit.

In some measures the Willard Group foreshadowed work that was to be carried out via the G20 and beyond. One illustration of this harbinger role came with the recommendation of one of its working groups that a Financial Sector Policy Forum be established, opening the way to the creation of the Financial Stability Forum which took shape in April 1999. Yet the innovation of looking forward to more inclusive forms of collective action was mixed with the discipline of orthodox solutions that looked back. With issues such as "crony capitalism" in mind, a second working group recommended that the IMF work on a Transparency Report indicating the extent to which an economy meets internationally recognized disclosure standards. A third working group laid out the conditions for dealing with orderly workouts for excessive indebtedness and pushed countries to "make the strongest possible efforts to meet the terms and conditions of all debt contracts in full and on time."[10]

It is not surprising that the tilt toward accommodation on the part of the G20 was filtered through its entrenched club culture. In procedural terms the champions of the G20 were ahead of the curve in their concerns about inclusiveness. Martin, for instance, gave ready access to Anwar Ibrahim, the Malaysian finance minister, before his imprisonment, and took the message seriously that the lessons, rules, and prescriptions from the IMF were problematic for the global South. Nonetheless, in the gestation period toward G20 Finance, inclusion was wedded to efficiency. As one of Martin's close advisors stated, "It was clear that the plain, ordinary regulatory apparatus that we had internationally was not working very well."[11]

Martin's own determination to move past the technical focus and ideological parameters of the Willard Group initiatives was made clear in his public declarations. This sentiment is well captured in the speech he made to the Interim Committee of the IMF in September 1999:

> These steps contribute important improvements to the international architecture. As we have seen over recent years, however, we

still need a forum that can provide a broad overview and that can address issues that go beyond the responsibilities of any one organization or that involve more than financial regulation *per se*. The crises of the last two years have ... shown that what happens in emerging markets matters in a big way to everyone. There is therefore a need for an ongoing forum that includes not only industrialized economies, but key emerging and developing economies as well ... Canada therefore supports the formation of a new mechanism for ongoing consultation on matters pertaining to the international financial system—the new G-20 ... The group will be a forum where Ministers can talk candidly about important policy issues, in a format that encourages spontaneity.[12]

As indicated, though, this bias toward efficiency—or for that matter legitimacy—was not shared by key members of the club. The push for innovation came from Canada and the United States with increasing support from the United Kingdom (mainly through Chancellor of the Exchequer Gordon Brown). The forces of resistance came from Europe generally and Germany and France more specifically, who viewed this campaign (rightly) as having the potential for creating momentum toward reform in the international financial institutions. If there was a contagion effect on the problems in the financial system there was also a contagion effect in terms of problem solving. As Robert Rubin, the Treasury Secretary in the Clinton administration before Summers, put it, "What you had was really very Eurocentric ... and it didn't make a lot of sense."[13]

It is this narrative, with a focus on the underlying tensions between the innovators and the resisters, that is at the core of the anecdotal accounts of practitioners. For Martin the key part of the strategy for change was a division of labor in which he (and Summers) took on the Eurocentrism in the push for the G20 and Brown concentrated on international financial institution reform.

Although the reform of international financial institutions took much longer to animate, the establishment of the G20 of finance ministers and central bank governors in September 1999 marked an authentic breakthrough in global governance. Formally at least, it was a forum that placed priority on equality of membership. There was to be no veto power, votes or shares. The hosting function was to be done on a rotating basis. There would not be any permanent secretariat tied to one country. Efficiency required opening up the club to new members with equitable rights and obligations. As Martin declared in July 1999, just before G20 Finance came into life, "It is not reasonable to expect sovereign governments to follow rules and practices that are 'forced' on them by a process in which they did not participate. Therefore, whatever form the renewed global financial architecture ultimately takes, all countries must 'buy into it' and take ownership. Only then will the framework have legitimacy."[14]

The extent of this breakthrough on non-G20 countries—that in Martin's words they were to "be at the table and be part of the solution"[15]— should not be minimized. The establishment of the G20 set a precedent by opening up membership on a procedural basis to pivotal countries of the global South. Not only did a large group of countries from all quadrants of the globe enter the G20, but these countries gained some significant forms of ownership of the forum. The informal culture of the G20 provided countries from the South with a sense of "we-ness." The distribution of the hosting function showed that the G8 was willing to share this trapping of power.

The creation of G20 Finance had attractions especially for a country such as China without significant defects. It enabled an informal mechanism for dialogue among systemically important countries within the framework of the Bretton Woods institutions. China thus received greater status and access without moving away from the rest of the rising, emerging, and developing countries on its own. As one prominent Chinese economist commented, "broader representation is crucial. The G20 is designated to fulfill this need for representation from emerging markets."[16]

At the same time, the advantages generated by the G20 Finance in terms of problem solving did not mean that all of the legitimacy issues were dealt with. Notwithstanding the expansion of membership, there was a still an inner circle of decision makers. Martin became the first chair of the new G20. Brown in turn took on the position of the chairmanship of the IMF's policy advisory committee, the International Monetary and Finance Committee, keeping this role until he became prime minister in mid-2007.

The G20's initial hosting functions were also maintained in the inner circle. The formative move toward the G20 in April 1999 took place in Washington. The subsequent ministerial meeting in December 1999 was held in Berlin, chaired by Martin (although Martin and Germany's finance minister Hans Eichel were formally the co-hosts). It was only after the start-up phase was completed that the hosting function was spread more widely (India 2002, Mexico 2003, China 2005, South Africa 2007, Brazil 2008).

This in-between status strained the boundaries in terms of legitimacy. Besides indicating that there was still a divergence between G8 and non-G8 countries inside the G20, it reinforced the notion that the more the G20 was successful in operating as a harmonized club, the more it differentiated between insiders and outsiders. Both conceptually and practically, it provided some credence to the view of Gerry Helleiner that the G20 was a forum for de-legitimization, not re-legitimization.[17] While the status of pivotal countries such as China, India, Brazil, South Africa, and Mexico was enhanced, other countries became increasingly marginalized. The obvious candidates for this downward slide were the small, poorest countries. To this list of "losers" in the process could also be included traditional "middle" states in Western Europe such as the Nordics and the Dutch as well. These countries were far from poor but they often acted as the voices for that constituency, claiming the status of good international citizens.

Transcending or trapped in the legitimacy gap?

The ongoing gap in the nature of representation in G20 Finance fuelled critical speculation about the purpose of the forum. Even some laudatory commentators asked questions about whether G20 Finance was a means of imposing a US approach by other means. This was backed up to some extent at least by interviews with pivotal players in the Clinton adminis-tration. Rubin is quoted most notably for saying that although Martin was "a very strong voice" for reform, the United States was the driving force behind the scenes.[18] In other words, the United States wanted to deliver the outcome of reform without the impression of unilateralism. An ex-Canadian official confirms this point to the extent that the United States wanted reform without taking the Europeans head-on over the issue: "There was a sense that this would be better if it wasn't a com-pletely American initiative. So Paul [Martin] became the guy who was front and centre, and Canada more generally, in organizing this."[19]

Criticisms by scholars were more far ranging, with the legitimacy gap serving as a connecting theme. For some, the focus would be an extension of the interpretation that the establishment of the G20 was shaped by the United States as the leader or hegemon in its own self-interest. Robert Cox puts this view across in a broader context: "the dominant state takes care to secure the acquiescence of other states according to a hierarchy of powers within the inter-state structure of hegemony. Some second-rank countries are consulted first and their support is secured. The consent of at least some of the more peripheral countries is solicited."[20]

Others adopted a perspective that took in not only the motivations for the establishment of G20 Finance but (dealing with the practi-tioners on their own terms) whether the forum did what it was set up to do in terms of efficiency. A cluster of these analysts argues that the G20 brought some tangible benefits but needed improvement. Tony Porter showcases the sophistication of the model, with the substitution of greater legitimacy for the disciplinary practices of the past. However, he reinforces the image of the G20 and related bodies as clubs rather than a networked approach. In doing so he distances himself from the critical perspective that highlights the mutually supportive roles of states and powerful market actors, as conceptualized, for instance, in Cox's *nébuleuse*,[21] a transnational process merging finance officials, international financial institutions, and other actors in various financially dominated discourses, in order to enhance the extent to which states are forced to adjust to the needs of the global economy. In Porter's view, the creation of the G-20 "increased the autonomy and distance of their member states relative to business rather than increasing their linkages. Private associations, such as the International Institute of Finance, which was created by the world's largest commercial banks and involves itself in global policy matters on their behalf, played no significant role in the creation."[22]

The distinguished economist Gerry Helleiner adopted the view that the creation of the G20 in a process "led by the United States ... represented a small step towards improved global governance in that it expanded discussion of some international financial issues beyond the bounds of the G-7, within which decision-making power continues to be closely held." Despite the opening up of these opportunities, this forum was held back by its deficiencies. Foreshadowing some of the later criticisms about the G20 at the leaders' level, his main point is that the G20 was a forum that bypassed the majority of developing countries, which albeit "virtually ignor[ed] ... [made] earlier continuing efforts ... to interest the G-7 and other industrial countries in initiating a process of discussion of international financial governance issues which had at least some superficial similarities to the current G-20." Such overtures were made by the G24—a committee of developing country finance ministers established in November 1971—at the Halifax G7 summit, and at a full-fledged G24 ministerial meeting called in the wake of the Asian crisis in February 1998.[23]

Still others are more positive, in the sense that they judge the G20 to have opened the parameters of debate about the financial system. Jacqueline Best, for instance, credits "top-down" forums—epitomized by the G20—for engaging in the search for normative answers about the purpose for which the financial system should be constituted.[24] On a point that coincides with later thinking on the need for a G20 at the leaders' level, Michael Hodges indicates the ability of forums such as the G20 not only to set agendas and raise attention to issues, but also to mobilize domestic decision making, namely to "light fires under civil servants and bureaucrats."[25]

This positive impression meshes with the reflections of additional practitioners and academics. In the words of two Australian analysts:

> ... the G-20 highlights the importance of policy learning and transfer, the role of epistemic communities, and the discursive and policy activism of increasingly autonomous organizations. According to insiders ... the G-20 offers a forum for widening existing mind-sets and policy paradigms. An intellectual soil-tilling exercise in this regard occurs in the run-up to annual ministerial meetings by way of several prior deputies meetings as well as workshops, study groups, commissioned research, and background discussions, which help set the agenda and frame issues.[26]

Returning to the club orientation of the G20, however, a theme that stands out in many of the critical assessments of the forum is the limits of substantive innovation. An illustration that is used to reveal these restrictions is the consensual acceptance of the benefits vis-à-vis capital account liberalization. Above all, these sorts of parameters were noticeable in the midst of the Asian crisis in which the proposals put forward by a "financial stabilization" camp, which generally looked to more interventionist/Keynesian measures to restrict the speed and volume of speculative financial flows, were ignored.[27] Again in a rehearsal of what was to come later with the ascendancy of the G20 at the expense of the UN, the suggestions in a UN report that viewed capital controls as a viable option, received no buy-in within the G20.[28]

Transcending a technical orientation

The commonplace understanding of G20 Finance in its start-up years was that it concentrated almost exclusively on technical issues. The orthodox bias in its approach can be gauged from a summary of the discussions held during its first meeting in Berlin in December 1999:

> Ministers and Governors at this inaugural meeting discussed the role and objectives of the G-20, and ways to address the main vulnerabilities currently facing their respective economies and the global financial system. They recognized that sound national economic and financial policies are central to building an international financial system that is less prone to crises. They noted the importance of strengthening national balance sheets to help cushion against unexpected shocks. They encouraged steps to strengthen sovereign debt management, and greater attention to the impact

of various government policies on the borrowing decisions of private firms.[29]

To be sure, critics have some basis for their contention that the G20 at this stage reverted in some respects to the agenda of the Willard Group with a focus "on enhancing accountability and transparency, strengthening financial systems, and managing financial crises is quite striking."[30] That said, the prospect of G20 Finance moving beyond these limits was always in train. A good signal that the broadening out approach would work came with the defeat of those European countries that preferred to utilize the G20 to deal with issues where there was no consensus in the IMF. Certainly, Martin continued to anticipate this broadening out approach. As he stated after his appointment as chair of G20 Finance, "There is virtually no major aspect of the global economy or international financial system that will be outside of the group's purview."[31] He repeated the assertion subsequently to a Canadian parliamentary committee.[32]

To highlight the point that the G20 was not just a narrow, technical forum, the 2000 meeting in Montreal focused on the opportunities from and challenges to globalization.[33] The so-called Montreal Consensus addressed specific issues such as income distribution and social protection. The momentum in this direction was accelerated by the tragedy of 9/11, after which the G20 agenda inevitably shifted toward the links between finance, security-oriented priorities and, to a limited extent, the targeting of "root causes" for such attacks. The 2001 meeting in Ottawa and the 2002 forum in New Delhi targeted the fight against the financing of terrorism, with the G20 putting into place an action plan with special attention to freezing terrorist assets. As a reflection of the strengths of the root causes argument, the 2003 meeting in Morelia, Mexico focused on global poverty. Reflecting a growing frustration with orthodoxy, the G20 sought to expand its scope to encompass poverty reduction, development assistance and the UN Millennium Development Goals.

Another current that swept through that forum was that, just as the financial issues addressed by the G20 were transnational in nature, so were many other issues that needed to be tackled by the G8. This larger cluster included terrorism, climate change, energy security, and health governance. None of these issues could be solved if it was left only to the traditional "steering committee" of countries through the G8.

Martin linked his functionalism theme—a recurrent refrain in Canadian foreign policy—to instrumental legitimacy as the motor of reform. Health governance in the area of infectious diseases (an issue that made it onto the G20 agenda in 2000) stood out: "[the] rapid spread [of this issue would] immediately tip the balance in terms of a reformed G8 [because of] the threat of a global pandemic."[34] Globalization, according to Martin and other key policy entrepreneurs, needed to be "shaped" in a more effective manner on its social as well as economic dimensions. The equity rationale was compelling. The main argument, though, which also prompted a call for an extension of G20 Finance into a leaders' forum, was based on instrumental necessity. As the current OECD secretary-general (and former Mexican finance and foreign minister), Ángel Gurría put it bluntly, "the different fora that deal with globalization are not working."[35] In moving past the technical agenda, Martin also sought to go beyond the exclusive state-based club orientation of the G20. Although the impact of the move should not be exaggerated, the decision by Martin to meet civil society organizations before the 2000 G20 finance meeting in Montreal—and to take those voices to the meeting itself—deserves recognition. Moreover, it seems quite clear that Martin wanted to do more to build a network of dialogue (and potential support) for the G20 but could not find agreement to do so from his more club-like partners.

The catalytic effect: turning the G20 into a leaders' summit

The visionary component of the G20 does not end with the mechanisms inherent to that forum. What elevates the G20 toward a higher stratum as an innovative initiative is its ongoing catalytic quality. Its experience was crucial in pushing Martin into firm advocacy of ambitious summit reform via the notion of an L20. In terms of style, the experience of G2O Finance profoundly conditioned both the why and the how of the elevated approach that Martin wanted to adopt in a new leaders' forum. As opposed to the popular impression and stigma of the G8 as talking shops, Martin and other finance ministers saw the G20 as a vehicle for action. Getting the right members—with individual as well as collective leverage—was a crucial ingredient, but building a culture of delivery within this group was also vital. As he explained in an interview, if the member countries "are big and powerful enough ... deliberations lead to real decisions." The G20 action plan against terrorism was rapidly adopted. "So that it isn't simply, let's discuss, it's, let's discuss and make a decision and implement it. And the G20 was able to do that in this particular case. I think you're going to see more and more of that."[36]

Although an idea that found solid traction in the think tank world, the notion of an L20 was not seamlessly translated into action. It is worth examining some of the key differences between G20 Finance and a G20 summit at the leaders' level that raised the bar of difficulty.

One significant difference was the co-leadership between the main policy entrepreneurs: Canada, Germany and, crucially, the United States. Taking its leadership status seriously, the Clinton administration responded to the Asian crisis by embracing institutional reform. The administration of President George W. Bush was far more resistant to this form of new multilateralism. Bush shared some of the same issue-specific concerns (notably avian flu) but this did not translate into support for an L20. When Martin tried to make the call for an informal meeting of the L20 leaders on the margins of the UN world summit in New York in September 2005, intended to review efforts on the Millennium Development Goals, Bush could not be brought "onside."[37] This "ambivalent" response (a response repeated on several occasions through the course of the L20 initiative) sucked a good deal of the momentum out of the initiative, notwithstanding Martin's enthusiastic campaigning among key leaders of both the G8 (Prime Minister Junichiro Koizumi, a policy entrepreneur himself, with a very different style than the Japanese bureaucracy which remained opposed to the L20 and low key on the G20), and those from putative L20 countries (President Hu Jintao and Premier Wen Jiabao of China, and President Lula da Silva of Brazil).

A related issue was the difference in the policy ambit between G20 Finance and the proposed L20. There were obvious rivalries among the countries/ministers doing the running on the G20. A good example of this came in the jockeying for position between Canada and Germany in the run-up and during the proceedings of the first G20 meeting in Berlin. Yet the strong level of consensus among the key policy entrepreneurs was striking as well. Although there was some disagreement in terms of the membership of the G20—over the inclusion of Saudi Arabia, Egypt, Turkey, Korea, and Australia, for example—this did not in any way impede the process of institution building. On the one hand, firm consensus built up on which countries should be involved based on economic capacity. China and India were obvious choices in this category, but Saudi Arabia, with its massive oil and financial reserves, was also included on this basis. On the other hand, there was agreement about which countries needed to be brought in because they might be part of future financial crises. In this category were included Argentina and Turkey.

At the same time characteristics that reflected the closed-club nature of the G20 forum emerged. An important sub-group of finance ministers displayed a close affinity in the orientation of their policy entrepreneurship. This group included Martin, Brown, and South Africa's Trevor Manuel. When other colleagues faced adversity, moreover, this group rallied to their cause as in the case of the imprisonment of Anwar Ibrahim.

Building consensus on the L20—or an alternative model of reform—has proven more elusive. The G8 process has intricacies well beyond those found in the G20. Whereas the latter forum has maintained a policy-driven agenda, the former is as much about style as performance: photo ops are more important to leaders than finance ministers. So are unrehearsed informal exchanges, often related to domestic politics. Lonely at the top, leaders can share confidences as a peer group during G8 summits.

This is not to minimize the power of leaders to take decisive action. Leaders can make a difference across the range of issues on the G8 agenda, whether on Africa's development, or aid and debt relief, Kosovo, or macroeconomic issues. What should not be overlooked, though, is the hold of the international/domestic two-level game.[38] If the international arena grabbed their attention, they still looked at global issues through particularistic local lenses.

At first glance Martin's visionary commitment to the L20—as an extension of G20 Finance—appears to be an exception to this rule. As an existing member of the exclusive club, Canada arguably stood to lose, not gain, by any dilution of the G8 through an L20. Yet even in Canada's case, the initiative played to some fundamental concerns that had both international and domestic dimensions. An L20 project could win Canada favor among ascendant economic powerhouses and markets of the twenty-first century. It also could play well with various diasporas, especially the extensive Indo-Canadian and Chinese-Canadian communities. More generally, "another worthwhile Canadian initiative" held attractions as it cultivated Canada's reputation (popular among a considerable proportion of the electorate) as a policy innovator and good international citizen.[39]

Conclusion: from visionary policy innovation to reactive political opportunism

This chapter demonstrates that the logic of extending G20 Finance to encompass a leaders' summit, as opposed to replacing it, was building up prior to the 2008 global financial crisis. By 2007, an assessment written for the South African G20 Finance concluded that the forum had made some strong progress on microeconomic reforms, such as the adoption of international codes and standards by the member countries and the work to disrupt terrorist finance networks.[40] On the other side of the ledger, however, the report suggested that the G20 had reached some limits. Although it had built a shared set of principles around the global economy, it had been "less successful in putting these broad policy objectives into operation," and had been unable to resolve "major international macroeconomic issues," such as "global imbalances and further trade liberalization."[41]

This chapter also reveals, however, that the push for reform at the apex of global power did not move in a straight, rational line. Over time, unfortunately, an air of opportunism began to hover over proposals for institutional reform. Martin's peer group examined these proposals in light of both the impact of and the constraints on the G20. A good illustration of this attitude came from Hans Eichel, the German finance minister (1999–2005):

> There is a need to reinforce the growing sense of responsibility of all members for their respective regions and for the world economy as a whole. On this basis policy co-operation could be broadened as well. This applies both to the number and frequency of meetings and to the division of labor by subject matters. If the G20 continues to develop along these lines and becomes even more effective, I think we could in theory expect to see G20 comprising the Heads of State and Government set up some time in the future.[42]

What is striking about the wave of calls for institutional reform—above all, on the reconfiguration of the G8—from around mid-2005 onward is their disconnection from the experience of G20 Finance. Politically, this is not surprising, in that all these calls have come from leaders who have not been ministers of finance (and in certain cases, such as in the United Kingdom, where the minister of finance has been a rival for power). Diplomatically, though, it means that calls for G8 reform often go hand in hand with either trips to the countries that are invited to join and/or as "carrots" to enhance bilateral relationships. A good example of these instincts may be viewed through the efforts of France's President Nicolas Sarkozy. In declaratory terms, he tended to voice support for a country (India and South Africa, for instance) during official tours of those countries.[43] In operational terms, he added specific countries (Egypt was the most obvious one) to coincide with other initiatives, as on the Mediterranean community. Such actions open up the issue of membership well beyond the parameters of the G20.

This concern about opportunism, reform for political not policy reasons, it must be added, is used also by financial bureaucrats who want to maintain the status quo. Beeson and Bell, for instance, quote the governor of the Reserve Bank of Australia that converting the G20 into an L20 would be a mistake that would "undermine or transform the underlying dynamics that revolve around longer-term consensus building." Leaders have "to go home with some great triumph in their bag, and so the focus becomes on what is deliverable ... It is less likely that you can actually work hard over a number of years on quite important fundamental things."[44]

Above all, the question of timing has to be factored in. The G20 Finance as rehearsed in this chapter was created because of a crisis. This fits fully the schemata of how new forms of institutional structures—and representational privileges—come into being.[45] The sense of urgency concentrates the mind of state officials. Moving through the cycle from the establishment of the G20 to its extension into an L20 was pushed by a catalytic vision. What was lacking was a catalytic or triggering moment, where the process of reorganization could move across the decisive point in terms of political or diplomatic support. A major pandemic might have triggered such a break with the status quo, as did the Asian financial crisis in the case of the G20, but to the credit of lower-level bureaucrats and experts (who took the burden of responsibility of handling these health governance issues on the ground), this sort of episode did not escalate to the point where leaders had to take control of the agenda.

The direct line between the G20 and G8 reform has thus been eroded, in the sense that there is little current perceived opportunity for a "big bang" reform of the G8 with the inclusion of the G20 roster of countries. Instead of initiatives being pushed for G8 reform with this set menu of countries simply being carried over from the G20, suggestions of countries to be brought into an enlarged G8 were made on an à la carte basis or with a smaller constellation of countries.

It is these alternative design options that lie at the core of the discussion in Chapter 3. If in some way a detour from the central analysis of the book—the shift from a G20 Finance to a G20 at the leaders' level—under conditions of crisis, these alternative designs reveal both the richness of the debate about reform of global governance and the differing views among G8 countries about what reform should look like. The L20ish reform drive was the maximalist approach but, as evident in the initiatives for reform that took shape via the G8 "outreach" process, there were also on offer other, more minimalist approaches. As explored in Chapter 3, the Heiligendamm Dialogue Process—initiated by Germany's Chancellor Angela Merkel—was based on functional notions. That is to say, it rested in the belief that cooperation in specific areas (innovation, investment, development assistance, and energy policy) would develop into further forms of trust and cooperation.[46]

As also analyzed in Chapter 3, the number of countries attached to some other initiatives replicates features of the G20/L20. The best illustration of the staying power of this formula is the incorporation of the

MEM (major emitters meeting) dealing with climate change within the 2008 Toyako G8 Summit, a process that supplemented the so-called Outreach 5 of the Heiligendamm Process with the addition of Indonesia, South Korea, and Australia.

What is clear through all these debates and alternative options is that policy entrepreneurs retain the capacity to surprise academics. Motivations can be teased out and institutional and policy ramifications located in retrospective fashion, and obstacles remain easy to detect. What is much harder to discover, though, is when and where initiatives can be launched and gain traction in the global architecture. As elaborated in Chapter 4, the G20 at the leaders' level came into being suddenly as a reaction to a distinctive set of shocks, but it was based also on a catalytic notion of leadership. The L20 proved a fascinating laboratory for taking this spirit of reform to the apex of power. Although stalled and morphed as an initiative at least for the moment, the prospect for another burst of activity along similar lines was still available. It awaited just the "right" or, in terms of public policy performance, "wrong" galvanizing conditions. Only then did the big bang idea of elevating G20 Finance to the leaders' level trump the limited but still interesting options of reform described in Chapter 4.

3   G20 competitors as reform options

- The O5 in economic and diplomatic context
- G8 outreach
- Constraints on the O5/G8 model for reform
- The Heiligendamm process
- The G8+O5 vs. the G20
- Cementing the BRICS
- Conclusion: contentions on G criteria

This chapter shows that there were alternative options to the straight-forward elevation of G20 Finance to the leaders' level. With hindsight, the approach in which a leaders' summit was called in a direct modeling of G20 Finance was logical. Yet, as we discuss in some considerable detail, taking this prototype "off the shelf" was not a foregone conclusion. In competition with this approach were other possibilities, the main rival option being to build on the G8 framework, in which countries privileged via a process of outreach were brought directly into the embedded leaders' summit. This choice was very much an incremental variant. The G8 club stayed at the core of global governance. It just got bigger. The attractions were in its simplicity. Few critics could disagree that the five big outreach countries—China, India, Brazil, Mexico, and South Africa (O5)—merited graduation to the G8.

The disadvantage came from the embedded dynamic via the G8. The O5 countries had become engaged in an extension of the outreach process through the Heiligendamm process. Yet they continued to feel frustration and even resentment about their status by doing do. One of the fascinating and unanticipated effects of the "outreach" process was the consolidation of a small group of big countries from the global South into new habits of working together. If not the only dynamic behind the formation of BRICS (Brazil, Russia, India, China, and

South Africa), this chapter highlights how the awkwardness of the Heiligendamm process supported a move to this parallel forum.

Moreover, as this chapter will also illustrate, this option contained some disincentives for some G8 countries also. The G20 approach left more wriggle room for the United States to add other countries to their liking, and only them. Indeed, the fact that the G8-O5 model was driven by European countries, most notably France, accentuated the pushback from the Americans. Ultimately the embedded option was dismissed by the Bush administration. However, the question of the right formula, if any, for G reform was kept alive, being neither resolved nor abandoned throughout the Heiligendamm process, with a clear and decisive choice coming only with the financial crisis. Given the protracted period of debate over this issue, this alternative choice deserves serious scrutiny. The incremental option, as scrutinized in this chapter, extended the process of innovation in global governance even as it was overtaken by circumstances.

The O5 in economic and diplomatic context

The O5 lies in between the BRICS construct and the wider G20 membership. This group therefore covers not only the core BRICS countries—with Russia already in the G8 at the leaders' level—but also Mexico. Even before the financial crisis a strong argument was made that the global economy could no longer be managed—or globalization reshaped—without the presence of the O5 countries. This governance gap was magnified in the developmental and social arenas. As India, China, Brazil, and South Africa especially extended their functional reach in these domains, was it proper or practical to leave the O5 out?

The dramatic rise of the BRICS was rehearsed in the Introduction. Whichever configuration of rising powers is used within the context of global governance, it is difficult not to start the discussion with their apparent economic emergence. In the context of this conceptual chapter, the O5 create a new triangular formation in the world.[1] They form a distinctive post-bipolar triad of state types: a "first world" club of highly industrialized nations of the North represented in the G7, a "second"-tier world of emerging economies the core make-up of which is the BRICS, and an extensive and heterogeneous "third world" (previously concentrated in the G77) of the rest—a new three-world structure.[2]

Amid many differences, the common features of the O5 countries include large populations accounting collectively for more than 40 percent of the world's total, with rapid urbanization, low wage rates, episodes of high growth, growing inflows and outflows of foreign direct investment, high rates of growth of trade and, consequently, fast accumulation of foreign exchange reserves, growing domestic demand as a result of increases in individual incomes and overall economic development, fast growing demand for energy, and the attributes of regional hubs. There is often a substantial variation in these indices between different countries of this group. For example, China's long-standing high economic growth stands in contrast with Mexico, South Africa, and Brazil, where the growth of economies is more episodic and volatile. As we saw in Chapter 1 (Table 1.1), while the growth rates of the emerging powers tend to be unstable, they are, for the most part, significantly higher than those of the G8 and match or surpass the world average.

At the same time, any discussion of the economic successes of the O5 members cannot omit questions regarding the sustainability of the economic growth in these countries. Apart from economic indices and forecasts, environmental constraints will present a major challenge to the sustained growth and fast economic development of the emerging powers. As reflected in the recent Copenhagen, Cancún, and Durban conferences, the core members (constituted in the BASIC group made up of Brazil, South Africa, India, and China) are firmly recognized as pivotal countries when it comes to issues related to environment, pollution, and climate change. Indeed, in terms of carbon dioxide emissions, it is clear that the emissions from these countries will, on average, grow faster than those of the G7 both in aggregate and per capita, but still not match the G7 total per capita emissions well into the foreseeable future, if ever.

The economic logic of this model is complemented by an even more convincing diplomatic-cum-regionalist or strategic logic for focusing on the O5. All of the O5 countries have demonstrated an impressive global (if not yet quite globalist) reach in terms of their diplomatic profile, shifting from club to network diplomacy.[3] The stretch of China's international influence has been well documented.[4] For example, Beijing's concerted "charm offensive" toward Africa has been conducted not only bilaterally but also multilaterally through the convening of the impressive Forum on China-Africa Cooperation in November 2006.[5] Similarly, New Delhi hosted its first India-Africa Summit in April 2008. India has become a hub of diplomatic interaction—network as well as club diplomacy—as representatives of India's old and new friends vie for attention and deals, particularly reflecting its recent strategic partnership with the United States. Prime Minister Manmohan Singh was chosen to speak on behalf of the South in Bandung, Indonesia, on the 50th anniversary of the creation of the Non-Aligned Movement (NAM). Brazil under President Lula da Silva launched a number of high-profile diplomatic initiatives, ranging from leadership on the G20 developing countries via the World Trade Organization (WTO) and the proposal for a global fund against hunger, to a push on biofuel diplomacy using its sugar cane-based ethanol production. South Africa shares an innovative partnership with India and Brazil—the India-Brazil-South Africa (IBSA) Dialogue Forum—as well as playing a strong role in the G77, the African Union, and the New Economic Partnership for Africa's Development (NEPAD). Mexico has combined its membership in the North American Free Trade Area (NAFTA) with an ascendant role in the Organisation for Economic Co-operation and Development (OECD).[6]

The attraction of a limited, stable, and equivalent-status group suggested in the O5 model is reinforced by its simplicity. Procedurally, this model cuts out much of the debate about membership for an extended G20 beyond a core grouping. Certainly there are benefits of sticking to small numbers, in that the difficulty of reaching consensus on complex issues (hard enough with a G13) would potentially increase with a G20. The ability to solve crises—as the United Nations (UN) has often found out—is not enhanced by simply building a more inclusive decision-making process.

Operationally, the case for the inclusion of these core countries can be made on grounds of both efficiency and legitimacy. As noted at the outset, all of the core O5 countries are members of G20 Finance composed of finance ministers and central bank governors. They fit the profile of classic, big, emerging markets or regional powerhouses, all of which are becoming increasingly integrated into the world economy.[7]

This structural strength goes hand in hand with diplomatic prowess. As suggested by John Humphrey and Dirk Messner in their innovative work on "anchor countries," the size of the economies of these hub countries must be blended with their capacity "actively [to] participate in global dialogue" that is crucial for this analysis.[8]

G8 outreach

The response by the G8 to this pattern of economic growth and rising diplomatic profile has been an opening up through a diffuse pattern of outreach. At the Evian Summit in 2003, France chose to showcase members of the Big Five—with the leaders from China, India, and Brazil (along with those from other G20 potential members including Mexico and Saudi Arabia). At Gleneagles in 2005, the United Kingdom, with a similar model in mind, invited the same core countries (albeit without Middle East representation) to discuss climate change.

A similar framework was used in key ancillary bodies. Most noticeably, the G7 forum of finance ministers has been opened up to the upper echelon of the same group. The finance ministers from China and India attended the two 2005 meetings, in St Petersburg and London.

So entrenched had this hub approach become that it operated with little critical comment. At the societal level, protestors have targeted many aspects of the G8—and on at least one occasion (the 2006 Melbourne meeting) of G20 Finance—for criticism, but the outreach component had slid under the radar. The main focus for reproach was not the inclusion of these countries but, rather, when this core group appeared to have been excluded. French President Jacques Chirac publicly rebuked the United States for not being more inclusive of these regional hubs at the 2004 Sea Island Summit: "We cannot discuss major economic issues nowadays without discussing these issues with China, with India, Brazil, South Africa."[9]

If inviting the O5 appeared to have become a habit at the generalized level, it was not so at a more specific level. Italy and Canada took what might be termed an Afrocentric approach. At the G8 summits that they hosted—in Genoa in 2001 and Kananaskis in 2002 respectively—they picked a form of representation that emphasized the attendance of leaders from the African continent and the implementation of the NEPAD agenda. Japan at the 2000 Okinawa Summit took a similar line, inviting Algeria, South Africa, and Nigeria into the mix (with Thailand added in as well). Britain's Prime Minister Tony Blair played the Africa card as well at Gleneagles, combining Big Five participation on climate change with African participation on debt relief and development assistance.

Other countries took a divergent track. As mentioned, the United States did things its own way at Sea Island in 2004, moving from an approach that downplayed outreach altogether to one that placed the emphasis on West Asia. The response rate, however, proved modest for this invitation: Afghanistan, Bahrain, Iraq, Jordan, Tunisia, Turkey, and Yemen accepted, but Saudi Arabia, Kuwait, Pakistan, Egypt, and Morocco declined. So the Bush administration scrambled in the last six months to bring together a blend of African states to Sea Island.[10]

As noted, however, the O5 had a number of strong advantages over the other models, not only in terms of economics but also with regard to diplomacy. The behavioral or functional range of each of the Big Five members on the diplomatic axis is far greater than the other developing-country members of the G20. Confirmation of this elevated status accorded the Big Five countries has come out in the rotation of the presidency of the G20, in that India was tasked with this role in 2002,

Mexico in 2003, China in 2005, and South Africa in 2007, with Brazil taking over in 2008 amid the central moment of the financial crisis.

Constraints on the O5/G8 model for reform

For the G8 and O5 to emerge as competing forums would have been a tragedy. Instead they somehow had to be combined into one grouping that, for political, representational, and legitimacy reasons, also included at least one Islamic nation. If there was an opening for the O5 countries to be the model for G8 reform, there continued to be severe obstacles to progress along these lines. Inside the G8 there remained some considerable opposition to any major reform. One of the major functional initiatives of the British government during its presidency was the creation of a "G8 Plus Five" process to connect the energy and environment ministers of the G8 and the O5 outreach group.

The potential of this initiative was ready to be captured. However, Russia, during its time as president of the G8, did not nurture this process, marginalizing it at the St Petersburg Summit in 2006. Japan also downplayed the role of the O5 outreach group during its presidency in 2008, crowding them out on the third day at Toyako with the addition of Australia, South Korea, and Indonesia for the Major Emitters Meeting (MEM-16). "Variable geometry," in which countries with substantial interest in or capacity to contribute solutions to a particular issue can be invited to the table in addition to a core group of across-the-board global policy heavyweights, is a superficially attractive option to resolve pressures to expand membership. Hokkaido demonstrated the mistaken allure of variable geometry. Hard feelings were generated by different leaders being marched in and out for various parts of the meeting depending on the subject being discussed. Configurations involved the G8, the G8 +O5, the MEM-16, and the African guests. Variable geometry is a recipe for dissonance and non-cooperation. The premium should be on repeated pre-summit consultations and post-summit reporting as alternative and less damaging means for effective participation besides being at the table.

Outside the G8, the presence of South Africa as the sole African member of O5 remained controversial. Another point of controversy came because of the absence of any Islamic country. This mode of participation was at the core of the US approach to outreach at the 2004 Sea Island Summit. Even with the dual approach of the Blair government—with both core O5 and African representation—the United Kingdom found itself in a position where it had no major Islamic representation at Gleneagles (a missing element that was made more glaring by the London bombings on 7 July 2005).

Notwithstanding these deficiencies, there continued to be solid counter-arguments as to why the model of G8 reform should not be stretched too far to gain additional representativeness. Paul Martin contemplated adding either Egypt or Nigeria, or both, from the Islamic, sub-Saharan Africa, and Arab worlds, to the G20 model. However, the concept that he was convinced was right built on the G20 Finance model, with Indonesia, Saudi Arabia, and Turkey in and Nigeria and Egypt out.

The remaining flaws of the O5 model paled as well by contrast with those offered in alternative designs. Klaus Schwab, the executive chair of the World Economic Forum,[11] made proposals for a Partnership 21, along the lines of the five permanent members of the UN Security Council (P5), which would include a highly rigid decision-making structure. The International Task Force on Global Public Goods suggested an expanded version of the L20/G20 that, if commendable in other ways, was overcrowded with a Global 25.[12] Such a large group would have the drawback also of tilting the balance toward legitimacy at the expense of efficiency.

Martin laid out his L20 framework for all to see.[13] This was highly commendable as a model of global governance, with impressive intellectual endorsement in a variety of think tanks from around the globe. Yet, in the absence of urgency, the "big bang" approach to reform did not garner immediate diplomatic impact.

Incrementalism—if far less attractive as a normative device for reform—gained momentum from 2005 to 2007. It allowed different champions, whether Britain's Prime Minister Blair or Germany's Chancellor Angela Merkel, for example, to hand off some elements of ownership as they moved in and out of the presidency of the G8. It also avoided direct confrontation with the resisters. Instead of trying to address all of the detailed issues of modalities, the focus was a neo-functional one with an emphasis that reform is required if the major questions of the day (be they energy, climate change, health, development, or global economic imbalances) are to be addressed adequately and effectively. An excellent illustration of this perspective comes out in one of the frequent references to G8 reform made by President Nicolas Sarkozy of France:

> The G8 must continue its slow transformation, which got off to a good start with the Heiligendamm process. The dialogue conducted during recent summits with the top leaders of China, India, Brazil, Mexico and South Africa should be institutionalized and scheduled for an entire day. The G8 can't meet for two days and the G13 for just two hours. That doesn't seem fitting, given the power

of these five emerging countries. I hope that bit by bit, the G8 becomes the G13.[14]

The Heiligendamm process

By the 2007 Heiligendamm summit, it was clear that major international challenges could not be addressed without ongoing cooperation of the large countries of the global South. The formalization of the Heiligendamm process tried to accomplish this goal, albeit doing it within clearly set boundaries.[15] Although it was clear that Germany did not want to "prescribe to future presidencies whom they should invite,"[16] the formalized dialogue was a way to encourage the resisters to invite the O5 (at least for the duration of the arrangement). One of the main objectives in promoting the Heiligendamm process by Germany may have been its drive to take a leadership role, especially in global climate change debates.[17]

In initiating the Heiligendamm process, Chancellor Merkel made it quite clear that "We don't want to turn the G8 into a G13." Rather, she explained to her parliament in May 2007, "without the emerging economies, progress on issues such as climate change, the world trade round and intellectual property rights is unimaginable."[18] Even so, the idea of establishing a dialogue between the G8 and the O5, and of creating a secretariat within the OECD (a choice that left some important developing countries more than a little uncomfortable, as the OECD is generally viewed by them as itself an elitist Western club) to manage the developing contacts between the G8-O5, suggested that the G8 was already reinventing itself "as a vehicle for informal problem-solving between the most powerful countries of today and tomorrow."[19] The G13 in effect emerged through the back door.

Owing to the strong resistance within the G8, however, the process was very much steered from the G8 without much input from or consultation with the emerging countries. The basic structure relied on a Steering Committee and four Working Groups (co-chaired by G8 and O5 countries) on investment (USA and Mexico), energy (Canada and India), development (France and South Africa), and innovation (Britain and India)—topics of most interest to the G8—were included. Migration and governance, preferred topical areas of the O5, were not included. With the obvious exception of Mexico, the O5 are not members of the OECD, viewed as the "rich countries' club."

In addition to increased legitimacy of the G8, the dialogue in informal atmosphere was intended to create trust, bring more understanding of common responsibilities pertaining to global issues and to explore avenues for stalled negotiations in other international forums, most notably the Doha Round.

Good intentions of the German host notwithstanding, several mishaps at the launch of the Heiligendamm process as well as the general approach to the process as "outreach" did not contribute positively to the onset of the process. The most infamous incident was the release of the communiqué which announced the establishment of the Heiligendamm process without any input from the O5 and before the emerging powers actually joined the G8 meetings.[20] India's Prime Minister Manmohan Singh's remark—"We have come here not as petitioners but as partners in an equitable, just and fair management of the global community of nations, which we accept as reality in the globalized world"[21]— was seconded by a hopeful statement from China that the G8 Outreach will not be used as "a means of exerting pressure on developing countries."[22]

The first two years of the Heiligendamm process were financed by the German government with very modest support from Japan, the G8 host in 2008. More out of default than design, Italy, host of the 2009 G8 Summit but without a clear vision for the summit, tried to revive the flagging process. Still a low-key process, the slightly redesigned Heiligendamm process was put on life support until the French presidency in 2011. The entire second day of the l'Aquila summit was given over to a meeting between the core membership and the O5, with final reporting of the Heiligendamm process. Not without consequence, Egypt was added to this mix (which brought similarities to the earlier idea of transforming the G8 into a G14, including the O5 and Egypt as a representative of the Arab-Islamic countries).

Following the final report on the works of the Heiligendamm process presented in l'Aquila, it was decided to continue for another two years in a somewhat more flexible format. New topical issues were put on the table, including a strategic approach to development and its social dimensions, assistance to vulnerable states, food security, and others. Cosmetic changes were also made to the operations of the Steering Committee. Most importantly, however, there was a change of vocabulary from the Heiligendamm-defined "outreach" (a term strongly criticized by the O5) to l'Aquila "partners."

Although all of the O5 countries became engaged in the process, this incremental process was unlikely to have resulted in wider reform without a global shock such as the financial crisis. On the O5 side there was simply too much baggage attached to the G8 and the process of outreach. Traditionally focused on the formal, more inclusive structures (such as the UN), China never actively sought full membership in the G8. If comfortable with the language of dialogue, cooperation, and partnership, it had serious reservations about a tight embrace. In addition to protecting its developing-country status, China was wary of full membership in the G8 so as to avoid potential attempts at "socialization" by the Western powers and the possibility of pressures on domestic policies to which Beijing is very sensitive.[23]

As opposed to the other O5 countries, for India and Brazil in particular, potential membership in the G8 was never considered as important as permanent membership of the UN Security Council. Enlargement of the G8 was seen as somewhat of a "consolation" prize (and a stepping stone toward it) after the failed campaigns aimed at Security Council reform that foundered at the largely disappointing UN world summit in 2005. Both India and Brazil also have a very strong self-image rooted in the developing world, yet, like China, they do expect more recognition of their growing role in the world. India and Brazil alike question the current global governance architecture and push for comprehensive reforms. India has been the most critical of the Heiligendamm process and the general approach of the G8 to the emerging powers. Indian diplomats were making it very clear that, even though India is a champion of the global South, the country is very much entitled to equal status in the G8.

If still somewhat awkwardly, South Africa has always been thrust into taking on the status of being the representative of the "African cause" or "continental voice" on the international stage. It has been considered also the ideal partner in Africa for the G8, despite strong reservations to such a designation coming from within the African continent. As much as South Africa strongly supported the Heiligendamm process as a suitable opportunity for expanding the dialogue, the process was seen only as one of the elements for improving the wider relationship of Africa with the rich countries. A major challenge for South Africa's diplomacy was how to navigate the dialogue with the G8 so as not to be accused of "selling out" by its own region and improve its legitimacy on the continent. Another challenge for South Africa is "the interplay of three factors: costs, capacity, and global constraints." These are factors that no developing country, and no African country in particular, can ignore.[24]

Finally, Mexico was the outlier in the process, although interestingly one that assumed a very active bridging position in the Heiligendamm process. As a member of the OECD and NAFTA, Mexico had shed the developing-country identity in the mid-1990s. Still, skillful diplomacy, leveraged by a Mexican Secretary-General of the OECD, rather than leadership based on merit, has facilitated the role of Mexico as a convener of the O5.[25] The G8 dialogue was an opportunity for Mexico to realign its foreign policy more with the South and try to push migration as a major topic for debate within the G8-O5. It was also another avenue for Mexico to try to go around unsuccessful regional attempts of bridging the North and South American continents that significantly damaged Mexico's relationship with Brazil. In similar fashion the O5 provided Mexico with a good venue for mending its strained relationships with China and India, given their direct competition in the US markets.

It is important to note that despite the individual and collective criticism and reservations on the part of the O5 toward the dialogue process with the G8 started formally in Heiligendamm, it was a complementary step to earlier initiatives. The O5 finance ministers joined with their counterparts from industrialized countries in 1999 to form G20 Finance. All the countries in the O5 have struggled with their own identities both to deepen their ties to the G8 and, at the same time, keep their status and identity as champions of the global South.

An unintended but very interesting consequence of the Heiligendamm process was the self-endorsement and solidification of the O5 grouping. Over the past decade, the emerging countries have been grouped in different configurations, from BRICs to IBSA, to BASIC (at the 2009 climate talks in Copenhagen), and then BRICS again with South Africa formally joining the four BRICs in 2011. The cluster has not been presenting consistently just one identity. However, with the exception of the IBSA commission, the O5 has been the most enduring and operational grouping. It has met regularly since 2007, it has issued joint statements both prior to as well as following G8 Summits, and it has also shown limited attempts at coordinating (or at least discussing) positions in international negotiations. However, as we shall see shortly, the BRICS may be consolidating as an annual summit process now.

More substantially, although not framing the ultimate outcome, the O5 in the context of the G8 institutionalization created the impetus and the pressure point for change. If the G20 had not been called, it was clear that a G13 or G14 would have been the forum of choice when it came to President Sarkozy's turn to host the G8 in France during 2011.

The G8+O5 vs. the G20

Indeed, a strong case can be made that the O5 serves as a better model for reform than the G20. In terms of functional legitimacy the G8 plus O5 stands up well to scrutiny. There is a good deal of credibility in terms of representation. China, India, and Brazil are clearly in an elevated position of their own, but Mexico and South Africa act as valuable additions. South Africa looks better as one African country out of 13, or one sub-Saharan African country out of 14 than one out of 20. Mexico's location as either a North American country or a country of the Americas offsets to some extent the over-representation of the European countries. On effectiveness, each of the O5 has some impressive elements of global reach. Even Mexico (OECD/NAFTA) and South Africa (NAM/G77/Commonwealth/Cairns Group) have a high degree of institutional profile.

Just as importantly, each of these countries has the state capacity available to deal with the array of complex issues. Although China, India, and Brazil stand out by this standard, each of the O5 possesses strong bureaucratic features. Mexico chaired the O5 through a sherpa (a personal representative) appointed by the Foreign Ministry. South Africa displayed a good deal of technical acumen at the bureaucratic level through the O5 process.

By way of comparison, the G20 has some notable flaws. One is that the original G20 finance ministers' model had included what can be termed "problem" as opposed to "solution" countries, at least as defined as being debtor countries. Against the background of financial crises of the late 1990s, Argentina and Turkey stand out as particularly illustrative cases of traditional debtor countries being invited to be at the table.

These instrumental advantages, nonetheless, were trumped by a combination of contextual disadvantages of the O5 with respect to the competitive model of the G20. At a psychological level, the O5 bore the burden of being created as an element of outreach rather than being present at the creation (of the institution if not the idea) of the G20. This burden became acute when Japan failed to recognize the Heiligendamm process or O5 group in Toyako, going back instead to outreach. This ensured that there was little appetite in any of the O5 countries for any initiative that smacked of being a G8 appendage.

In terms of leadership, the O5 became identified with a European construct both incrementally (through the Heiligendamm process) and transformatively (through the call for an extension of the G8 through a G13 or G14). Italy had an opportunity to move from the Heiligendamm process to the G13/G14 but missed the chance, preferring to go wider rather than the more selective route. Sarkozy was unlikely to repeat this unproductive approach. In these circumstances, the United States had a multitude of reasons to push for the big bang on its own terms (and turf) rather than waiting for 2011 in France. It preferred to be an initiative-maker instead of an initiative-taker.

On the more technically oriented start up of the G20 Finance meeting, the United States was prepared to share ownership. The initiative was a joint activity between the Clinton administration (with Larry Summers and Robert Rubin as key players) with a small group of finance ministers, initially Paul Martin of Canada but with Germany's Hans Eichel, South Africa's Trevor Manuel, and others added to the mix. On the pivotal issue of G8/G20 transformation, however, the United States wanted to be the prime driver.

This pre-emptive move allowed the United States to be seen as rewarding allies. In general geopolitical terms this meant the inclusion of countries such as South Korea, Indonesia, Australia, Turkey, and Saudi Arabia into the mix, instead of having them left out in the G13/14 constellation. Functionally, it allowed a composition that included the MEM grouping, viewed as being vital to US President Barack Obama's initial approach to tackling the climate change agenda.

Jumping ahead of the financial crisis as the major catalyst for change, the G20 big bang even at the time of crisis allowed Obama to send a signal to Sarkozy and some other Europeans that there were alternatives to their preferred ways of doing things. In terms of process, there was quite clearly a sense of frustration about how Italy had handled the G8 hosting function. By going wide in terms of numbers and agenda, l'Aquila was about everything and nothing. Obama dealt with the G8 in a cursory manner, treating it as an interlude between his more significant political trips to Moscow, the Vatican, and Ghana.

Finally, turning back away from US to O5 motivations, the sense of solidarity among these counties can be exaggerated. Each of the O5 members has very distinct national interests and identities. Each sees its "bridging" role between North and South in quite different ways. Each has a very dissimilar neighborhood and club membership.

When the necessity arose, the model of the G20 assumed an ascendant position over the G8 plus O5 model. In a significant symbolic display President Lula da Silva handed out Brazilian football jerseys with the number "5" jersey at the l'Aquila summit as a display of apartness from the G8. However, symbolism was trumped by the logic of a G20 as the world was confronted by financial crisis in 2008. Differentiated but incremental processes gave way to a collective form of big bang action.

Cementing the BRICS

That said, the combination of the stalled momentum in the G20 and growing self-confidence by the BRICS as a powerful and cohesive grouping could reshape the balance between the two informal groupings in the composite architecture of global governance as sketched in the Introduction. The fourth BRICS summit, held in New Delhi on 29 March 2012, could mark a watershed. The grouping's summit advanced from a mere talk-shop opportunity to sketching the outlines of an alternative configuration of global governance. Potentially the BRICS coalition represents a powerful challenge to the US-dominated architecture the apex of which consists of the UN Security Council, the World Bank,[26] and the International Monetary Fund (IMF).[27] For the first time, the sense of frustrated entitlement found expression in some concrete ideas on how to break through the frozen configuration of global privilege and power. The BRICS have put down markers that they intend to use their demographic and economic clout to challenge and change the way the world is governed through formal multilateral machinery and informal groupings.

The global financial crisis has discredited the Washington Consensus on deregulated neoliberal capitalism and shifted the balance between states and markets. The mindset that privileges Western powers and their biases is trapped in the old paradigm and fails to recognize the new realities. The global financial crisis, as President Lula da Silva bluntly put it, "was created by white men with blue eyes."[28] In comparison to most Western economies responsible for the crisis, the BRICS have exemplary budgetary and fiscal performances. The BRICS blamed the European and US central banks for "aggressive policy actions" to stabilize their domestic economies, which had spilled over into emerging market economies by generating "excessive liquidity" and fostered "excessive capital flows and commodity prices."[29] Deliciously turning the tables, they called for the advanced economies "to adopt responsible macroeconomic and financial policies, avoid creating excessive global liquidity and undertake structural reforms to lift growth that create jobs."[30]

The World Bank has a decidedly outdated North-South and donor-recipient rather than development partners orientation. The Delhi Declaration called for a study of the feasibility of creating a new South-South development fund. Finance ministers are to report back on this at the 2013 summit in Russia.[31] Although this could eventually rival the World Bank, for now it is presented as a complement, to assist with infrastructure and other development projects that fail to attract World Bank or IMF funding. The five countries renewed demands for the leadership of the World Bank to come from developing countries and for expanded voting rights for developing countries in the IMF as well as an increased lending capacity of the Fund.[32] They took initial steps toward facilitating South-South trade in local currencies, thereby reducing the role of the dollar as the global currency.[33] The lowered transaction costs, it is hoped, will stimulate intra-grouping trade. Although intra-BRICS trade has grown by 28 percent annually, the ambition is to double the volume to US$500 billion by 2015.

The increasingly confident BRICS resent calls for "responsible" stakeholder policies as efforts to subjugate their worldviews to the global North's priorities (as a responsible actor, you will do what we say), and generally take an instrumental approach to international governance. Charles Grant argues, for example, that China and Russia are instinctively suspicious of the very notion of global governance as a self-serving Western concept. They are still strongly resistant to international interference in internal affairs, preferring informal gatherings of big powers and regional institutions to formal multilateral machinery.[34] The other BRICS would likely share the sentiments on global governance as being essentially unequal and unfair, and on the importance of non-interference in internal affairs.

Nonetheless some caution needs to be interjected about the robustness of these contours of transition in the international hierarchy. Their biggest common interest is in global economic governance. The most serious drag on the prospects of the BRICS being a major force in global governance is not resistance by the old order but the serious differences of interests among the group's members. BRICS is a rare, if not unique, phenomenon: a diplomatic grouping that follows an acronym coined by a private-sector analyst. It is not the product of diplomatic negotiations based on shared political values or common economic interests. For a turn of phrase by Jim O'Neill of Goldman Sachs in 2001, a grouping was born in 2009.

The BRICS are still at a very early stage of development. In all of them, domestic priorities and problems trump club solidarity. The April 2010 Brasilia summit was shortened into a one-day event when Chinese president Hu Jintao went home early to deal with a major earthquake, which killed more than 600 people in western China. In June, another BRIC summit around the Toronto G20 was cancelled completely when President Lula da Silva stayed home because of the massive floods in northeast Brazil.[35]

With long and not always settled borders, India and Russia have problems with China. China's hyper-competitiveness inflicts material harm on Brazil. India is vulnerable to shock while South Africa's place at the table may make political sense but is economically indefensible. Two of the five are authoritarian states, although all the three democracies have a tradition of reticence in global democracy promotion efforts. They are divided on reform of the UN Security Council,[36] with China's interest lying more in a bipolar (G2) than a genuinely multipolar (G20) global order. All five have a greater stake in bilateral relations with the United States for reasons of market power, investments, and high technology. The lack of common values and interests leaves them open to the dismissive comment of being "bricks in search of cement."[37] Moreover, in 2012 Brazil and India seemed to be stuttering economically, which would undercut the very basis of their recently added global clout.

Nevertheless, BRICS is a useful grouping for the countries to share and learn from one another's development experiences, something in which the G8 have absolutely nothing of any use or relevance to offer. Politically, the Delhi Declaration signals growing self-consciousness by the five BRICS that they have global weight and mean to begin using it. The statements on Syria and Iran mark out a clear "product differentiation" from the dominant transatlantic policy on contemporary global controversies.

Conclusion: contentions on G criteria

As showcased in this chapter, composition of a new, influential, high-level group at the core of global governance is very contentious. There are no logical criteria. Should the poorest be included? Should it comprise regional groupings? Is Africa under-represented in the G20—Nigeria is not included. President Jacques Chirac promoted Algeria's candidacy, preferring another Francophone country. Should the smallest be represented? The landlocked? In effect, anyone excluded will be irritated. The challenge is to devise a grouping that maximizes both legitimacy and effectiveness.

Size is contentious. The larger the group, the more legitimate; however, the larger the group, the less likely that it will be effective. Twenty is a large number, given the need for informal give and take, and with the practical barriers to communication across languages and cultures. The larger the group, the fewer the number of significant countries that feel unfairly barred from the table. The advantage of the L20 is that it emerges from an existing group.

The symbolism of the L20 held considerable appeal. The L20 initiative did not have the look of the "coalitions of the willing" put together on an ad hoc basis. Nor does it have diplomatic connotations associated with established institutions (an exclusive membership and/or veto power). The focus on leaders networking could generate spill-over into a wide number of subsidiary and interconnected networks. In the past, endorsements of the concept have come from groups as diverse as the World Economic Forum, the Helsinki Process on Globalization and Democracy, and the UN High Level Panel on Threats, Challenges and Change.

As we will focus on in Chapter 4, in 2008 the L20 idea became reality, emerging from chrysalis in President George W. Bush's announcement convening leaders from the G20 Finance countries, along with the heads of the UN, the World Bank, and the IMF. As we will see in Chapter 5 and Chapter 6, the G20 at the leaders' level is now functioning. Success in one issue will lead to reconvening on the next global crisis. The original assumption behind a long-running project involving collaboration between two Canadian institutions—the Centre for International Governance Innovation in Waterloo, Ontario, and the Centre for Global Studies in Victoria, British Columbia—was that the first meeting of the L20 would be called to respond to some specific crisis.[38] Leaders would agree to meet again and would add items to the agenda. An obvious next subject for the G20 is climate change. Other possibilities include post-conflict instability and nation-building, or restarting the moribund Doha trade round.

Good ideas are necessary for advances in global governance, and the ideas developed in the L20 project—emphasizing the need for reforms at the top to go beyond incremental reforms—showed their superiority over the model favored in the "Outreach"/ Heiligendamm process, which as evidenced in this chapter still had a structure of inequality built into it. The processes traced in this chapter, however, remain relevant as providing an in-between stage among policy makers. As exhibited in Chapter 4, the legacy of this model (with a preference for a G12, G13, or G14) did not fade away completely even after the 2008 financial shocks. Still, as we demonstrate in Chapter 4, the G20 became the main game in global governance in the post-crisis world.

4 Financial crisis as catalyst

From Washington to Pittsburgh

- The 2008 global financial crisis
- The allure of alternative designs
- The evolution of the G20 in practice
- Improvised crisis diplomacy
- Competing interpretations of global governance
- Variable or eroding forms of leadership
- Conclusion: moving past the first tests

This chapter depicts the manner by which the G20 at the leaders' level came into being as a direct consequence of the global financial crisis (GFC) of 2008–09 and the ongoing financial instability left in its wake. We focus particularly on the theme, whereby under this catalytic force the G20 moved into the putative position as the premier forum for global economic governance.[1] The immediate impact of the G20 as a "crisis breaker" was palpable. From the initial leaders' summit in Washington, DC (November 2008) to the second in London (April 2009), and the Pittsburgh summit (September 2009), the G20 generated a number of major initiatives, most notably big domestic stimulus packages, and promises of new resources for the International Monetary Fund (IMF), the World Bank and other multilateral development banks. By the time of the London G20 summit, countries had raised their commitment to spending up to a combined 1.8 percent of gross domestic product (GDP).[2] The London summit supplemented this with the largest pledge in history, worth over US$1 trillion. The collective desire to prevent a repeat of the crisis also produced additional reforms in the international institutional architecture, most notably through the move from the existing Financial Stability Forum, founded in 1999 by G7 finance ministers and central bank governors to promote international financial stability, to a reconfigured Financial Stability Board (FSB).

Still, even with this big bang dynamic, this chapter contends that a number of open questions remained. Looking back, alternative designs still had some support among key policy makers and needed to be put to rest. There continued to be forms of organizational competition. Taking the G20 "off the shelf" was not quite as easy as it looked after the fact. As noted, an extension of the G7/8 + G5/6 model remained in play as the financial crisis struck, supported by its hyperactive champion President Nicolas Sarkozy of France. However, the United Nations (UN) and the claims of universalism also provided an alternative model to the self-appointed concert model, as did the growing consolidation of the BRICS (Brazil, Russia, India, China, and South Africa), as noted in the last chapter.

Looking forward, beyond its immediate role as the primary locus for collective action on the crisis, a major debate arose about whether the G20 would be able to move beyond the crisis committee stage and catalyze a reordering in global governance. This view privileges the G20's ability to act as a new form of "steering committee" with a membership beyond the countries encompassing the post-1945 settlement and its add-ons in the 1970s (through the creation of the G5 and then the G7) and the post-Cold War era (the G8). Key emerging powers have been added to the old establishment that was previously restricted to North America, Western Europe, and Japan.

As illustrated in this chapter, the innovative quality of the G20 rests on two very distinct strands of activities and tests of accomplishment. The first test of the G20 is as the proverbial recession "buster" in the immediate aftermath of the GFC. A vital focus of this effort would continue to be to maintain the momentum of the stimulus packages and then wind them down through a coordinated exit strategy. However, another related test that came to occupy a considerable amount of time and effort revolved around getting the reconfigured regulatory regime right. While the crisis was exposed after severe market failure, it was brought on by successive policy and regulatory failures.

One of the most impressive aspects of the G20 has been the sheer weight of its convening power. To highlight the G20's concert mode, however, is not to overlook its contested nature both on practical and normative grounds. Although the G20 took on a dominant role, it did not do so without having to overcome some important obstacles. One was a deep-set skepticism that it could perform what it set out to do. The influential *Financial Times* columnist Martin Wolf asked, "Will the G20 rise to these exceptional challenges? No, is the answer."[3]

Before examining in more detail how the G20 operated in the manner it did, the dynamic about how the G20 moved to occupying the center stage first requires some attention. As this chapter underscores, the G20 merits attention in large part to its improvised nature. Other core institutions come into being through a protracted process of thinking and action, even if they have done so through crisis conditions, notably war. The G20 came into being in a month after the 2008 financial crisis hit. Yet, no less than other institutions, this intensity of response was facilitated by the possession of an "off-the-shelf" model in place.

The 2008 global financial crisis

The financial crisis roiling the world in 2008 was the result of serious shortcomings in domestic financial governance that highlighted gaps also in the global governance of international finance and capital. Both the Asian crisis of the 1990s and the 2008 market collapse demonstrate the need for efficient, effective, and transparent regulatory and surveillance instruments and institutions. The immediate roots of the crisis lay in the excessive and less than transparent leverage of complex securities and derivatives that introduced one degree of separation too many between the virtual and real economy. The US regulatory regime governing its financial and banking worlds can euphemistically be described as light, incomplete, and fragmentary. Even the high priest of market capitalism, Alan Greenspan, the former chairman of the US Federal Reserve, was moved to confess during Congressional hearings that he "made a mistake in presuming that the self-interests of organizations, specifically banks and others, were such that they were best capable of protecting their own shareholders and their equity in the firms."[4]

Thus the causes of the crises lay in domestic governance imperfections and the solutions entailed domestic government and market responses. One after another, led by Britain's Prime Minister Gordon Brown, governments underwrote massive bailouts either by buying toxic debts and/or injecting capital into banks in order to stabilize financial markets and provide liquidity to keep credit lines open.

The role of global governance institutions was to contain the contagion. Only a new regulatory regime will reassure many countries that the balance has been restored between the risks and benefits of integrating with an open world economy. To borrow language from the climate-change context, all countries have a "common but differentiated responsibility" for the stability of the global economic and financial systems. Countries such as China and India have limited access to current global decision-making channels and sharing the responsibility for managing the global order. The idea that they will continue to integrate with the world order on terms and following norms set by the West is quaint and archaic, in particular when China is the chief US creditor. In order to be made responsible stakeholders in the management of the regime and the outcomes that come from it, they need ownership of the process. One way to promote the idea in the United States is to characterize the Chinese and Indians as accepting the iconic US philosophy of "no taxation without representation."

The allure of alternative designs

If the G20 ultimately gained ascendancy, the first site for debate about the institutional implications of the crisis was the UN.[5] Speaking in the UN General Assembly on 23 September 2008, US President George W. Bush tried to set a reassuring tone that the crisis could be handled by actions at the national level and that his administration was on top of efforts to manage the situation. The theme he emphasized was interdependence, not coordinated action: "We have taken bold steps to prevent a severe disruption of the American economy, which would have a devastating effect on other economies around the world." The administration and Congress were working on a bail-out package, he added, "and I'm confident we will act in the urgent timeframe required."[6]

Sarkozy upped the ante by calling for an immediate summit aimed at moving toward a form of "regulated capitalism" to replace a world financial system that had become destabilized. Pointing to a G8-plus meeting, Sarkozy said that it was the duty of leaders of those states most directly concerned to meet to examine the lessons learnt: "The 21st century world cannot be governed with the institutions of the 20th century." Moreover, "The global nature of this crisis means that the solutions we adopt must also be global, and decided upon within legitimate, trusted multilateral forums." Therefore, he concluded, "Let us act so that our international institutions are more coherent, more representative, stronger and more respected."[7]

A follow-up meeting was held in Washington on 8 October in which Sarkozy (accompanied by President of the European Commission José Manuel Barroso, and Christine Lagarde, then the French finance minister and later the IMF managing director) tried to move Bush toward an enlarged G8 with pivotal emerging states, albeit significantly not a full-fledged G20.

In the meantime, though, a number of other events shifted momentum away from the G8-plus format toward the G20. The first and most decisive was the unanticipated attendance of Bush and Treasury Secretary Henry (Hank) Paulson at the G20 finance ministers and central bankers at an emergency session during the annual meeting of the IMF in Washington on 11 October. After that event it was reported that, "Bush said he had come because the crisis had spread globally and was so serious that he planned to expand the discussions to solve the crisis beyond the G7 to the G20."[8] Significantly, Paulson writes in his memoirs that he had proposed a G20 meeting before Sarkozy's visit in an effort to deflect the French approach which the "White House suspected [was an effort] to pull off a publicity coup on our home turf."[9]

A second, albeit indirect, momentum-builder toward a G20 was the public endorsement by Gordon Brown for the need to move on a plan of "coordinated action" as the way forward.[10] While not an explicit endorsement of the G20 notion, Brown had a number of incentives to move in that direction. Not only did he have a longstanding connection with G20 Finance, but his year of hosting the forum was coming up in 2009. His concern with building "a new Bretton Woods ... a new international financial architecture for the years ahead" accentuated his personal/ideational rivalry with Sarkozy. As a key minister and advisor to Brown put it later in his memoirs, "the G20 was Gordon's chance to show his strength and skills on the world stage, as a former finance minister unrivalled in his knowledge of the global economy. If we succeeded, we would not only demonstrate the appeal of our policies, but also Gordon's gifts as a leader."[11]

Third, Australia's Prime Minister Kevin Rudd advised Bush, just before he and Paulson met with G20 Finance, that any initiative must go beyond the G7 or indeed a G8-plus. Rudd argued that, "the better vehicle for a coordinated response to calm the markets and toughen financial regulation was the broader G20 grouping, including G7 members plus China and a range of other nations from South America and the Middle East, as well as Australia."[12] Australia's championing of the elevation of the G20 meshed in turn with the strong support for the forum by both Korea and Indonesia.

Whatever the precise mix, all of these forces combined to prioritize the G20 over the G8-plus model. Bush might have been a "lame duck" but on this issue he did not act as one. Fearful that the Sarkozy approach would gain traction, he made it clear that he wanted the summit to be bigger and more inclusive than the G8-plus model. As John Kirton puts it, the US approach was to "go slow, go long, go limited, go light," whereas France's was to "go fast, go short, go wide, go deep."[13]

Still, defeat on the structure did not mean that Sarkozy's bid to shape the G20 format had faded. Combining his personal energy with French diplomatic assets, Sarkozy moved successfully to bolster the already large European delegation at the first G20 summit with the additions of Spain and the Netherlands, invited in an ad hoc fashion without official member status. Sarkozy also tried to wrest back some of the momentum by his extremely verbose press conference after the summit, a performance that was in marked contrast to Bush's minimalist style.

The other option that Bush deflected was the choice of the UN itself as a universal "crisis committee."[14] The UN initially embraced the notion of a G20, with suggestions that Secretary-General Ban Ki-moon offered the UN's New York headquarters as the summit site. However, even after another such invitation, this overture was declined by the Bush administration. Instead of establishing itself as a central component of the G20 model, therefore, the UN became gradually marginalized from the process. Although Ban did attend the Washington G20, a considerable distance appeared between the UN and the G20 approach on the eve of the summit. In a news conference on 11 November (the G20 being on 14–15 November), Ban emphasized the need for "inclusive multilateralism" with a focus on protecting the wellbeing of the developing countries, as well as major UN development goals, including climate change, food crisis issues, and financing for development.[15] The Secretary-General is an invitee at the G20 summits but, in keeping with UN protocol itself, does not have equal status to that of heads of government/state and so plays a secondary role at the G20 table.

If laudable as an overall objective, this strategy was overtaken by the items on the G20 agenda. To some extent, this distancing trend was reinforced by the response of specific members of the UN General Assembly. Rather than working more systematically to integrate its agenda into that of the G20, the General Assembly became the main site of institutional resistance to the G20. In principle, the main source of contestation came from the move by the General Assembly president (Father Miguel d'Escoto Brockmann, Nicaragua's foreign minister) to convene a panel of experts, chaired by Joseph Stiglitz, in contradistinction to the G20. Organizationally, the main alternative focal point became the UN Conference on the World Financial and Economic Crisis at the end of June 2009.

Diplomatic support for greater inclusion within the G20 process, far from disappearing, increased over time. By distancing itself (or being distanced) at the outset from the G20 process, nonetheless, the UN marginalized itself from a policy perspective. As one UN document noted, "The absence of the UN from these processes and meetings puts it at a decided disadvantage in policy discussions, even on development issues. Moreover, the UN continues to be marginalized from all G20 macro-financial discussions despite their importance for sustainable development and social progress."[16]

The evolution of the G20 in practice

Unlike traditional "like-minded" groups, the logic of the G20 is not so much bound up with norms but with process and delivery. As in classic forms of new "settlements" from the past, the public image of the G20 is that of leaders sitting at a table with their counterparts from other big countries, with their advisors behind them. This image also is in line with the interpretation that the financial crisis has brought about the return of the state.[17] Yet, although in its core composition the G20 is a concentrated club of states, central to both its role as crisis committee and steering committee, it possesses some features of the networked approach due to its links not only to the international financial institutions and the FSB, but also to other layers of technical experts in both the public and private domain.

The intensity of the G20's style presents as well a mixed picture. The technical orientation of the G20 puts the onus on a painstaking, detailed approach, with participation through a number of working groups requiring impressive expertise and stamina. Certainly this side of the G20 is important, both in its own work and through "outsourcing" to the IMF and the FSB. At the same time, nonetheless, the G20 dynamic contains striking new elements, with state officials no longer trapped in traditional scripts. Indeed, one of the most striking things about the G20 process is the degree of improvisation taking place. To be sure, these techniques sometimes go hand in hand with quiet (or closed) diplomacy. However, this should not discount the levels of hyperactivity featured via the G20. Unlike past eras of financial and economic crises, it is the extremely rapid timeline that stands out in the project.

Diplomacy cannot in turn be divorced from global governance. Intertwining the G20 in this way to a larger shift in the rules of the game puts considerable weight on a rebalancing function between North and South. These debates move in turn to explications about who won and lost by how much in the G20 dynamics. Postwar settlements make this definition clear. States gain or lose territory and access to the negotiation table and negotiated institutions, such as permanent membership of the UN Security Council. Diverging from this script, the G20 was formed as a response to an immediate economic crisis rather than after a war. Yet the exclusionary practices used to create its membership ensures that there remain both winners and losers.

In many ways it is this familiar element that is dominant. A G20 appears to have the logic that there are 20 members (with 19 countries and the European Union—EU) around the table, an extension of the G20 finance ministers and central bankers. Looking more closely, however, this model is eroded if not completely broken. Rather than being limited strictly to 20, the seats at the table increase to over 30. Moreover, the status of many actors around the table is highly ambiguous, both at the state level (Spain as a permanent guest!) as well as with respect to the presence (or absence) of international organizations.

There is the need then to provide a more nuanced gradation in levels of "winners" and "losers" in the G20 project. In keeping with the focus on process, it is the major actors across the North/South constellation who grab the bulk of the attention. In the North this brings the debate back to the contradictory role of the United States. At first glance, the opening of the "concert" to the big countries of the global South would indicate that the United States is the biggest loser. After all, it was the prime underwriter or even the hegemon of the previous order. The "Made in the USA" causation of the economic crisis—via the sub-prime mortgage meltdown and the collapse of Lehman Brothers and Bear Stearns—reinforces this declinist representation.

This straightforward view, though, gets blurred owing to the degree of US diplomatic leadership. As noted above, even as a "lame duck" president, Bush could act as an effective convener of the first meeting of an elevated G20—the leaders' "Summit on Financial Stability and the World Economy"—in November 2008 in Washington, DC. Following that, even amid all his domestic preoccupations, President Barack Obama orchestrated the major moves on the consolidated design of the G20 prior to the Pittsburgh summit in September 2009.

Alternatively, China appeared to be the big winner of the G20 ascendancy, even lending credence to the notion that China was part of a new, informal G2 inside the G20 project.[18] Yet, as with the United States, any stark conclusion must be tempered. Consistent with the realist framework, Beijing's move into the "concert" has accentuated the image of China as a *demandeur* inside the system, either by itself or in combination with India and Brazil. Another positive externality of the G20 is that it embeds the G2 within a larger, multilateral setting.

The alternative image of China posits it as the blocker of demands by other countries in the G20. From the outset China made it clear that it would not discuss global imbalances or its exchange rate policy. There were also sound instrumental reasons for China embracing the G20. It shared with other members a desire to stimulate global economic growth and was keen to cooperate because it depended so heavily on exports. It was also hard hit by increases in unemployment (20 million workers lost their jobs in the early months of the crisis).[19]

The number of countries involved in the G20 is highly salient to the question of winners and losers. The Vienna settlement (1815) was mainly negotiated by Great Britain, Austria, Prussia, and Russia, although "lesser" powers also played some part. Paris 1919 played to a similar formula, with a big three or four (when Italy is included with the United States, Great Britain, and France). Yalta and Potsdam in 1945 were owned completely by the new big three, the United States, Great Britain, and the Soviet Union. If it is true that the other major meetings were open to a wider cast, the decision to institutionalize the P5 revealed the power equation at the UN conference in San Francisco in 1945.

From this point of view, the G20 is quite different. The sense of equality among the core members allows for some distribution of convening and hosting functions. As *The Economist* declared, "The old order has effectively acknowledged that the rest of the world is too important to keep from the room."[20]

Yet the "rest" must be nuanced. To be sure, it is the big ascendant powers that command the most attention. Yet significantly, within the G20 there is also the second tier of states who can be considered to be "rising" as well. One of the key elements of the Obama administration's strategic vision before Pittsburgh was to be seen as rewarding regional allies. In geopolitical terms this meant the inclusion in the forum of countries such as South Korea, Indonesia, Australia, Turkey, and Saudi Arabia, instead of having them left out in the alternative G14 constellation. Functionally, it allowed a composition that included the Major Emitters Meeting (MEM) grouping, vital to Obama's original approach to tackling the climate change agenda.

Improvised crisis diplomacy

What stands out about the crisis committee accent put on the G20 process is the speed of the project. Certainly it is the improvised nature of the G20 that distinguishes it from other forms of collective action during earlier salient moments of crisis. The World Monetary and Economic Conference in London in the midst of the Great Depression only took place in June 1933, long after the start of the great Wall Street crash in October 1929. Likewise, the Cancun North-South conference took over a year to get off the ground, from early consultations in May 1980 to the actual summit in October 1981.

There are of course limits to how far the historical comparisons between London 1933 and Washington, DC on 14–15 November 2008 can be drawn. The G20 operated in a very different context than the 1933 London conference. For one thing, the G20 finance forum (along with the G8 summit process and outreach sessions with the so-called

O5 of China, India, Brazil, South Africa, and Mexico) had established a system in which ministers and officials were used to meeting with one another on a regular basis.

The other big difference is the embedded nature of the international institutional architecture facilitating the G20 process. One of the unanticipated results of the G20 upgrade is the revival of the IMF. In the week before the G20 leaders' summit, Bush and Paulson sat down with IMF delegates at their annual meeting.[21] Not only did the IMF dramatically move back into lending activity, but it was deemed to be the most appropriate body to establish an early-warning system for crises, with the argument that the Fund would do a better job than private-sector analysts and forecasters (including ratings agencies) with potentially severe conflicts of interest.

Nonetheless, the basic point that needs to be made is that when the crisis came in 2008, the established institutionalized format was deemed to be inadequate by the United States and other pivotal countries. This sense of inadequacy is captured by the remarks of Guido Mantega, finance minister of Brazil and chairman of the G20 Finance, in October 2008. Rather than suggesting that the G20 Finance forum, which Brazil was to host in the coming weeks, served as the best vehicle for dealing with the financial crisis, Mantega called for a new form of improvisation to deal with "the most serious financial crisis perhaps since the crisis of 1929," which "demands quick answers, immediate answers." Unfortunately, "there is no agile structure prepared to deal with emergency economic problems. That is what we have seen at this time ... We have to turn this G20 into a forum or a tool of some kind that can provide answers to immediate problems and coordinate its actions better amongst many countries."[22]

Not only was there no pushback or disagreement from the club insiders; in fact they shared the sentiment. Paulson commented that, "If you look at the global financial architecture, I don't think it reflects the global economy today." He was responding to a question whether the G7 should be expanded to include developing powers such as China, India, Russia, Brazil, and Mexico. "It's a big world, and it's a lot bigger than the G7," he added.[23]

Gordon Brown and several other G7 leaders also supported the idea. They called for a major global meeting to redesign the world's finance system and rewrite the rulebook of global capitalism. Brown argued that while the "old postwar international financial institutions are out of date ... the same sort of visionary internationalism is needed to resolve the crises and challenges of a different age," as had been demonstrated at Bretton Woods. He proposed "cross-border supervision of financial institutions; shared global standards for accounting and regulation; a more responsible approach to executive remuneration that rewards hard work, effort and enterprise but not irresponsible risk-taking ... the renewal of our international institutions to make them effective early-warning systems for the world economy," and a rejection of "the beggar-thy-neighbor protectionism that has been a feature of past crises."[24] He warned that, "We are in the first financial crisis of the new global age ... We need to recognize that if risks are globalized, then responsibilities have to be globalized as well."[25]

It was this sort of improvised action, albeit with greater output in declaratory statements as opposed to tangible operational activity, that the Bush administration produced in November 2008. Unlike the American stance in 1933, hosting such a meeting indicated that international cooperation was not to be subordinated completely to national self-help. In this "near-death" scenario localized political and policy procedures would not be enough to stop the hemorrhaging set off by the combination of market and policy failures.

Obama's subsequent endorsement helped to consolidate the project. This sense of continuity amid all the attention to "change" is made apparent by the extended utilization of improvised techniques. To be sure, this style was muted at the London G20 where Obama was content to let Brown and his team do most of the substantive running as host for the event. Indeed, with the exception of Larry Summers (as director of the National Economic Council at the White House), few within the Obama administration were focused on the G20 until Pittsburgh.[26]

Still, Obama's constructive contribution on specific issues, most notably his behind-the-scenes mediation work on the sensitive issue of whether or not Macau should be included in the list of "tax havens," can't be overlooked. After some one-on-one meetings, Obama was able to get the parties to agree to use the word "note" rather than "recognize" with respect to the list of tax havens drawn up by the Organisation for Economic Co-operation and Development (OECD) and endorsed by the G20.[27]

The high-water mark for Obama's improvised style, though, came in the run-up to the Pittsburgh summit in September 2009. By that time a sense of summit fatigue was setting in, given the intensity of the G20 process since it began in November 2008. Furthermore, there was no end in sight to summitry à la carte. South Korea was pushing for an early G20 summit, and as noted, France was contemplating a G14 instead of a G20. What the Obama team—led by Michael Froman (whose own improvised style can be measured by the fact that he was willing to conduct an interactive briefing session with US bloggers at the London G20) as G20 sherpa (a personal representative) and deputy national security advisor for international economic affairs—did, therefore, was to push for a rationalization of the process.[28] Another G20 was paired up with the regular G8 summit to be held in Canada in mid-2010. South Korea was pushed back in terms of its hosting ambitions, but received ample compensation through receiving the co-hosting position with Canada of the mid-2010 G20, along with a stand-alone event in Seoul in November 2010.

Competing interpretations of global governance

While its perceived value as a crisis committee brought it into being, ideational pressure for the establishment of a new "steering committee" for global governance has been consolidated beyond its early champions.[29] It quickly became conventional wisdom that it was now the G20 and not the G8 that was the hub of global economic governance. In Barry Eichengreen's words:

> No one who is serious about coordinating a global monetary and fiscal response to the deepest recession since World War II thinks that this is something that the G7 can engineer. Whether the task is developing ideas, reaching consensus on their desirability, or moving from ideas to implementation, the G20 which has working groups active in all these areas is where the action is.[30]

Supportive references either implicitly or explicitly stating that the G20 should serve as a steering committee became commonplace in the post-crisis atmosphere. Brown, host of the London G20, was one strong advocate of this design. Talking to the media before the Pittsburgh summit, Brown declared that, "What we are trying to do is to create a new system of international economic co-operation around the world. It's never really happened before. We've had the G8, we've had all these organizations. We've got this one chance to make a huge success of international economic cooperation."[31]

Analysts at some of the most influential American think tanks made the point just as keenly. C. Fred Bergsten, director of the Peterson Institute for International Economics, stated that the G20 had become "an effective steering committee for the world economy."[32] Stewart Patrick, at the Council on Foreign Relations, reprised the theme of "present at the creation" in terms of a big moment of institutional reform, with the G20 lying on cusp of a "new economic order."[33] Colin Bradford, at the Brookings Institution, interpreted the G20 as filling a crucial gap in governance, between states and markets: "Not having a global steering committee means that the world's free market is the only governance mechanism. And that has already failed the people."[34]

The key ingredient in all these positive interpretations is adaptability. The G7 leaders' summit held some core merit beyond its role as an informal steering group for the world economy. Such advantages hinged on the G7's like-mindedness, connecting not just "rich" countries into a single club but countries that shared common attributes in political systems and values.[35] Galvanized by the financial-economic crisis, these characteristics were subordinated in the G20 creation to other attributes centered on size and stake in the economic system. Right of entry into the "steering committee" was not based on political acceptability but on economic weight.

This fundamental reorientation was based on a number of basic assumptions. The first was that big rising states—and China, India, and Brazil in particular—were reformist and not revisionist.[36]

The second consequently predicted that because of this position, these big three emerging market economies could be trusted to be "responsible stakeholders" in the system.[37] Such an approach played down like-mindedness as the determinant for club membership with respect to economic global economic governance. In its place the G20 privileges pragmatism. That is to say, if accorded the status as club insiders, the rising states will not act in a zero-sum manner but allow "deal making" negotiations with trade-offs.

As much as anything, this faith in pragmatism would be a crucial test for the sustained progress of the G20. The economic trauma surrounding the planning for the November 2008 summit concentrated minds and cut down the blame game about who or what caused the crisis. However, amid various, though uneven, signs of recovery, disagreements among the members of the G20 surfaced shortly thereafter. This is true on specific issues (bankers' bonuses being the prime example) that divide the old establishment, especially the "Anglo" world and continental Europe.

Still, the range and intensity of possible tensions is much greater not only between the United States and China, but between the United States and India and Brazil. Basic differences persist on matters such as development and the definition and promotion of "democracy" in international affairs. Some informal bargains occurred before the Pittsburgh summit, most notably in the trade-off between putting both international financial institutions' reform and "imbalances" on the table. This sort of deal making is far more difficult after a return to "normalcy" once the crisis has abated. Under pressure to modify their domestic policies, the big countries from the global South take on the role of spoilers, with an eye to blocking initiatives that harm their interests.

Variable or eroding forms of leadership

Much of the success of the G20 has continued to hinge on US leadership. Yet the center of gravity of the global power structure is arguably no longer in the United States, a transition that reflects the erosion of US leadership capabilities both in terms of normative credentials and its geopolitical weight-cum-clout in world affairs.

Nor have any other of the big "rising" states moved to fill this leadership vacuum. China continues to play the long game in the G20, playing up the visuals of its rise but maintaining a flexible position and hedging its bets. It is comfortable in the G20 as it never was in the context of the G8 "outreach," but it has a variety of other options as well, both global and regional.

This hedging approach allows China to deal constructively with the United States on specific arrangements for the G20. What it precludes is China over-promising. There are some areas where China, along with the other rising powers, has shown leadership,[38] even in the context of the outreach group (for instance on food security). When it wants to, as in its announcement of its massive stimulus package ($586 billion) ahead of the Washington G20, it can compel attention by the sheer scale of its ability to act on its own behalf. Yet China's hybrid status as both a rising and a developing state mutes the range of out-in-front leadership activities that it is willing to take, a disinclination that may be reinforced by the more domestic orientation of its growth model.

Brazil's approach echoed some of China's hedging strategy, in that it possessed a comfort level with its rising status in the G20 that it never could obtain through the "outreach" process of the G8. Far more rapidly and vocally than China, however, Brazil combined its ambition with a scathing critique of the pre-crisis rules of the game. Guido Mantega, Brazil's finance minister, as noted above, promoted an upgrade of the G20 as a problem-solving mechanism, but he could push (along with President Lula da Silva) for this type of reform on grounds of equity. This more normative stance was based on legitimacy, in that the G8 was not a representative body. No longer was Brazil willing, Mantega stated, to be part of the outreach process: "We refuse to participate in a G7 as coffee drinkers, either in the first part of the meeting or in secondary parts of the discussions." To this critique was now added the efficiency argument. The crisis was "Made in the USA," a situation made more deficient because the United States has its hand on the tiller of the "Washington

Consensus" (the economic orthodoxy pushed by the Washington-based financial trinity of the US Treasury, the World Bank, and the IMF), dishing out stern advice to other countries on how to manage their economies.[39]

Do other countries have the will and capacity to take on innovative forms of leadership? European leaders, notably President Sarkozy of France, were the notable *demandeurs* for a summit to combat the financial crisis. In terms of longer-term influence, nonetheless, the position of Europe appears weaker. The EU pushed with some considerable success the assault on tax havens. It did so, though, with the support of the United States. The other issues at the top of the European agenda (bonuses for bankers) remain a political sideshow to the core regulatory agenda, and it is on those main-game regulatory issues that Europe has demonstrated most palpably a form of non-leadership, with national cultures and interests trumping collective action. Moreover, the success of the EU in gaining multiple seats at the G20 has rebounded to Europe's detriment in two ways. The first is that other states want seats as well (most notably Poland). The second is that a reaction has set in about over-representation. As on IMF reform, pressure will grow for European membership in the G20 to shrink, not expand.[40]

Where there may be the will and the capacity to fill the gaps in leadership is among states below the top tier. To some extent this is leadership through the extended provision of a convening power. A prime illustration is the role of South Korea. Notwithstanding a structural weight below that of not only China but Japan, and India, Korea raced ahead to grab the right to host the first G20 outside the "Anglo" world. In doing so it played up its "bridging" role with respect to its evolution from a developing country to a developed (OECD) state. Although not alone in its ambitions, Korea's unique brand is important here (punctuated by the close relationship between the Korean state and corporate giants such as Samsung). At odds with the image of concentrated concert power, the increasingly fragmented nature of the G20 has allowed members outside the G8 and the BRICS to make their own distinctive imprint on the institution.

Conclusion: moving past the first tests

As this chapter argues, the G20 passed the first (stress) tests in synchronized fashion. Despite debates about definitional issues, a striking degree of coordination was established concerning national and international stimulus packages. Notwithstanding the protectionist flavor of "Buy America" and other types of procurement programs, borders were kept open with no return to the beggar-thy-neighbor autarchic "solutions" of the 1930s. Regardless of the intensity of the diplomatic process, it took at least a year before any signs of summit fatigue set in.

Passing these first tests, however, does not ensure that the G20 has become consolidated at the apex of global governance. On the contrary, as displayed in Chapter 5 and Chapter 6, some degree of backtracking on the G20 promises has become apparent, due either to exhaustion and complacency, or to ideological and policy concerns about the promises. The United States could be instrumental in bringing the G20 into being, but it was no longer strong enough to impose its will on others. Notwithstanding the impression that it was concert power in action, increasingly the image of the G20 was that of a fragmented—and possibly fraying—institution.

As in other institutions the lack of a command and control structure exacerbated the fragmentation of the G20. Big is difficult especially when—as noted in the concluding chapters—there are not only so many interests and identities around the G20 table but so much delegation to other institutions, above all the IMF and FSB. Still, even if raising the level of difficulty, the central take-away from this chapter is precisely the need for commitment by the G20 members as equal members in an innovative and central form of global governance. This commitment was readily attained under traumatic crisis conditions. It was much harder to maintain over a longer and more uneven set of circumstances.

5 Consolidating or fragmenting the G20

- Crisis committee or hub of economic governance?
- Hub and spoke institutions
- A tight hub or a loose vehicle for caucuses?
- The 3G and bridging the legitimacy gap
- Conclusion: moving forward or losing its grip?

The shifting global order may be witnessing a parallel shift from a command-and-control model to a consent-and-cooperation model of global governance, with limits and caveats to both models as idealized depictions. The image of the G20 has been that of a pivot of concerted global cooperation. In structure this forum appears to have the character of a "constructed focal point" by which policy direction is coordinated among key actors at the hub of decision making.[1] Some observers have emphasized the thickness in the degree of control and command that the G20 exerts throughout the world. Anders Åslund, for example, sees the G20 as a new form of centralized "concert of powers" with a high degree of global authority, dictating to others.[2]

At odds with this representation of the G20 as a command-and-control type of institution, however, are some important features of the G20 that signify an incompleteness of design. Rather than being a thick, finished project, this forum displays in many ways an open plan that projects institutional thinness and fragility.[3] If by definition the G20 is the group of the world's economic and geopolitical heavyweights, it has also been sensitive to avoid giving the impression that it speaks for the rest of the world.

This chapter highlights a number of key areas in which this incompleteness is projected. The first centers on the central purpose of the G20. At the Pittsburgh meeting the dominant scenario was that the G20 had metamorphosed to become the primary hub of global economic governance. This opened the way for the G20 to move to focus on an expanded domain of issues, with an orientation toward not only the immediate agenda of "recession busting," but also additional areas stretching from finance and climate change to development.

Still, what appears clear is the extent to which the G20 has shrunk and not expanded its own agenda. Such a concerted orientation showcases the G20's key (and impressive) role as a crisis committee and the prospect that it could move into the role of an embedded steering committee. The "go-to" standing of the G20 at the moment of crisis in practical policy terms meshed with the need for a fundamental rearrangement in the distribution of the share and stakes of global political and diplomatic power. At its core, the G20's attraction—but also the source of its heightened stakes in institutional performance—came with the recognition that the two tests (as crisis committee and hub of economic global governance) were inextricably linked. As John Lipsky, the deputy managing director of the International Monetary Fund (IMF), put it at the time of the Pittsburgh summit, "This movement to the G20 and away from the G7 is recognizing economic realities. You can't talk about the global economy without having the major dynamic emerging economies at the table."[4]

The danger, nonetheless, is that such an extended focus on keeping up the momentum, and then winding it down through a coordinated exit strategy, distracts attention from the more ambitious objective of embedding the G20 as a steering committee over a much wider policy agenda. Although we touch on this dilemma in this chapter, we leave a fuller discussion of the tensions between the crisis committee and steering committee over a much wider agenda to Chapter 6.

The second area of incompleteness centers on the primary organizational role of the G20. Until Toronto (when President Lula da Silva of Brazil missed the meeting),[5] all the invited leaders took their places around the table. Moreover, the G20 has had the ability to call in (or alternatively sideline) the attendance not only of individual countries, but also international and regional organizations. This stark display of its convening power does much to reinforce the image of the G20 as a new concert of powers, with a command-and-control position in global affairs.

Yet the hub image must be judged not only by its "club" but its "network" model, in that the G20 has offloaded many of its responsibilities to other bodies, most notably to the Financial Stability Board (FSB) and the IMF.[6] In doing so it has helped revive the IMF from its position of relative decline since the time of the Asian crisis in the late 1990s. In many ways this relationship strengthens the position of the G20, in that it provides the forum with amplified technical support. Yet it also opens up the scenario where the IMF's position could be strengthened to the point where it may be judged itself to be the hub institution. By way of comparison, the United Nations (UN) has moved from some initial signs that it was part of this wider G20 network to a somewhat disconnected relationship.

The third area of incompleteness centers on the relationship between the G20 and other G groups. The image of the G20 as a hub or "constructed focal point" assumes that the G20's ascendancy is of such a magnitude that other G groups are placed in a decidedly subordinate position or eliminated altogether. Yet, contradicting this supposition, other Gs have not withered away. This is especially notable in the staying power of the G8, but it is reflected also in the caucusing efforts by select states from the global South, encompassing states from within and without the G20. A prime example of a new dynamic emerging from the creation of the G20 are the activities of the Global Governance Group (3G) that is composed of an array of small countries that want to be engaged, both on principle and self-interest, with the G20.

These three areas do not exhaust the spectrum of debate about the G20. However, they do cut into the main sources of debate about the process and progress of the institutional format. The manner and the degree to which these issues are settled (or not) will influence not just the efficiency but the legitimacy of the G20 project. The discussion of these debates in this chapter will then extend into a fuller discussion of the successes and constraints of the G20 in Chapter 6 and Chapter 7.

Crisis committee or hub of economic governance?

The primary purpose of the G20 will only evolve with the clarification of its agenda. Under current conditions the logic of concentrating its efforts on its role as a crisis committee is unassailable. At the domestic political level, this focus remains the top priority for most G20 members. The infusion of massive amounts of public money both directly and indirectly (through increased funding for international organizations) has done much to resuscitate national economies after the profound financial shocks experienced in 2008.

Notwithstanding this success, though, the recovery process is still fragile with a number of problematic scenarios in train, including a highly differentiated road to recovery. Up to Toronto there was a built-in incentive for state officials to favor holding the course, with no stretching of the agenda until the commitments made in prior G20s (and Pittsburgh in particular) had been met.[7] The dominant message has largely been that governments needed to "finish the job" by implementing the stimulus measures they provided before putting on the brakes, which if done too abruptly or sharply, could push many economies back into recession.[8]

Diplomatically, this concentrated approach also had the advantage of not going too far in disturbing the consensus established through the G20 process. At the time of Pittsburgh in September 2009, there did appear to be the prospect that the agenda could open up in a more ambitious manner. Most notably, the issue of "imbalances" was placed on the agenda along with a renewal of the drive for reforming the international financial institutions (IFIs).[9]

Since Pittsburgh any such prospect for an enlarged consensus has eroded considerably. The relationship between China and the United States has been severely tested amidst charges of heightened protectionism and currency manipulation (as well as geopolitical maneuverings). More generally, the G20's willingness and/or ability to expand its mandate have been curtailed by the frozen condition of issues such as finance for climate change.

The momentum stalled. The Doha round of trade talks has gone nowhere. Trade and investment to fuel private sector-led growth and development have not been liberalized. Bilateral free-trade arrangements seem more likely than greater openness and liberalization under binding, treaty-based multilateral regimes. A 5 percent shift in IMF voting shares from the sclerotic established economies to the fast-rising ones is not strikingly dramatic. Paul Martin, the intellectual and political godfather of the G20 Leaders' summit, had warned that the G20 could not function as the world's new steering committee "under the old rule of sovereign rights without sovereign duties."[10] Unfortunately, after the sense of crisis dissipated, the gravitational forces of the system of sovereign states began to pull even the G20 countries back toward the pursuit of narrow self-interests.

All this being said, the institutional dangers of not progressing beyond the role of crisis committee need to be rehearsed. At its core, the G20 at the leaders' level was premised on the idea that leaders could do things that finance ministers, central bank governors and other state officials could not. They could mobilize resources. They could make difficult trade-offs between apples and oranges. They could demonstrate through their involvement that "they cared" through times of economic crisis.

Only during exceptional circumstances, however, do leaders immerse themselves in the continuous and deep details of public policy. A finance-driven crisis is one such instance, but there is a limit to this type of personal involvement. The agenda as it has evolved in the G20 process is very technical indeed, stretching the limit of intricate personal involvement. To be sure, one of the attractions for leaders of the G8 was its looseness, in that leaders could mix policy details with political talk.

The fundamental risk for the G20 if it does not expand its mandate, therefore, is that as the crisis recedes, an exit strategy will not only take place with some staged withdrawal of the stimulus spending, but in parallel some exit strategy will evolve for the leaders' involvement in the G20. Again, during times of crisis, leaders, either for economic or political reasons, pick up on issues that would otherwise be under the purview of cabinet ministers and their bureaucrats. This is certainly the case in the aftermath of the global financial crisis (GFC) that broke out in 2008. Leaders are keenly interested in all of the issues both as causes and effects of the crisis, whether bank bonuses, the regulation of hedge funds, new levies or taxation, and the establishment of "living wills" and other forms of regulatory reform.

The sustainability of such an involvement is questionable. With a return to "normalcy" (itself a contested condition) leaders will be attracted in turn to a more ordinary role. That is to say, they will want to site themselves as strategic steerers not as tactical doers.

Indeed, a sense that a return to normalcy was possible emerged as early as April 2009 amid the London summit. Mario Draghi, in his position as chair of the FSB (before moving to become President of the European Central Bank), stated in a report that:

> It appears that the worst scenarios regarding prospects for the global economy and financial system are no longer quite so prominent in the minds of market participants. This offers us a unique window of opportunity both for short-term actions to stabilize institutions and promote credit extension, and for implementing measures to strengthen the system for the longer term.[11]

Moreover, the space for the G20 for concerted efforts on the regulatory agenda was increasingly constrained. Over time the locus of control of policy initiatives in this domain has shifted back to the national level. The key turning point came with the decision of the Obama administration to sponsor the bill, "Financial Crisis Responsibility Fee," designed to recoup taxpayer funds and reduce risk-taking by banks. This unilateral US action complicated joint action through the G20 for an insurance levy or tax on banks, especially as some other countries also opposed such initiatives. Significantly, albeit with mixed motivations of their own, some prominent voices in the private sector—for example, John Varley, chief executive of Barclays,[12] and Stuart Fraser, policy chair at the City of London[13]—have criticized the United States for pushing ahead with its own regulatory reform at the expense of concerted action.

From this perspective, going bigger in terms of the G20 agenda has considerable allure. An atmosphere where a wide variety of issues and potential trade-offs between unrelated and dissimilar issues can be discussed will certainly keep the leaders' engagement far more than the technicalities of financial regulations and reform. Certainly, there will be limits on this going big approach. Above all, security issues many be off limits. Still, even with these constraints there is some space to expand the agenda.

Although concentrating on the core agenda of the G20, Canadian Prime Minister Stephen Harper (co-host of the June 2010 summit) highlighted the connection between setting a "credible plan" for an exit strategy with "consequences beyond the purely economic." In his address to the South Korean parliament in December 2009, Harper argued that problems from a lack of sustainable growth would eventually spill over to issues of environmental security as well as peace and security issues.[14]

South Korea, as the host for the November G20 summit, also emphasized the need for the forum to move to the stage where "global leaders aggressively coordinate their exit plans."[15] Beyond this, though, Seoul also sent a number of signals that it was contemplating stretching out the agenda for the G20 when it hosted the forum in November 2010. In his various "outreach" efforts, Changyong Rhee, South Korea's Secretary-General of the Presidential Committee for the G20 Summit, placed high emphasis on efforts to solidify the G20's role not only as the "premier forum" for crisis management but also for beyond-crisis economic cooperation. On top of follow-ups to Pittsburgh on recovery and exit strategies, a framework for sustainable and balanced growth, and the reform of IFIs, other issues such as trade, food and energy security, and climate financing were highlighted.[16]

As a collective entity, the G20's willingness to move beyond its global crisis committee role to embrace a wider agenda even extended to its reaction to the Haiti earthquake. Helped by the fact that the sherpas (personal representatives) of its member countries were meeting in Mexico, the G20 was able to act on a consensual basis with respect to this emergency: " ... we the G20 reaffirm our readiness and commitment to send immediate economic and in kind assistance to attend to the basic human needs of the Haitian population at this time of hardship."[17]

Hub and spoke institutions

When the GFC hit in full force in 2008, the G20 was in the clear ascendancy over other institutions, including the IMF. Indeed, a strong case can be made that of all the international organizations, the IMF suffered from the deepest legitimacy "deficit" over the past decade. One of the unanticipated consequences of the crisis was the re-emergence of the IMF as a credible and pivotal institution. Even so, in a number of declarations, the IMF continued to state that it is subordinate to the G20. The role that it plays was said to be that of helping the G20 states adapt their policies and to assess the wider implications of these policies. As the Director of the IMF's Strategy, Policy and Review Department contended that, "We see our role as a trusted advisor, with the G20 firmly in the driver's seat."[18]

On some issues, however, the IMF can be viewed as trying to move to strengthen its own ascendant position. By December 2009, it signaled that it was shifting its attention from "rescue efforts" to ensuring longer-term stability. Outlining its work plan for the next six months, the IMF said it would help countries devise strategies to withdraw excess liquidity. The IMF also sent some indications of more ambitious objectives. Managing Director Dominique Strauss-Kahn told the IMF Executive Board in December 2009 that the mix of innovative responses to the crisis was important, but he also went on to emphasize the enhanced systemic importance of the IMF, contending that "the formal mandate of the Fund may not fully capture what is expected of an effective guardian of global macro-economic stability."[19]

To be sure, if this activity demonstrated the ambition of the IMF, it also revealed the current limits of the IMF as a parallel (or even competitive) hub. It beat a retreat from the suggestion that it was conducting assessments of countries, on whether or not their economic policies promoted balanced economic growth, not as part of any formal surveillance role but only as "technical advice." Certainly there was no suggestion that the IMF had any legal right or technical mechanism for compelling changes in policy. All it could do was to plug the data provided by the G20 countries into a "raw" global scenario, assessing (after reconciling differences in macroeconomic projections) whether additional adjustments were necessary to reach growth objectives and ensure financial stability.[20]

At the Seoul summit in November 2010, the G20 leaders called for enhanced economic surveillance, urging the IMF "to focus on systemic risks and vulnerabilities." A former deputy secretary-general of the Organisation for Economic Co-operation and Development (OECD) notes that the G20 represents 85 percent of world gross domestic product (GDP), about the same as the OECD did when first created. By 2015 the OECD will represent only 50 percent of world GDP and only a few European members of the OECD are in the G20. However, the OECD has an efficient secretariat and therefore, according to him,

"Closer cooperation among the IMF, the OECD and the G20 would make enhanced surveillance even more effective."[21]

In comparative terms, however, the IMF has been able to locate itself inside the G20 nexus in a far superior manner than the UN. Even in areas of strength the UN faced a challenge from the G20 in terms of agenda expansion. The prime illustration of this type of situation where the G20 was being contemplated as a default option was on climate change. Having been left out of the US-BASIC (Brazil, South Africa, India, and China) meeting at the end of the December 2009 Copenhagen climate summit, EU officials alluded to a turn toward the G20. As the foreign minister of Spain, the country assuming the EU presidency, noted, "We need to change our negotiating strategy."[22]

A tight hub or a loose vehicle for caucuses?

The G20 brings together all countries with clout, size, and weight in the world economy. The three attributes in combination make them systemically significant. Although not every G20 participant satisfies all three criteria, every country that does so is included in the G20.

This is not enough to shield the G20 from charges that it too is a self-selected group based on size, wealth, and power. The image of the G20 as a tight hub or redesigned apex of power is premised on a fundamental change of identity and sense of interest of its members. What is so different about the G20 is that instead of like-mindedness as the cement binding the group, consolidation is achieved by deliverables derived from problem-solving on an issue-specific basis. The G8 was a club of the like-minded, essentially transatlantic with Japan co-opted in. The G20 is more representative of the global diversity of power, wealth, and values.

Such a privileging of pragmatism runs into two sets of problems. One, touched on earlier, is the problem that the individual countries in the G20 may prefer to subordinate collective action within the G20 to domestic policy preferences. This problem stands out in the Obama administration's Financial Crisis Responsibility Fee, but it is reflected as well in the decision of the Brown government to have a one-off tax on bankers' bonuses, the move by Australia to increase interest rates, etc.

The problem, however, goes beyond interests. It underscores as well the unsettled nature of a shared identity within the G20. The states can come together in the time of crisis but are they willing to make the G20 the "hub" of their primary focus in terms of diplomatic activities, never mind primary loyalty?

Canada (the 2010 co-host along with South Korea) bought solidly into the G20 project as a problem-solving mechanism. At Pittsburgh, Harper lauded the G20 substantive achievements as "historic." He noted that a year before stock markets were falling at a precipitous rate and financial institutions were collapsing in ways not seen since the 1930s, and "now we are seeing signs of growth." Conceding that the G8 was "not a sufficient group [anymore] to deal with major economic and financial issues," he acknowledged the G20 as an alternative forum had worked well as a crisis committee. Had it not been possible, for the first time in history, to get the leaders of the major economies in one room together and coordinate their policies, the result could have been very different.[24] Although a bit unwieldy, the G20 had thus proved its value since leaders first met in Washington at the height of the financial shocks.[25] At the same time, Harper emphasized in Pittsburgh that the G8 would not disappear. While it will no longer be the premier body on economic issues, he noted that the G8 also had an active problem-solving role in other areas like development and international peace and security: "We view it important that these kinds of discussions continue."[26]

The promotion of open democracy and individual liberty both within the original G7 members and also globally was accepted by the group at its very first meeting in Rambouillet, France in 1975. As John Kirton has argued,[27] the G7 was a major democratic concert that combined globally dominant power with the shared social purpose of democratic pluralism and market economy. The incorporation of a defeated but democratizing Russia (as it seemed or perhaps, more accurately, as it was hoped at the time) with the G7's transformation into the G8 was soon followed by a relative shift in power to some key emerging non-Western actors. That is, in a world of globalization and connectivity, political victory in the Cold War was followed by a relative economic decline in a globalizing, open, and tightly wired world in which other systemically significant actors had to be accommodated and incorporated at the top table of global economic policy making.

Since the Pittsburgh G20 summit in 2009, however, it is the privileging of like-mindedness that has gained momentum. This approach came to the fore of the G7 finance minister meeting in Iqalluit, in the Canadian territory of Nunavut, with its back-to-basics organizational style. The site of the meeting was small. Moreover, the agenda was to be stripped down, rebranded as a "fireside chat" style with no formal communiqué.

Amid the onus on convenience, with an enhanced comfort level, there was no escaping the fact that at its core this approach was premised on a heightened degree of like-mindedness. As one Canadian official was quoted as arguing, such an organizational format was considered to be the model for the ongoing structure: "There likely is merit in making sure those who are like-minded and who rely on each other for trade and commerce and investment have some sort of united front."[28]

This image of the G8 as a like-minded forum was enhanced further in the agenda-setting process. "Hard" security agenda issues have been given considerable attention, notably Iran and nuclear issues (including "dirty" bombs) and vulnerability of fragile states. Equally, though, high-profile "soft" issues have gained ascendancy, with a heightened focus on the UN Millennium Development Goals generally[29]—and maternal health in particular—through the provision of clean water, inoculations, and the training of health workers.

Looking specifically at the architectural implications of this dual structure, it is possible to see a scenario where—assuming the continuing existence of the G20 as a leaders' summit—the G8 becomes in effect a caucus group of like-minded states. Organizationally, positioning the G8 meeting before the G20 plays into this scenario. So does the focus of the G8 on developmental issues. The positive cast on this scenario would allow some move toward convergence on select issues. Internally, this type of caucus formation might drive greater coherence within the G8. Externally, development issues appear to be a good barometer about whether this structure is useful or not.

The negative spin, by way of contrast, suggests the hardening not of the connections but the disconnections between the G8 and the big "emerging" states in the G20. This interpretation of the scenario puts the emphasis on the competition between rival caucuses of the G20 membership. That is to say, a counterpart of the G8 caucus would become embedded via some extension of either the O5 from the Heiligendamm process or more likely the BRICS.

Nor, it should be added, is the G8 free of problems. Despite the image of like-mindedness, many big rifts divide the G8 members. One case in point is the issue of bank taxes, with several European countries, most consistently Germany and France, pushing initiatives to implement such measures and Canada and Japan resisting.[30] Another case comes on the divide between those G8 countries in favor of putting the emphasis on austerity over public finances and those that stress ongoing stimulus as the road to recovery.

Additionally, the idiosyncratic nature of G8 hosting needs to be mentioned. It was difficult even for the most ardent supporters of the G8 to retain faith about its viability when it was hosted by Italian Prime Minister Silvio Berlusconi in 2009. As one prominent journalist predicted, Berlusconi wasted an excellent opportunity to revive the G8 much earlier than expected:

> I would ... argue that the G8 was quite well-placed to see off the upstart G20—were it not for one thing. Next year it will be presided over by that one-man wrecking crew, Silvio Berlusconi, the Prime Minister of Italy ... After a year with Berlusconi in charge, I can confidently predict that the G8 will be a smouldering ruin.[31]

The fact that the G8 survived Berlusconi and its internal rifts is testimony to the difficulty of transition in terms of the architecture of global governance. With all its advantages, the G20 still faced the barriers that bigness imparted. On the one hand, the bigness within the G20 meant a decline in informality, an attribute much in tune with leaders' comfort zone. On the other hand, the G20 was not big enough to refute all charges and perceptions that it was an instrument of concert power.

Through some of its issue-specific targeting the G20 reinforces this impression. The classic case goes back to the "tax haven" or offshore financial corporate offices controversy. Without representation, small states concentrating on this type of offshore (or in some cases, onshore) activities found themselves in the firing lines of efforts to name and shame. Thus for both symbolic (exclusion) and instrumental (eroding competitive advantage) reasons, a number of small states began to combine in rival enterprises.

The 3G and bridging the legitimacy gap

Signs of mobilization along this line may be emanating though groupings such as the Global Redesign Initiative sponsored by Qatar, Singapore, and Switzerland within the World Economic Forum, as well as the Singapore-driven Global Governance Group or 3G. Both tap into a palpable sense of frustration that the G20 is not adequately reflecting the concerns of small states that are not its members, even though these states face the same challenges.

Led by Singapore, with its UN Ambassador Vanu Gopala Menon in a key role, the 3G has played a constructive role as a bridge between the G20 and the UN system. Its goal is to engage the G20 and help to shape its evolution so that broader community interests beyond the G20's members are taken on board. The composition of the G20 reflects the contemporary political geography of the world but is less than an exact mirror. It includes 10 non-Western countries, of which six are

Asian and three Islamic. A 20-strong global group in principle can be large enough to incorporate the world's diversity yet compact enough to foster personal relationships and build trust among them, but in the existing G20 Europe is over-represented while Africa is under-represented. The European bias worsened with the invitations to Spain and the Netherlands in Washington in 2008. To redress that, the heads of the African Union and the Association of Southeast Asian Nations (ASEAN) were invited to Pittsburgh in 2009.[32]

The 28-strong 3G,[33] conceptualized initially at the time of the London G20 summit in April 2009, has come together in the belief that by working collectively, the 3G members might channel their views into the G20 process more effectively. They have taken care to be constructive more than critical. Representing several small and medium-sized countries, the 3G has been particularly supportive of the formal participation of the UN Secretary-General in the G20 summits and preparatory meetings on behalf of the wider UN membership. Otherwise the G20 will suffer from consultative, inclusiveness, and transparency deficits.

Obviously the G7 is a more congenial setting for discussing sensitive political and security issues with more of a shared sense of political (liberal democracy) and economic (free market) values. However, the small size comes at the cost of representativeness and legitimacy. Having 55 seats at the table in Pittsburgh, however, seems to have gone way too far in the opposite direction: "Whoever organized it did not have a clue."[34] As the Americas, with a bigger total population and economic output alike than Europe (in 2008, 676 to 498 million people, and US$18.6 trillion and $17.3 trillion, respectively[35]), have a total of five seats at the G20 table, perhaps Europe's representation could be cut down to five as well.

The critique from a small-state perspective intersects with the embedded perspective of universalism through signs that the UN Secretary-General supported mobilization against the G20 not just in the form of the 192 initiative but in smaller groups. George Yeo, Singapore's foreign minister, commented during a well-publicized visit to Davos:

> The UN Secretary-General Ban Ki-moon supports our initiative and I think he should play a bigger role in those [G20] meetings because he represents all of us. The G-20 should not be exclusivist in its approach when it convenes meetings on particular areas of interest and must include other countries by using variable geometry for different subjects so that different countries can attend.[36]

A tangible sign that the 3G was able to bridge its leverage and the extension of legitimacy was through the rapprochement of the UN Secretary-

General's (UNSG) role in the G20. As noted, the Bush administration had chosen the IFIs over the UN in an explicitly exclusionary fashion. What the G20 was instrumental in doing was to re-insert the UNSG into the G20 process, if not as a primary actor then at least in a connected/ supportive manner. This re-insertion was done above all through persistent lobbying in the run-up to the Toronto 2010 summit, due to concerns that UNSG Ban Ki-moon would be excluded from the summit. A second achievement in instrumental results, due to 3G pressure and in combination with other forces (including the push by South Korea as host), was the acceptance by the G20 of a formula for non-member participation, enabling the summit host to invite up to five guests. Although mainly directed at the settlement of the question of regional representation, the 3G was the main beneficiary of the decision of this G20 just before the November 2010 summit to introduce a "G20 plus five" approach, with the Korean preparatory committee explicitly stating that this decision had been made because "we finally agreed that we needed to have a better geographical balance."[37]

Conclusion: moving forward or losing its grip?

Post-Pittsburgh, as described in this chapter the G20 became characterized by an unanticipated looseness and fragility rather than a consolidated quality in its organizational architecture. As a crisis committee the G20 can be lauded. Faced with an emergency the G20 quickly established itself as the pivotal go-to forum. As a more extended project, however, more questions than answers appear.

Of course decisive moves could be made to allow a transition in the G20 from crisis committee to a bona fide hub of global economic governance. Pittsburgh demonstrated that such moves are possible, given some degree of concerted will and diplomatic skill. Such moves need a ripeness that combines a sense of need with some sense of relief that the meltdown associated with the economic shocks of late 2008 has passed. Movement into this condition was further complicated, however, by the appearance of the "euro" crisis from the beginning of 2010 with a focus on the deficiencies of quantity and quality of bank capital, liquidity and leverage of a number of European countries beginning with Greece and moving on to Ireland, Portugal, and Spain (the "PIGS"). The outset of this ancillary crisis meant that the core issue of "exit strategies" meant to be pivotal to the agenda of the Toronto summit was put off until Korea.

Beyond the implications of the euro crisis for European integration, this situation also provided credence to those who pointed to a decoupling of growth and recovery on a global basis. Whereas Europe was foundering (with Germany the noticeable exception), Asia and Brazil grew appreciably, fuelled by the Chinese stimulus program and consumer demand in the other big countries of the global South.[38]

Quite clearly, then, the G20 entered into an different in-between period in which initiatives are possible but only within a more restricted environment, due not to the appearance of more formidable domestic political constraints but the association of identities and interests with other international forums apart from the G20. These limitations do not induce defection but straddling and hedging behavior.

Such issues, while complicating the analysis, however, do not necessarily have to be judged fatal. If the G20 represented a new steering committee it could not achieve this form via tight control. In terms of intensity it needs to take a flexible approach to the regulatory agenda, allowing a more pluralistic model that accepts (but has surveillance) over different national models.

In terms of scope, the G20 needed to showcase its network as much as its club personality. As noted at Seoul, leaders decided to limit non-member invitees to five, of which two had to be from Africa. The fact that the G20 has facilitated the renewal (and reform) of institutions like the IMF and the FSB should be viewed as a positive benefit, not a threat. Again, however, issues of overlapping mandates need to be dealt with.

In a similar manner organizational questions surrounding the relationship between the G20 and the G8 should not be treated as either/or. The G20 will consolidate its leadership mantle if it shows instrumental legitimacy, that is to say by working effectively. A sense of like-mindedness points to the sustainability of a G8, but any escalation of a competitive relationship with the G20 is unlikely to help achieve greater efficiency for the G8. Rather than pushing to tighten the organizational format, the best approach may be to increase the looseness, encouraging the engagement of a number of other caucus groupings. As it is, there have been calls for an East Asian or Asia-Pacific caucus within the G20.[39]

As part of the global rebalancing of the moral world order, an obvious question is: who will define the norms of responsibility? One of the best definitions was provided by Robert Zoellick when he was Deputy Secretary of State: "Responsible stakeholders ... recognize that the international system sustains their peaceful prosperity, so they work to sustain that system."[40] As China, India, and Brazil emerge as important growth centers in the world economy, the age of the West disrespecting the rest's role, relevance, and voice is passing. A much-needed global moral rebalancing is in train. Westerners have lost their previous capacity to set standards and rules of behavior for the world. However, will the non-G8 members of the G20 become "responsible stakeholders"? One possible precedent is Japan. Although it was not a partner in designing and establishing the post-1945 international institutions, it became fully integrated into the global economic and security orders, recovered prosperity, and acquired a major stake in the stability of the international system.

Looking at the West versus the rest narrative within the G20, as also in the larger multilateral system, there are significant differences of worldviews and values on the right balance between states and markets; on the nature of, reach of, and limits to state sovereignty with respect to international surveillance of economic policy instruments and performance as well as the use of force to quell domestic unrest and challenges to state authority; and on the sources of domestic legitimacy as expressed in demands for democracy and respect for human rights and dignity of the individual person.[41]

So far, the signs are that the new players in the global bloc are more interested in the status and trappings of power than in assuming the burdens of leadership that come with the territory. Nor is it clear that they have the institutional capacity to connect national aspirations of rapid economic development and political stability to breaking global gridlocks on such issues as climate change, nuclear security, and agricultural trade. Besides, free-riding is actually a very rational strategy of maximizing benefits and gains and minimizing costs and pain.

Of the newer, non-Western members of the G20, China is probably the most committed to an externally oriented strategy of economic and diplomatic engagement with other actors, to consolidate stability, expand markets, and secure access to the vast resources required to sustain China's growth and development.[42] Many developing countries have benefitted concretely from growing Chinese involvement in building physical infrastructure, especially transportation and buildings; technical assistance in building public health infrastructure; financial and industrial training; and so on. The contours of China's future foreign policy will be shaped by the demands and sentiments of the Chinese people, by the studied deliberations and conclusions of the intellectual and political elite, and by the post-2012, post-Hu Jintao and Wen Jiabao leadership.

Brazil adopted a markedly assertive foreign policy under President Lula da Silva, positioning itself as a natural Latin American leader, opening several new embassies and consulates and investing considerable political and diplomatic energy in projecting Brazil globally. Just as importantly, Brazil showed a capacity and willingness to distinguish itself from US and Western policy, if necessary by standing up to Washington, for example in the joint initiative with Turkey to resolve the standoff with Iran over its nuclear program.

In part the Brazil-Turkey initiative, which drew a positive response from Iran but was quashed by the UN Security Council, reflected growing self-confidence among the new emerging powers. In part also it reflected growing concerns about US dereliction of duties in providing global public goods and underwriting international order.

As the only Southeast Asian member of the G20, Indonesia can be a bridge between the G20 and smaller developing economies and use its seat at the table to push for issues of relevance to them, such as strong, balanced, and sustainable growth to reduce and eliminate poverty; the eradication of corruption; food security; commodity price stability; the creation of a global financial safety net as a second line of defense against future economic shocks; and reform of IFIs to give more voice and vote to developing countries.[43] Even more interestingly, G20 membership has helped to instill self-confidence in Indonesia as a global diplomatic player beyond, but without undermining, its Southeast Asian identity.

Similarly, calls have been made for South Africa to push the African development agenda with a focus on issues like debt relief, market access, aid, and improved access to health services and medicines.[44]

Such a revamped organizational design, nonetheless, should not at all mean a decline of ambition. On the contrary, focusing less centrally on the details of being a crisis committee allowed a greater emphasis on getting its functions as a steering committee right. Paul Martin as finance minister of Canada (1993–2002) was the political entrepreneur responsible for creating G20 Finance and chairing its first three meetings in Berlin (1999), Montreal (2000), and Ottawa (2001). He can also accurately be described as the political godfather of G20 Leaders, a concept he pushed and advocated as and after being prime minister of Canada (2003–06). His views therefore carry weight. He argues that the G20 "has begun the needed transition from global crisis responder to modern diplomacy's steering committee." Furthermore, success in the transition will depend, first, on the G20's ability to make globalization work for everyone, including non-G20 members; and second, on its capacity to contain the contagion resulting from the interdependence of countries on a broad range of issues. "In both instances I believe the answer lies in the G20's ability to demonstrate that the protection of sovereignty in today's world is directly proportional to the degree it is shared."[45]

As we will explore in Chapter 6, however, the positive elements of a looseness of design come up against some formidable constraints in practice. The expectation that the G20 could move smoothly to a steering committee role was premised on the assumption that the G20 could deal effectively with its original core mandate as a crisis committee. This task was made much more difficult by the protracted and uneven extension of the financial crisis. It was one thing to face obstacles about sovereignty over a broader range of issues. It was another thing completely to be bogged down in the "recession-busting" dynamics amid increasingly divergent views about how to deal with these aftershocks.

6 The G20 between the dynamics of innovation and constraint

- Reviewing and previewing the G20 summits 2008–12
- Expanding the G20 substantive agenda
- Conclusion: between a crisis committee and a steering committee

The G20 at the leaders' level stands at the center of a process of innovative design with respect to global governance. In many ways this was a design that privileged stability—the need for the old order to re-shape itself if it was to survive.[1] Yet it also contained elements of equality. Only with a bold leap that addressed the representation issue head on, and bridged the global North–South divide, could the question of legitimacy as well as inherent effectiveness gaps be addressed. The tensions and divisions in the G20 have not morphed into a straightforward replica of the traditional North–South split but rather are cross-cutting issues. This phenomenon comes out strongly on issues such as bank taxes, where the resistance of Canada, Australia, and Japan was joined by China, Brazil, and Mexico. It is also witnessed in the debate over imbalances where Germany and Japan are linked with China as "surplus" countries versus the "deficit" countries (above all the United States).[2]

The recognized champion of this reformist model was Paul Martin, successively finance minister and prime minister of Canada between 1993 and 2006. In a speech at the Woodrow Wilson Center in Washington in April 2004, Martin articulated the genesis and the framework he had in mind:

> … an approach I believe to be worthwhile would be to look at the lessons learned from the Group of 20 Finance Ministers that was formed in the wake of the Asian financial crisis that began in 1997. We foresaw an informal gathering of Finance Ministers, representing established and emerging centers of influence, and coming from very different political, economic, cultural and religious traditions.

We wanted to bridge the "us" versus "them" mentality that bedevils so many international meetings, and it has worked remarkably well— because peer pressure is often a very effective way to force decisions. We believe a similar approach among leaders could help crack some of the toughest issues facing the world.[3]

Ideally, therefore, the G20 contained elements of advances toward a cosmopolitan order, in which countries from most of the major regions and cultures would obtain representation. Not only could the G20 offer instrumental delivery, it could do so explicitly as a forum of "unlike" actors, fully reflective of a diversity of voices. Instrumentally, although continuing to come up against serious barriers pertaining to competitive national interests, the G20 can be situated as a forum in which participants have the potential to make a genuine effort to find solutions that can be accepted by others on the basis of openness to learning and deliberation.[4]

As the G20 moved from concept to practice, galvanized by the financial shocks of late 2008, many of these claims became embedded in the project. As David Held has argued, the G20 featured "an unprecedented successful attempt by developing countries to extend their participation in key institutions of global governance."[5] During its first year, as demonstrated in Chapter 4 and Chapter 5, the G20 elicited considerable praise as a new institution of global economic governance. From the first Washington G20 leaders' summit in November 2008 through to the third Pittsburgh summit in September 2009, it helped policy makers manage the global financial crisis in a much more cooperative and effective manner than their counterparts in the era of the Great Depression. The G20 leaders were also applauded for actively launching important international reform initiatives to address key causes of the crisis, notably global imbalances and regulatory failures.

In contrast to the successes of the initial summits, the Toronto summit in June 2010 and the Seoul summit in November 2010 present more mixed if not completely sober experiences. As the urgency of the economic crisis diminished, the sense of common purpose that united the G20 leaders seemed less present. Caio Koch-Weser, former managing director of the World Bank and Germany's secretary of state for international finance, notes that although the London summit made important decisions, the G20 "has been fragmenting and diluting" since then. It gets bogged down in the news agenda of the day. Instead of wasting time drafting headline-grabbing communiqués on the global issues of the day, he believes, the G20 would do better to establish a small secretariat to focus on structural issues, such as current account imbalances.[6]

By the time of the Seoul summit in particular, the G20 became caught up in a number of bitter disputes such as those over the "currency war," both in terms of US charges of Chinese manipulation of the RMB and US quantitative easing, and global imbalances and the debate over current account targets. The media increasingly adopted a much more skeptical view than their earlier glowing reviews of the G20's role as a crisis committee. The new mood was summed up by the *Financial Times*, which concluded that the Seoul G20 demonstrated "how not to run the world."[7] This pessimistic mood, moreover, was not dispelled in the lead-up to Cannes: "Whether it can move from platitudes to policy on the eurozone and on global imbalances will be the test of its relevance as a body, even if it has already shown itself to be short of the world's premier global economic forum."[8]

The formidable constraints on the G20 should not be ignored. Due to the embedded constraints of collective action, as Stephen Krasner predicted, the Seoul G20 "stumbled" over a wide number of impediments before it.[9] Yet in terms of both agenda and form, this stumble does not translate into a collapse of the G20 project. The constraints should not, therefore, be exaggerated to the point where the G20 is viewed as having lost its capacity to act as a hub of global governance. Amid all the high-profile tensions and abundance of competing voices and interests,[10] there are glimpses that the G20 is moving—albeit slower than some observers expected—from a crisis committee to a steering committee at the apex of power. Among its successes are:

- it has cut through the traditional boundaries of North-South;
- it has mobilized both national and international fiscal stimulus packages;
- it has prevented a repeat of 1930s-style protectionism;
- it has served as a platform to build a new regulatory regime through the Financial Stability Board (FSB), invoking mechanisms for benchmarking and peer pressure;
- it endorsed the new strengthened bank and liquidity standards developed by the Basel Committee on Banking Supervision at its request;[11] and
- it has negotiated policy trade-offs and facilitated compromises, including quota and vote reform for the emerging economies in the International Monetary Fund (IMF).

In this chapter we review both the capacity of the G20 for innovation and the hold of constraints in two different, albeit connected, ways. On the one hand, we go through the dynamics of the G20 summits in chronological order. This summary is intended to provide a concise analysis of both the major achievements and limitations of these meetings. On the other hand, we probe the option of the G20 moving beyond the crisis committee functions, increasingly dominant in the review of more recent G20s, to a steering function with a much broader ambit beyond dealing with the immediate consequences of the financial crisis.

Reviewing and previewing the G20 summits 2008–12

Washington, London and Pittsburgh, November 2008–September 2009

Convened at the height of and in response to the global financial crisis (GFC), the inaugural G20 leaders' summit held a double significance. It reflected the emerging global power configuration and it symbolized the need to have emerging powers seated at the table. At Washington, London, and Pittsburgh in 2008–09, the top priority for the G20 summits was a massive package of budgetary stimulus. Accepting its role as the premier economic steward for the world, the G20 focused on restarting global economic growth through coordinated fiscal stimuli and additional resources for the IMF to provide lines of credit and facilitate flows of capital; restoring financial stability and correcting global imbalances, particularly between excessive export dependence and anemic domestic spending; avoiding competitive devaluations and protectionist measures; and instituting better financial market regulatory mechanisms to avoid a repeat of the threat of financial meltdown.

Its shift from a crisis response mechanism to a forum for addressing systemic reforms has been less dramatic. On the economic front, it has sought to tackle global imbalances, particularly between the heavy export orientation of China and the conspicuous lack of consumption savings in Japan and the United States. Reforming the financial regulatory regime has also been a priority item on the G20 agenda, including a 5 percent shift in IMF quotas from industrialized to developing countries.

At their first meeting in Washington in November 2008, ironically at the initiative and under the chairmanship of the global governance-phobic US President George W. Bush, leaders agreed in principle to avoid protectionism and coordinate policy responses to the great financial crisis. Faced with a predicted global economic contraction of almost 3 percent, and apprehensive of a resulting slew of protectionist measures, world leaders committed themselves to refrain from new barriers to trade and investment, new export restrictions, or World Trade Organization (WTO)-inconsistent export stimulus measures.

At the second summit, in London on 12 April 2009, G20 leaders from the North and South acted to ensure recovery, repair the financial systems and maintain national and global flows of capital through coordinated expansionary fiscal and monetary policies. That is one, not insignificant, explanation for the more rapid recovery than anticipated. The "Standstill Provision" was extended through 2010. The agreements were honored despite an anticipated downturn in global trade of almost 10 percent. The US$5 trillion-worth of concerted fiscal expansion by the 19 major economies of the world, surpassing the 2 percent of gross domestic product (GDP) target set for implementation by 31 March 2009, was unprecedented in scale and scope.[12] Financial markets recovered, economic activity restarted and green shoots of financial recovery could be detected in several places.

The more enduring significance is that, grasping that a global economy requires global governance and that such governance is possible only through global cooperation, the world's leaders agreed to a broad reform agenda. In addition, the leaders agreed to new domestic and international initiatives to improve the oversight, surveillance, and regulation of financial markets and institutions, and to reform the IMF and give it additional resources to strengthen its central role in the international monetary system. Greater resources were promised to the IMF to strengthen its financial crisis management role, and decisions were announced to reform the financial regulatory system and underwrite global capital flows. They thus recommitted to an open trading system described by Pascal Lamy, director-general of the WTO, as "an insurance policy against protectionism."[13]

Once Washington announced that it would be hosting the third G20 summit, in Pittsburgh in September, the already scheduled G8 summit in l'Aquila, Italy for July was rendered inoperative as far as any major economic decision was concerned. At the time, the third G20 summit in Pittsburgh was hailed for marking a critical transition from crisis to recovery. The focus in Pittsburgh accordingly was to put in place policy and institutional measures that would prevent a return to crisis, through reforms to the world's premier economic and financial systems. Earlier promises were reiterated and the task of monitoring progress on financial regulation was assigned to the FSB, an upgraded model of the previous Financial Stability Forum. Most importantly, the world's great and good designated the G20 as "the premier forum" for international economic cooperation.

The two central elements were a new Framework for Strong, Sustainable, and Balanced Growth, on the one hand, and reforms of the financial regulatory and supervisory instruments, on the other. For the first time ever, a large number of countries representing 85 percent of the world's economic output agreed to work together to assess one another's economic plans with a view to consistency and mutual implications, to come to a consensus on best practice for the necessary reforms to redesign the global economic governance architecture, and to modify existing and adopt new policies to rebalance global demand in order to promote strong and sustainable growth for all. The Pittsburgh reforms included rules on more capital to back lending (equity ratio) and to minimize leveraged trading.

After Pittsburgh, as the G20 moved out of "its heroic phase," some momentum and urgency was lost.[14] The June 2010 summit in Toronto degenerated into running battles between an extraordinarily large number of police and protestors, and that will likely be its defining and enduring image.[15]

Seoul, 2010

The G20 meetings in Seoul, South Korea in 2010 and Los Cabos, Mexico in 2012 were important for the symbolic shared ownership of the G20. The November 2010 meeting in Seoul was the first time a G20 leaders' summit was held in an Asian country and a non-G8 country. Its modest impact on Western media commentators largely reflects that it spoke mostly to developing country concerns. Europe agreed to give up two seats in the 24-member IMF executive board to emerging market economies. Having earlier asked for stronger new bank and liquidity standards to be developed by the Basel Committee on Banking Supervision, the G20 endorsed these in Seoul. Of particular interest was the Seoul commitment to better reflect emerging market perspectives in developing financial regulatory reforms, for example the authority and capacity to supervise local branches of foreign financial institutions, or tools for mitigating the impact of excessive capital flows (a dispute over which had led to a standoff between Malaysia and the IMF during the Asian financial crisis of 1997). With Argentina, Brazil, China, Indonesia, and Russia among those countries to have placed some restrictions on capital movements in and out of their jurisdictions, and steered by the G20, the IMF has taken a more relaxed stance toward this as a regulatory tool than was the case in the 1990s or early 2000s.

Befitting their developing-country status, the non-G8 members succeeded in putting on the G20 agenda the issues of economic development, infrastructure for growth, development aid, and financial safety nets. This was important because although the G20 is a club of the world's economic heavyweights, somewhat counter-intuitively it also includes the world's majority of people living below the extreme poverty line of $1.25 per day.[16] The Seoul Development Consensus not only sidelined the Washington Consensus on neoliberalism, but it also moved the development debate in rich countries beyond merely the design and level of aid packages, to focus instead on structurally important pillars of development like education and skills, infrastructure, domestic mobilization of resources, private sector-led growth, social inclusion, and food security. In other words, it returned to looking at successful models of development from outside the West, including, of course, South Korea which wants to promote itself as a bridge between the industrialized and developing worlds. Western precedents, values, and benchmarks are being quietly shelved in favor of more pragmatic, individually tailored policies for the specific economic and social conditions of each country. Perhaps this could be taken one critical step further by using the G20 to redesign the multilateral architecture for development cooperation between North and South, including questions of inequality in and among nations and the distributive outcomes and gains from globalization.

The G20 working group on development, co-chaired by South Africa and South Korea, self-evidently speaks to developing-country concerns. It builds on the Seoul Development Consensus which in turn is based on South Korea's successful transition from a poor developing country to an Organisation for Economic Co-operation and Development (OECD) member, with an emphasis on growth-led development through physical infrastructure, employable skills, and access to finance and investment. A World Bank paper suggests that there would be considerable benefits to extending the emphasis on infrastructure-led growth to all economies.[17] Because this will require a coordinated effort to remove policy and market failures and an annual $400 billion–$650 billion shortfall in infrastructure financing,[18] the topic is worthy of being elevated closer to the top of the G20 agenda.

The G20 set up a High-Level Panel on Infrastructure in recognition of the key role of infrastructure in eliminating bottlenecks and underwriting growth. Its brief is to tender advice on how to improve the institutional and enabling environment for infrastructure investment and to recommend innovative ideas for financing infrastructure projects, especially in difficult environments like sub-Saharan Africa. With stabilization of post-conflict countries, the world's fastest-growing young population, and vast tracts of arable land, Africa does offer an enticing prospect for growth and development if the G20 can restore confidence in global recovery and identity synergies between industrialized and developing economies for mutually beneficial partnerships.

While this extends the G20 ambit from the core mandate of aggregate global growth, the working group on anti-corruption, co-chaired by Indonesia and the United Kingdom, takes the group still farther into good governance. Follow-up discussions on employment, food security, and health will take it into the realm of social policy. Climate change financing and technology transfer would see it intruding into energy security even while not straying too far from its core economic mandate.

The G20 working group on corruption is a useful illustration of how a summit process can spark tangible measures and progress on a key policy agenda. Its action plan called for ratification of the United Nations (UN) Convention against Corruption (which all G20 countries have signed, though a few are yet to ratify), the enactment of laws against foreign bribery and the creation of stronger national anti-corruption agencies. This shows the potential for synergy between the informal G process and the world's organized multilateral machinery. The UN-centered multilateralism and the loosely structured G20 as a forum of informal cooperation can be mutually reinforcing if done right. The G20 working group also recommends cooperation with the OECD, the enactment and enforcement of anti-foreign bribery legislation, the creation of strong and effective national anti-corruption agencies, whistle-blower protection, the confiscation of illicitly acquired wealth and assets, and the denial of safe haven for corrupt officials and leaders. That is, a modest investment of time and attention by leaders can leverage significant action and progress on outstanding policy issues.

However, Seoul also anticipated some difficulties down the road. The trade-surplus countries rejected the notion of binding commitments to stimulate domestic demand, so the leaders delegated the task to the IMF, and the task of making recommendations on how to regulate banks was left to the FSB. Washington also brought pressure to bear on China at Seoul on artificially pegging the value of the RMB too low to the dollar. However, the United States came in for criticism too, for the expansive policy (quantitative easing II) announced by the Federal Reserve just ahead of the Seoul summit. (As we saw in a previous chapter, the BRICS—Brazil, Russia, India, China, and South Africa—returned to this criticism in much more forceful language at their New Delhi summit some months later.) In the end the leaders agreed to refrain from competitive currency devaluations and move toward a more market-based exchange rate system. As both issues—trade imbalances and currency rates—have strained relations between Beijing and Washington for decades, it would have been highly optimistic to expect a new institutional setting to overcome the underlying division of interests.

Cannes, November 2011

If Seoul in 2010 was important for the symbolism of Asia as the driver of global growth, Cannes in 2011 was even more poignant for the symbolism of Europe as the sick man of the world going cap-in-hand to Asia. The G20 summit in Cannes on 3–4 November 2011 was held at a time of a faltering global economy, downward revisions in economic growth projections, a deepening sovereign debt crisis in Europe, and rising global unemployment. Because expectations were not high, however, the disappointment at the meager outcome was muted. The internal European problem of the economic-cum-political crisis in Greece effectively hijacked the G20 agenda to rebalance the global economy, underwrite financial stability and tackle urgent new issues like food security, but perhaps the lasting image and fitting metaphor will be that of the Europeans going cap-in-hand to China to bail out their governments and financial institutions, and being told to find their own solutions.

The November 2011 summit in France was inevitably overshadowed by the continuing crisis in the eurozone. In the world economic and financial survey issued ahead of the summit, the IMF noted that the outlook had become more clouded, with weakened and uneven global activity, sharp fall in confidence and growing downside risks. The structural problems afflicting the advanced economies had proven to be more intractable than expected and their expansion was forecast to be weak and bumpy. However, the prospects for the emerging market economies were still robust, provided that global financial volatility did not escalate, the European crisis was contained within the eurozone, and the United States struck "a judicious balance between support for the economy and medium-term fiscal consolidation" to put public debt on a sustainable path and implement policies to sustain the recovery.[19] Of course, protectionist pressures had to be resisted.

When the G20 met, the multiple and overlapping fiscal, banking, and institutional design crises had the potential to spill over from Europe to the rest of the G20.[20] The European leaders agreed to adopt a new set of measures—reducing Greek debt, a bank recapitalization target, and leveraging the European Financial Stability Facility (EFSF)—to calm financial-market volatility and stabilize the situation, although ending the crisis may take some time and require deep reforms. This helped the G20 leaders to avoid having to offer money themselves, instead resorting to standard communiqué language of the need for enhanced global financial stability and strong but balanced global growth.

One solution that was floated, albeit more in hope and desperation than any expectation, was for China to be the savior, and perhaps also

India and Brazil, if to a lesser extent. Their interests now extend well beyond their borders and they have real stakes in a stable international economic order. As rising powers, their expansion could offset the transatlantic contraction in the United States and Europe while assistance to Europe would help to strengthen a multipolar global economic order. Or perhaps China could buy sovereign bonds of at-risk countries like Greece, Spain, and Italy, thereby reducing their exposure and averting their default. Participation in any rescue plan for the eurozone would demonstrate that China had become a responsible stakeholder in the international economic order. With China-EU trade at more than €350 billion, China as Europe's second-biggest trading partner, and Europe as China's biggest, maintaining a multipolar global economic system and the euro as a reserve currency is clearly in China's self-interest. In return, China could also try to increase its voting weight in the IMF by acquiring some European voting shares.

However, given that China's share of the world trade is still only one-third that of Europe and the United States, this seemed far-fetched. In addition, the structural composition of imports is different, with more than half of China's imports being raw materials and intermediate goods that are then processed into goods for export. Indeed the GFC forced the Chinese authorities to confront their dependence on an investment- and export-led growth model. In response, they attempted to reduce the impact of the financial crisis through fiscal stimulus of accelerated infrastructure investment, and a monetary stimulus through easier credit, especially for housing. The risk of this was feeding a property bubble. Moreover, Chinese authorities are only too conscious that they still face immense challenges of internal social problems, regional imbalances, and inefficiencies. Internationally, while China may conceivably end up playing a balancer role between the United States and the European Union (EU), its main preoccupations have been to limit the role of the US dollar as the world's reserve currency and to reform—but not overthrow—the international monetary system.

Canada's Prime Minister Stephen Harper and Finance Minister Jim Flaherty insisted during and after the Cannes summit that IMF funds, and those of China and Brazil, should be saved for crises that could afflict the developing world. In their view, the European countries were wealthy enough to find the necessary resources and tools themselves without dipping into the world's credit. They thus rebuffed European calls for the IMF and cash-rich emerging economies to contribute to the €1 trillion EFSF and help construct a monetary firewall against further debt crises.[21] This was consistent with Canada's position prior to the summit. In an opinion article, Harper made it clear that Europe had to take "immediate and decisive action to resolve sovereign debt and banking system issues" that would restore market confidence. The G20 must focus on medium-term debt and deficit reduction plans to implement the Toronto summit commitments, increase exchange rate flexibility, undertake financial sector reforms, and resist trade protectionist measures.[22]

The result of the differing worldviews on the role of the G20 vis-à-vis the eurozone crisis was to leave a void. As an influential German analyst noted, whereas the G7 had failed to prevent financial crises in the previous decade, in this decade the G20 was failing to solve them.[23] Because of deficiencies in the institutional architecture, leaders make promises of comprehensive solutions at summits but fail to deliver afterwards. Europe had created a monetary union without the necessary fiscal and political underpinnings. Because of inter-sectoral and cross-issue linkages, fiscal rules by themselves had proven an inadequate insurance against fiscal irresponsibility, private-sector imbalances and weak banking systems. The economic logic of a monetary union backed with a central bank, a common European bond market, and labor and product market integration had been buried under national preferences and European treaties. Neither the EFSF nor even the IMF was equipped to deal with crises in countries the size of Italy. At both the European and global levels, the choice may be to create a new institutional framework with new rules and compliance mechanisms, or to accept reverses in monetary integration and financial globalization as the necessary consequences of a failure to agree on and implement fundamental reforms.

The G20 may be the right forum for this but so far, it has to be said, it has failed to deliver. The Cannes summit practically admitted that the decade-long Doha round of trade talks had failed; made no effort to reform the international monetary system; and came up with an action plan that merely reaffirmed strategies already in place.[24] Wolfgang Münchau's assessment, noted above, complemented and updated that of Len Edwards, Canada's G20 sherpa (personal representative of the prime minister) from 2008 to 2010, that the G20 had effectively been missing in action for the year leading up to the Cannes summit, in contrast to its visible role in tackling the global financial crisis aggressively from 2008 to 2010.[25]

Los Cabos, 18–19 June 2012

Mexico in 2012 was the first time a Leaders G20 was held in a Latin American country. Although this book was completed before the summit, some comments can be offered. Writing ahead of the 2012 G20 summit in Los Cabos, Lourdes Aranda, Mexico's G20 sherpa, wrote:

> In a short time, the G20 has become the mechanism par excellence to co-ordinate economic policies, promote improvements to the international financial architecture, and contribute to a stable environment that is conducive to growth and development in all countries. It is the best tool we have to overcome, in an orderly fashion, the global economic challenges that we currently face.[26]

Mexico had been diligent in preparing for the summit. While working groups prepared papers on growth, the international financial architecture and financial regulation, finance ministers focused on stabilizing the eurozone, global recovery, agriculture, employment, and business. Most interestingly, Mexico also organized a meeting of the G20 foreign ministers and put consultation with the academic community on an official footing, through the Think20 meeting.[27] There were also other outreach activities to additional sectors like the business community (B20), youth (Y20), trade unions (Labor 20 or L20) and civil society more generally (Civil Society Dialogue).

The meeting of G20 foreign ministers in Los Cabos in February 2012 might well mark a watershed in the transition of the organization from a grouping to fix the world's financial-economic problems and woes, to one addressing peace and security issues in general. The timing was crucial, with post-Gaddafi Libya in strife, the UN Security Council in disarray over the intensifying crisis in Syria, and war clouds gathering on the subject of Iran's nuclear program. Potentially, 2012 was "a defining moment for the G20, one that will either demonstrate or destroy its capacity to be an effective steering committee for the global economy."[28] The meeting did not, and no single meeting can, resolve these issues, but it did highlight that the G20 is indeed the world's only meaningful forum that brings together all the countries with geopolitical and economic clout. A refusal to use it as a discussion forum for foreign ministers and leaders on all the great issues of security, development, and human rights would be an act of willful negligence. They can and should explore areas of convergence on emerging and evolving norms, like the responsibility to protect, including when to invoke it and how to implement it; on best practices with regard to the ongoing demands for post-conflict reconstruction and growing need for disaster prevention and recovery efforts; on the unresolved search for effective prophylactic as well as ameliorative measures to deal with climate change; on the growing threats of food, water, and energy security; and on the ever-present threats of global health pandemics and nuclear catastrophes.

Expanding the G20 substantive agenda

The G20's defining characteristic is that established and emerging powers are brought to the same top table as peers. The benefits and demands of such a grouping cannot be limited to the economic and financial sector, but must also embrace political, military, and social policies. Precisely because the big global issues are very complex, bold policy innovations are less likely to generate forward movement than a gradual narrowing of differences that builds a head of cooperative steam and a track record of steady progress.

Although the protracted nature of the financial crisis has imposed severe limitations on how fast and how far the G20 can move forward to the steering committee functions, from the very start there has been some space available to do so. At the very first meeting of G20 leaders, in Washington in November 2008, the joint communiqué committed the leaders "to addressing other critical challenges such as energy security and climate change, food security, the rule of law, and the fight against terrorism, poverty, and disease."[29] The Pittsburgh communiqué in September 2009 incorporated elements of climate change and energy policies into the recovery agenda. Thus it did not address climate change as such, but the financial aspects of dealing with it without compromising the need for sustainable economic growth.

Against the push for broadening the G20 agenda is the argument that the group should remain lean, focused, and disciplined with a tightly structured agenda. The temptation of agenda expansion has afflicted too many other organizations and forums. The leaders should take up only those issues—and never too many at any one time—that require and can be shifted with heavy lifting by them. The G20 is best suited to provide strategic direction and guidance, not technical fixes. Some governments and analysts fear that its agenda will be overloaded, relative to implementation capacity and attention span, if major issues like poverty elimination and economic development, climate change and energy security, or health and food security are added prematurely. Early expansion of the agenda can come only at the expense of focus and impact. Even the G20—indeed particularly the G20 as a leaders' summit—has a finite bandwidth. Before adding an item to its agenda, hard questions must be asked. Will the extra time and effort of leaders be worth the likely gains and results? On the principle of subsidiarity, can any given issue be handled better nationally or by ministers and/or officials below the summit? On the principle of complementarity, can it be addressed more efficiently and effectively in another forum, for example a regional or multilateral organization?

One worry about extending the agenda is that any move beyond its core economic concern would infect the G20 with the "Christmas tree effect," whereby it would be weighed down with too many items. However, not all issues are ever going to be of equal importance at every summit. On some issues a modest amount of leaders-level attention can be leveraged into significant work by lower-level officials. If the G20 is to move to being the hub of global economic governance—as advertised above all at the Pittsburgh G20—it must be more than a crisis committee. It must do more than correct private wrongs stemming from the financial meltdown. It must support a wider agenda based on public goods. If it is to be consolidated beyond a crisis committee, the G20 as an institution must ramp up its ambition. As countries recover lost ground and the G20 works itself out of its first major job of strengthening the international regulatory system, a much longer list of tasks and responsibilities begins to emerge. While systemically important, remedies undertaken to address private greed in global commerce—through better regulation and institutional reform—do not provide succor for the poor in the countries affected by the reverberating crisis and unrepresented in the G20.

The changes in economic power and trade balances will have a significant impact on political and security affairs. For this reason, too, it would appear to be unrealistic to believe that the G20, particularly if it succeeds in institutionalizing itself as the premier global economic forum, can avoid being "infected" by political and security affairs that also need global steering from a compact group with clout.

If the G20 were to expand its agenda, Bruce Jones suggests, as well as the G20 Finance, another supplementary mechanism might be a G20 Foreign Ministers to coordinate policy and another national security advisors' meeting to cooperate on terrorism and nuclear nonproliferation.[30] As noted above, Mexico did precisely this in Los Cabos a few months ahead of the leaders' summit.

Development

One topic with the potential to divide along the North–South axis is the very issue of development itself.[31] Some developing countries have an interest in obtaining G20 recognition of capital controls as a legitimate policy instrument to manage excessive global liquidity and rapid high-volume financial flows, the consequences of which can be devastating for smaller economies. They have long resisted Western suggestions for codes of conduct that would curb capital controls.

One of the significant achievements of the Korea G20 was to start the dialogue if not the deliverables in this direction, with the host country advocating a vision of development through sustainable, balanced, and enduring growth. The G20 is potentially an extremely useful site for debating alternative models of growth and development to lift masses of people out of debilitating poverty and a life without much human dignity. In *Asian Drama*, Gunnar Myrdal described Asia as a continent trapped in unequal exchange with the West.[32] One of the major strands of development theory held that the only solution for developing Asia was to adopt state-led and -directed industrial policies, Soviet-style planning, frontier protection for import-substitution policies, and infusions of foreign aid (capital and expertise).

Asians were deeply displeased with the IMF's crisis management in the Asian financial crisis of 1997–98. An important shift in the global economic order has occurred in the decade since. As Razeen Sally noted in the 2011 Hayek Lecture, today's Asian Drama is "the exact opposite of Myrdal's diagnosis and prognosis," a dynamism unleashed by the liberalization and deregulation of internal market, external trade and services, of product and factor markets, and of domestic and foreign investment.[33] Asia's success, in turn, was at the heart of the uniquely successful combination of globalization, growth, and prosperity in the 1980–2008 period. The divergence in economic performance between the developed and emerging economies in the face of the financial crisis since 2008 has accelerated the long-term trend toward convergence between the West and emerging markets, especially in Asia.

After the 2008 GFC, the resulting loss of faith in Western prescriptions led many countries to look for an alternative model to replace the discredited Washington Consensus on the free-market, pro-trade, and globalization policies promoted by the Washington-based financial holy trinity of the US Treasury, the IMF, and the World Bank. Some developing countries wanted to discard it in favor of a recipe for faster growth and greater stability. They began talking of an alternative "Beijing Consensus" of a one-party state, government-guided development, strictly controlled capital markets and an authoritarian decision-making process that can think strategically for the long term, make tough choices and long-term investments, and not be distracted by daily public polls.[34] Yet the idea of "a" China model is questionable,[35] with the country being too diverse in terms of regional and related cultural differences to amount to a single coherent model. Nor can other countries adopt a Chinese economic model without also establishing a communist party or similar political system. China's development experience, with its unique path dependence, would be exceedingly difficult for other countries to replicate.[36]

China's continuing rise and the more recent economic successes of Brazil and India, combined with the recent US-sourced GFC, have revived interest in the notion of a "developmental state," with differing needs, strategies, and growth trajectories than the so-called "Anglo-American" model.[37] The defining question is which approach to balancing relations between citizens, society, market, state, the global economy, and the international normative order, can produce the greatest gains in performance and results delivery. China, Brazil, and India do offer potential development lessons from the last three decades for other states. They are all strong proponents of purposive state intervention to guide market development and national corporate growth, rather than of relying on market-led growth. They have promoted the principles of increased state intervention for market regulation, greater balance between the real economy and the virtual economy, and between reliance on the national market versus international markets. The logic behind state intervention is protecting, as much as possible, sovereign national development ("economic sovereignty"), even while seeking integration into the world economy.

Yet another alternative is the so-called Seoul Development Consensus, adopted by the G20 at the Seoul summit in November 2010. This shifts the spotlight away from foreign aid toward investments in infrastructure, education, health, technology, and manufacturing. It puts the emphasis on private sector-led, poverty-reducing economic growth and job creation that is inclusive, sustainable, resilient, and balanced. It promises to address food market volatility, exclusion from financial services, and corruption. Diplomatically this initiative is an attempt to consolidate a new middle in the G20. With good reason the core of the G20 debates is almost entirely a source simultaneously of both cooperation and tension between the old and new establishment—that is to say, between the G8 on one side and the BRICS or the Outreach 5 (O5: Brazil, China, India, Mexico, and South Africa) on the other.

Food

A top priority, as France as host of the 2011 G20 recognized, is the issue of global food security. Price fluctuations in commodities and agricultural supplies have the most severe impact on the world's poorest people.

A report by the Commission on Sustainable Agriculture and Climate Change on global food security concluded that urgent action is needed to avoid irrevocable damage to sustainable and agricultural production by 2050.[38] Several different global threats—climate change, population growth, unsustainable use of resources—are converging and thereby intensifying the crisis of food security. Of the 7 billion people in the world in 2011, 0.9 billion were undernourished, 1.5 billion were overweight,

1.4 billion lived on less than $1.25 per day, 2 billion lived in dryland areas, and 1.5 billion were dependent on land that is degrading. In addition, 1.3 billion tonnes of food produced for human consumption is lost or wasted annually. To meet the looming threat, the report says a transformation is needed in food production, distribution, and consumption systems.

Since 2008, both the G8 and the UN have targeted this issue but have suffered from deficiencies respectively of its restrictions of membership and streamlined delivery due to organizational fragmentation. In any case, with the existing bodies like the Food and Agriculture Organization (FAO), the World Food Programme (WFP), and the International Fund for Agricultural Development (IFAD),[39] mandated to alleviate hunger, grow and distribute food as needed, and enhance agricultural productivity, the G20's role is essentially limited to promoting coordination, encouraging transparency of reserve stocks and injecting political impetus.[40]

Health

Another top-level issue is global health,[41] for the planet is "united by contagion."[42] Among the "dark" sides of globalization are the rapidity with which some diseases can spread to become global pandemics; the emergence of new, deadly, and highly contagious diseases; the lack of border defenses to protect against them; and the greater vulnerability of poor countries and poor people owing to risible preventive and negligible therapeutic care.[43] The back-and-forth movement of people in large numbers as business travelers, tourists, traders, soldiers, migrants, internally displaced, and refugees; the modes of transport they use; the incubation periods that ensure that most outbreaks develop symptoms only after borders have been crossed; and the jump across plant, bird, and animal species of some diseases all add up to a deadly cocktail of exotic diseases that cross borders free of passport and visa regulations.

Over the last decade, the world has witnessed three potential scares in particular: Severe Acute Respiratory Syndrome (SARS, 2002–03), Ebola (2000–08), and avian influenza (bird flu, 2005–06). In combination with HIV/AIDS,[44] they pushed to the very top of the international agenda the question of the global governance of health, which lies at the intersection of the security agenda with the fear of deliberately caused outbreaks of global pandemics and spread of highly infectious diseases; the economic agenda that embraces both the negative impact of poor health on development prospects and poverty eradication programs, and the costs of the health sector in advanced countries; and the social justice agenda that posits health as a social value and human right.[45] Poor health in turn exacerbates many other challenges of development. A sobering study estimated the cost of non-communicable diseases from 2010 to 2030 to be $30 trillion, or 48 percent of global GDP in 2010.[46]

Health is an investment in both human and economic development, essential to fighting poverty, and essential to both human and national security. Global health governance raises questions of allocation of resources, taxation, intellectual property rights, protection of traditional knowledge, social protection, women's and children's welfare, education, urban development, and tobacco and alcohol regulation. These can and should be addressed by leaders of key countries in a forum like the G20 to complement and underpin the UN system's convening power and normative and standard-setting work, including the legally binding International Health Regulations adopted by the World Health Assembly in 2005.

Climate change

Another issue that could still move onto the agenda, although perhaps more by default than design, is climate change.[47] While negotiations will continue through the UN Framework Convention on Climate Change (UNFCCC) process, climate diplomacy could potentially be forum-shopped to the G20 as it includes the principal players necessary for any agreement.

Based on scale, magnitude, and irreversibility, global climate change constitutes a critical policy issue. Urgent energy needs now for developing and developed countries have somehow to be reconciled with longer-term goals of halting and reversing carbon emissions and global warming. All sides must acknowledge their common but differentiated responsibilities, accept an equivalence of burden-sharing, see that all countries take national action and negotiate effective regulatory regimes aimed at stabilizing financial markets as well as global levels of carbon emissions. The problem will continue to worsen not because developing countries aspire to Western levels of affluence, but because they seek a minimally decent standard of living with affordable food, housing, and transportation, clean water, hygienic sanitation, and electrification. Westerners need to focus on questions of changing lifestyles and international redistribution; developing countries need to reorient growth in cleaner and greener directions. In order to understand one another's needs, aspirations, limitations, and constraints—financial, technological, social, political—their leaders need to be able to sit around a table and engage in an intimate conversation and, over time, learn to understand, respect and hopefully even trust one another.

Conclusion: between a crisis committee and a steering committee

Right from the outset there has been a tension between the possible ways forward for the G20. The G20 at the leaders' level was born out of crisis, as indeed the G20 Finance had been. As such the core mandate was to deal with the causes and consequences of the 2008 shocks. This approach put the onus onto a complex, albeit highly important, set of technical issues, with the main dynamic at the level of leaders being to mobilize domestic state officials and international organizations such as the IMF and FSB into concerted and effective forms of action.

Yet leaders are different. With some exceptions they are not experts on financial issues. Their strengths are in galvanizing actions across the domestic and international terrain. They can also make trade-offs if and when they are necessary. By this logic there is a huge incentive for many if not all leaders to expand the ambit of discussion and negotiation.

This chapter highlights the new in-between status of the G20 between the two functions of crisis committee and steering committee, the essential context for our concluding analysis that shifts the discussion from these central debates about operational motivations and dynamics back to wider conceptual and normative concerns dealing with legitimacy, leadership, and the logic of G20 multilateralism.

7 The G20 as the answer to the crisis of global governance

- Global governance in crisis
- Extending the G20's instrumental legitimacy
- Global leadership for a globalized world
- Conclusion: the fuzzy logic of G20 multilateralism

The noted philosopher of science Thomas Kuhn pointed out that science proceeds in revolutionary steps.[1] As the number and seriousness of empirical events that cannot be accounted for within the existing dominant theoretical paradigm grow, so the search intensifies for a new paradigm that can explain the growing range of observable phenomena. A central theme of this book is that we are at an analogous stage in global governance. The existing institutions and arrangements can no longer cope with the growing number, range, and gravity of the major global problems. Domestically, because everything is interconnected—think climate change—the leading role has to be taken by heads of governments, not individual cabinet ministers. Internationally, the accumulating anomalies need to be addressed urgently and collectively. As reflected by the emergence of the G20 at the leaders' level, the global financial crisis provided an opportunity to replace antiquated, creaking, and inadequate institutions with more efficient, effective, inclusive, and credible mechanisms and forums.

This concluding chapter attempts to put the G20 into a wider perspective of how it meets the needs for global governance. As rehearsed through this book, the delivery of this reformed institution was never assured until the traumatic 2008 crisis hit. Yet, because of prior ideational and practical activity, when the demand for change came the G20 could be delivered quickly and with an impressive amount of consensus. The impact of this dramatic move goes well beyond the supply of technical fixes that we have discussed in previous chapters. As outlined in this chapter, the implications of the G20 at the leaders' level stretch right across the conceptual and normative parameters of global governance.

Global governance in crisis

As noted in the Introduction, the principles and institutions of multilateralism are facing a crisis of confidence with respect both to legitimacy and effectiveness. The challenges of global governance are manifold.[2] The evolution of international institutions to facilitate cooperation and mute conflict lags behind the rise of collective problems with cross-border dimensions. The emergence of the G20 at the leaders' level on the back of G20 Finance confirms that the evolution of an existing informal intergovernmental process is more likely to occur than the comprehensive reform of existing formal organizations (such as the UN Security Council or the International Monetary Fund—IMF), or the creation of new institutions.

The most pressing problems are global in scope and require global solutions. The policy authority and coercive capacity for mobilizing the necessary resources for tackling them remain vested in states. There is a sharp disconnect between the distribution of authority in existing international institutions and the distribution of military and economic power in the real world.

There is a gap, as well, between legitimacy and efficiency. The UN's unique legitimacy flows from its universality, which also makes it a terribly inefficient and frustrating body for making, implementing, and enforcing collective decisions. Conversely, the small size of the G7/8 forum was meant to facilitate easy and highly personalized decision making but rendered its outcomes deeply unrepresentative of population, economic, military, and diplomatic power and influence, and therefore lacking both in legitimacy and effectiveness.

Thus issues of sovereignty, legitimacy, representation, and governance are central to the ongoing and necessary conversation among the influential members of the global North and South. Of all the existing or prospective institutions, the G20 provides the best forum for such a dialogue. In a world in which all politics is stubbornly local but most big-ticket problems are global, the G20 is uniquely placed to bridge the global governance gap.

The final global governance disconnect arises from the concentration of decision-making authority in governments and intergovernmental organizations, and the diffusion and dispersal of policy-influencing actors across all sectors of modern society. Civil society and business have a long history of engagement with international governance processes and institutions, but the policy research community does not. At the end of the day, however, the task of actually redesigning the existing framework of international order of course falls on the world's major leaders. Their challenge is to harness intellectual and political leadership that marries a noble vision for the future to the hard—not to say harsh—economic and political realities of today.

Against this backdrop, the key question is not whether the G20 exists at a ministerial or leaders' level, but if the addition of G20 Leaders to the mix of multilateral machinery will help the existing architecture of global governance improve its legitimacy and effectiveness. Its central hypothesis is that to deal effectively with world-scale problems in a post-unipolar world, the globalized world requires global leadership, in effect a steering group and agenda-setting committee at leaders' level.[3] Existing institutions and processes have proven incapable of dealing with key global issues, from financial crises to climate change, agricultural trade, and nuclear proliferation and disarmament. International institutions, processes, and mechanisms are limited by their portfolio boundaries. Global problems are cross-sectoral (going beyond the substantive mandates of individual ministers or organizations) and long-term (going beyond the electoral mandate of most governments). Heads of states and governments have a unique and indispensable role to play in resolving critical global issues. In the right circumstances, leaders—and only leaders—can transcend narrow national interests.

The G20 could be the vehicle through which key global issues could be addressed and resolved, but leaders do not solve complex problems among and by themselves at summits. Based on an intensive and inclusive preparatory process, they commit to act in their own countries, and they commit their ministers to act in concert with other countries' counterparts. Leaders commission work and agree to work together in international organizations, and they agree to collaborate on specific global or regional challenges. A leaders' summit communiqué can be an important priority- and agenda-setting document, laying out the leaders' own commitments, and new mandates for international organizations (for example, the Heiligendamm process remit to the Organisation for Economic Co-operation and Development—OECD), commissioning work and action. The communiqué sometimes announces the creation of new international mechanisms, open to membership by other countries. The summit preparatory process includes multiple meetings during which sherpas from each country refine problems being addressed and debate possible solutions. Sherpas produce a draft communiqué, which forms the basis for discussion and decision by heads of government.

Extending the G20's instrumental legitimacy

In order to defuse anticipated criticisms that the G20 is but a self-selected, exclusive club, the grouping must complement its core composition with a consultative network that reaches out to other governments as well as business, civil society, and think tanks. That is, its governance model should be to consult and cultivate, not command and control, so that others have and believe they have a genuine voice. The G20 is best placed to bring together all countries that count and are likely to count in the foreseeable future because of their weight (economic, financial, diplomatic, military, and/or normative). However, it cannot be even remotely representative of the smaller, deeply vulnerable, highly stressed, and frail countries and their populations: a G20 is not a G200. The excluded must be brought into the system so that their perspectives and interests are not unheard. This will make them more receptive to endorsing G20 policy responses and collective action in the globally legitimated institutional system of the United Nations (UN). To the extent that the contemporary web of global governance includes businesses and civil society organizations as actors and participants—as well as advocates, activists, dissenters, and spoilers—they too must be brought inside the tent through innovative institutional linkages. From pandemics to climate change, the Doha trade round, food and water security, nuclear nonproliferation and disarmament, and the world's financial health, three basic questions must be asked: who most caused the problem, who is the most impacted, and who can best contribute to solve (or prolong) it?

To curtail attacks on its credibility, a strong argument can be made that the G20 must go on the offensive and show that it has the functional capability to deal with these pressing issues on a global scale—and to do so in the welfare of both the represented and unrepresented. Moreover, by targeting this key set of public goods—food security, climate change, and global health—the G20 can deepen the nature of its policy networks beyond the ambit of states. It is in a strong position to develop innovative forms of financing between business and government and encourage transfers of knowledge, wealth, and technology. At the G20 ministerial meeting in Paris in February 2011, President Nicolas Sarkozy requested a report on financing for development from the Bill and Melinda Gates Foundation, including tax rates and coverage, official development assistance, private investment, and innovative financing. Although overshadowed at the Cannes November 2011 G20 by the euro crisis, such issue-specific initiatives along with the activities of the Business 20 (or B20) have the potential to become a source of both entrepreneurial and technical leadership for the G20.

G20–United Nations

The G20 should operate as the hub of a network not just of countries, but also of international institutions, recognizing interconnections among issues and fostering points of common interest. To be effective, such a hub-and-network model instead of a club node of global governance should be neither hierarchical nor bureaucratic. Instead, the emerging "new world requires multilateral institutions that are fast, flexible, and accountable, that can give voice to the voiceless with resources at the ready."[4] In Paul Martin's conception, on some issues the G20 leaders can take decisions themselves, as they did at the second summit in London in April 2009. On other issues, however, their role will be to communicate their agreed preferences to the actual negotiating forums so that the G20's priorities "infuse global institutions with the capacity to act."[5]

Loosely structured and informal multilateral groupings like the G20 and formal multilateral organizations centered on the UN are not just compatible with each other but may well depend on, support, and strengthen one another in delivering common goals. If the G20 and the UN are perceived and function as zero-sum alternatives, both will suffer on legitimacy and effectiveness. They must therefore build a positive-sum relationship. Bruce Jones has argued that synergies between the G20 and the UN could also be tapped by creating a caucus of G20 Permanent Representatives to the UN.[6]

In a sense the legitimacy of the G20 can be gleaned also from the fact that parts of the UN system were appealing to it as the forum of choice for advancing the UN's social policy agenda. Thus, on the eve of the Cannes summit, the Director-General of the International Labour Organization appealed to the G20 to focus on the plight of the world's unemployed and insecure workers, by raising investment in job-creating infrastructure projects from 5–6 percent to 8–10 percent of gross domestic product (GDP), facilitating access to credit lines for medium-sized enterprises as the main source of job creation, underwriting training, apprenticeship and up-skilling opportunities for the young, and building universal social protection floors.[7]

At the same time, one could argue that precisely because the G20 is not a treaty-based mandated multilateral organization, it should avoid excessive outreach and consultation. For that would risk confusing the roles of the two distinct types of forums and processes and would carry the bigger risk of the G20 usurping the role of the UN system and displacing formal multilateral organizations as the locus of universal collective action. In addition, as noted by Stewart Patrick, if through the

P5 (the five permanent members of the UN Security Council) experience, and particularly the US experience, the G20 eases and facilitates genuine global consensus, these countries might look favorably on a restructured UN Security Council with an expanded permanent membership. Conversely, however, if the G20 falls victim to the multilateral blockage syndrome, their instinctive suspicions of any effort to "reform" the Security Council will be doubly strengthened.[8]

Broader consultations

With non-member invitees and regional organizations, the G8 practice was continued of the host country using its discretion, but then the G20 agreed to establish an institutional framework with some common guidelines. There are indications that the G20 has settled on a formula for non-member participation, enabling the summit host to invite up to five guests, of which at least two must be from Africa, on a consensus of G20 members rather than its own discretion.[9] On the face of it this goes a long way to settling the regional representation. Nor does this move stop individual G20 members from initiatives with regard to engaging their own regional organizations. Indonesia may have led the way. In 2009, just before Pittsburgh, the Association of Southeast Asian Nations (ASEAN) established a G20 contact group comprising the organization's finance ministers, who can meet to draft common positions that can then be transmitted to the G20 by Indonesia.

A final key test for the G20 will be its ability to build a constructive constituency within civil society, an objective in turn only possible if the G20 moves from crisis response mode to an approach that privileges an expanded agenda appropriate for an institution deemed to be the hub of global governance. To develop practical solutions to real-life problems, the number of people at the decision-making table must be restricted to a size that permits a meaningful informal conversation to occur. However, concerns have been expressed repeatedly about the potentially "undemocratic" characteristics of any "exclusive" format. To increase the effectiveness, accountability, inclusivity, and credibility of decisions, G20 summits must provide for more effective articulation of information and positions from the international civil society, business, and policy research communities, as well as excluded countries. Success requires devising processes to engage civil society, ensure corporate input, and provide consistent and relevant intellectual staff support to the G20 process.

The G20 will also need to develop modalities to ensure that leaders receive credible and consistent intellectual support. A network of think tanks and policy researchers with cutting edge capacity could be brought together as part of the advance preparation of summit meetings, as was done by Mexico in Los Cabos in 2012. This is even more critical for developing and small countries. Unless the G180 (G200 - G20) are given a voice in setting the standards and the analytical and intellectual resources to avoid being overwhelmed by the superior technical capacity of the G20 countries, they will remain rule takers. Bodies such as the G24, which represents developing countries, as well as a network of adequately capacitated think tanks with policy access to government officials, have a critical role to play in ensuring that their voices are credible and heard in the corridors of global power.[10]

Moreover, to avoid the pathology of groupthink caused by a narrow policy elite that talks to insiders and the private financial sector, parliamentarians, civil society, and non-financial officials could be given entry points for access to international regulatory discussions, so that the technocrats are neither unaware of nor unresponsive to broader societal and community concerns and values.

Secretariat

The lack of a secretariat means an absence of continuity. As with the G8, the country in the G20 rotating chair assumes the responsibility and burden of providing all secretariat functions. The G8 process worked well with the use of a sherpa as a leader's personal representative, but even the G8 was criticized for breaks in continuity, gaps in institutional memory, and lack of any mechanism to monitor the implementation of promises made by the leaders at the summits. With many more members, the diversity of the types of members, and the greater call to reflect and represent the wider global community, the G20 will falter without more systematic machinery than its G8 predecessor. The tension between the need for standing official machinery in the form of a secretariat and the strong antipathy toward any more international bureaucracy will have to be reconciled if the G20 is going to be efficient in agenda preparation, logistical management of the summit process, technical support for leaders on the agenda items for discussion, and mechanisms to monitor the implementation of agreed tasks. Similar comments apply to the need to reach out to sectors beyond government officials, including nongovernmental organizations (NGOs), business groups, and think tanks.

The informal troika of past, present, and successor hosts has served as the functional equivalent of a G20 secretariat. Not all G20 members are equal in the quality and efficiency of their bureaucratic machinery and capacity. At some stage, the demands for institutionalization will inevitably require the creation of a G20 secretariat to "provide institutional memory, continuity for monitoring and follow-up of commitments, as well as to support outreach and consultation."[11]

Even the Heiligendamm process had set up a secretariat in the OECD for the systematic engagement of the Outreach 5 (O5: Brazil, China, India, Mexico, and South Africa) by the G8. The developing countries, including those in the G20, remain suspicious of the OECD as the rich countries' club. The obvious solution in that case is for one of the non-G8 members of the G20 to host the G20 secretariat.

Global leadership for a globalized world

The stimulus to the elevation of the G20 from a meeting of the top tier finance ministers to that of the top tier global leaders was a triple crisis of loss of confidence in markets, institutional capacity and political leadership.[12] Second, neither domestic nor international institutions are seen to have the capacity to avoid and manage financial, banking, and economic crises that have a cascading effect on one another. The G20, not the UN or the Bretton Woods institutions themselves, took the lead in shifting more responsibility through greater voice and vote to emerging economies in the IMF. It also took the lead in creating new World Bank trust funds to build new development-promoting markets by supporting investments in food security and financing clean and affordable energy. An institutional innovation like the G20 Leaders was required to restore confidence and trust, put markets and the financial sector to the service of the public interest, and make globalization work for people and not markets. However, for this, third, the G20 needs leaders with vision, conviction, commitment, and strategic empathy so that, without damaging their own economies or jeopardizing the future of their own peoples, they reassert public authority over national and global markets and connect and transcend national agendas to international goals and targets. Only global summits of the most relevant and the most capable can do this and prevent public welfare from being collapsed into the private interests of the market. As Paul Martin puts it, "The question to ask is not how to keep New York, London or German bankers happy, but how to keep the global economy healthy."[13]

The accumulation of global impasses means that some sort of a "grand bargain" will be required to break them: package deals involving diffuse reciprocity and equivalence of benefits whereby every party can claim to be a "net" winner and critics cannot easily prove relative losses to foreigners. This is why the deals can only be brokered by leaders, for only they can trade oranges for apples: ministers will look only to the apples or oranges that lie in their portfolio. This will involve at least three different but interlinked sets of actors. First, only technical experts can do the necessary thorough groundwork by way of advance studies, pre-negotiations and identification of options with attendant costs and benefits. Second, only heads of governments personally engaged and with sufficient familiarity and trust in one another can focus and deliver on the tradeoffs as a steering group on behalf of the world. Third, only universal organizations can authenticate and legitimize the grand bargains.

Yet the G20 suffers from a triple leadership hit: a dysfunctional and paralyzed US political system and process, a Europe distracted by a deep sovereign debt crisis, and an Asia reluctant to step out of the shadows to assume the mantle of leadership. Leadership consists of outlining a bold vision for the community as a whole and then inspiring individuals and groups to transcend their immediate self-interest in connecting both intellectually and emotionally with the shared vision. It calls for the capacity to set standards of conduct and benchmarks of progress, explain why these matter, and coax everyone into striving for and achieving these standards and goals. The dramatic challenges during and at the end of World War II produced a generation of statesmen who rose to the occasion for designing new institutions that have served their purpose well but have been overtaken by new circumstances. We need leaders who can rise to the challenges of the twenty-first century.

A central global challenge is the redefinition of sovereignty as responsibility. This is not necessarily limited to the domestic realm. Rather, the reality is one of systemic brittleness where shocks cascade across sectors and between countries. The contemporary international system exhibits systemic risks and vulnerabilities, both horizontally from one sector to another (the sub-prime crisis, mortgage meltdown, and crises in individual banks led inexorably to a global financial crisis), and vertically from firms and nations to the world. Sovereignty understood, and jealously guarded, as financial autonomy behind political frontiers becomes a risk multiplier for the system of sovereign states.[14]

Conversely, systemic resilience lies in supranational regulatory/ surveillance, coordinating and sanctioning mechanisms sans sovereignty. The damage from regulatory arbitrage—where financial institutions have shopped around for the weakest regulatory system—has been severe and worldwide. In other words, sovereignty entails global responsibility for the extra-territorial impacts of national decisions. Following from this, the G20 must be a steering group for the whole world, not an exclusive club of, by, and for self-interested members. Multilateralism must mean more than the pursuit of national interests by international instruments. In turn, these are the considerations that potentially make the G20 the best mix of efficiency, effectiveness, legitimacy, and representation.

Conclusion: the fuzzy logic of G20 multilateralism

While there is broad agreement that the world order is in flux and that the unipolar moment has passed, the nature of the emerging multipolar order remains fuzzy. US dominance may have eroded and its edicts may be increasingly contested, but its primacy remains indisputable. Will the new order be one of robust multilateral norms and institutions? Will the world revert to a balance-of-power system with the major powers forming and reforming security alliances and economic coalitions? Or will it be one in which, exceptionally in human history, there is no center of gravity or global guardian, as argued by Charles Kupchan:[15] a G-zero[16]? The G20 will clash horribly with any effort to resurrect a balance-of-power system, but it can be adapted to an order of multilateral institutions, or it can function as the hub of a new concert system. Since the Bush administration, a relatively weaker United States has retreated from the extremes but not the habit of unilateralism. The European Union (EU) remains committed to multilateralism but has punched well below its weight both diplomatically and economically.

The BRICS (Brazil, Russia, India, China, and South Africa) are in transition from dissenters and rule takers to becoming stakeholder-managers in the inchoate new global order. Nor are they united and cohesive. A big difference between Beijing and Moscow, for example, is that China is more comfortable with global governance institutions in the economic sphere, the rules-based regimes of which protect its interests as a dominant manufacturer, but, as a rising power, is less willing to be "Gulliverized" by international rules in the security sector. With Russia the equation is reversed.[17] The other BRICS are uncertain whether to join the privileged as insiders or as representatives of the excluded Others.

As laid out in Chapter 4 and Chapter 5, as a crisis committee, the G20 has achieved some considerable success. Faced with an economic emergency of epic proportions, the G20 quickly established itself as the pivotal go-to forum for collective response management. Through its dual existence, first as a forum of ministers and then as a leaders' summit, the G20 has shown itself to be capable of robust action. Rather than sticking to a set formula, when the global financial shocks hit the G20 capably reinvented itself. The challenge that lies ahead is not to let its successful steps taken in the past temper its ability to promote an extended array of bold and original solutions in the future.

The first three G20 summits were characterized by a unity of purpose which had dissipated by the time of Toronto in 2010 and has not been regained since. The G20 countries differ in their analyses of the nature of the crisis, the reasons for its persistence and hence also on the appropriate remedies and exit strategies. This is true of countries within the old G7 across the Atlantic, not just of countries from the North and South. That said, sharply differing perspectives on trade imbalances and exchange rate policies are particularly contentious between Beijing and Washington. Underlying these differences in analyses and prescriptions are the varying degrees of severity and persistence of the crisis in the different countries, the uneven speeds of their recovery, and alternative if not competing economic models and doctrines in terms of the relative roles of the state and the market, for example with respect to industrial and social policies. Consequently, the summit communiqués merely regurgitate lowest common denominator positions.

Another continuity from the G8 to the G20 is the promise-delivery gap between summit communiqués and implementation after summits. To paraphrase a comment made in a completely different context by David Fidler,[18] a pattern of high-level attention followed by anemic implementation would reveal a debilitating elasticity in foreign policy interests among the G20 countries which would gravely undermine sustainable progress on global problems.

As the G20 honeymoon has faded, it has had more difficulty shifting from a crisis response to longer-term systemic recovery and institutional reform mode. The 2010–12 summits revealed persisting differences among G20 countries on the impact of and recovery from the global financial crisis of the industrial and developing countries, on the pace and timing of exit from the stimulus packages, on the management of trade protectionism, on China's monetary and exchange rate policies, and on whether to persevere with the UN Framework Convention on Climate Change as the main forum for negotiating climate change after the failure of the Copenhagen Conference (the BRICS preference), or shift the issue to the G20 (the EU and US position). The G20 will likely face two, on the face of it contradictory, pressures. A failure to coordinate recovery and growth will undermine the credibility and reputation of the G20 as the premier forum for managing international economic affairs. Conversely, however, success in this task could increase pressures on the G20 to be the forum of choice for managing other issues and overload it with too many major intractable problems while the forum is still in its infancy.

Looking to the future, the scale of the damage caused by the global financial crisis (GFC) is such that it may take a generation to rebuild the global economic order that promotes sustainable and equitable growth, reduces global imbalances, keeps markets open for trade, and reforms the international financial system. The G20 can remain a prisoner of the past and function in effect as the old G7 plus others. Or it can make the transition to a more cohesive grouping in which the developing country giants move beyond being passive onlookers in global rule-making and reluctant followers of the rules made by the G7 club inside the G20 shell. For their part, the old G7 will need to refrain from perpetuating its ascendancy by defining "responsible" behavior as conforming to their priorities and preferences. In the shift to a genuinely shared rule-making G20, the ASEAN experience of coordinating domestic policy choices in member countries individually with policy responses among group members collectively can add to the EU's depth of experience in shaping the logic of collective action. It will require also the G20 to define the terms of the relationship among an evolving G6 of the United States, China, and India as significant individual country actors, and the EU, Latin America, and Africa as continental groupings.

There is also the question of cultural understanding and adaptation. The G20 could face tension between Western calls for decisive, results-oriented action and Asian preferences for building consensus through painstaking dialogue. The different actors with their respective political cultures will need to find a common comfort level on process as well as outcome.

Ongoing questions and challenges for the G20 include its lack of both constitutional authority and institutional capacity; its contentious and contested relationship with the formal UN machinery as the embodiment, custodian, and representative of the international community; and its untested capacity to incubate consensus and deliver on summit commitments and pledges. Will its implementation, accountability, and compliance mechanisms and performance prove superior or inferior to those of the G8 and the UN system? Its greatest comparative advantage over the other two paradigmatic institutional competitors is its core identity as the agenda-setting leadership forum of all the critical, systemically significant actors from both the global North and South. It should make the most difference, therefore, in those problem areas where leadership commitment is the critical variable (what David Shorr calls the discipline of "the pay grade test"[19]), where the primary obstacle to identifying policy overlap and convergence and reaching consensus is the unavailability or inadequacy of an appropriate forum, and where speedy resolution is essential. Conversely, if the chief impediment is a fundamental clash of interests, if the issues in dispute are technical more than political, then a fresh institutional setting is not the answer to the lack of common interest that overrides national or sectional differences.

Whether looking back between 2008 and 2012 (when this book was completed), or looking ahead to 2013 and beyond, the challenge for the G20 is to help the world manage the reality of intensifying inter-dependence among countries and growing interconnectedness among different issues. Today's threats and challenges can neither be addressed by countries acting unilaterally and in isolation, nor compartmentally within traditional bureaucratic stovepipes. Instead, they have to be tack-led collectively by all countries acting in a series of coordinated steps, if not in close collaboration, and simultaneously across the many different but interrelated sectors. One of the best examples of this is climate change.

It is easy but mistaken to conflate problems of substance—a sig-nificant and not easily bridged clash of fundamental interests—to lack of institutional forum or robustness. The principal bottlenecks to reso-lution of the Israel–Palestine conflict, the threat of a nuclear Arma-geddon, global warming, food, water, and energy scarcity are not the absence of the right institutional settings. The GFC and the protracted European sovereign debt crisis were the products of systemic imbal-ances and it would be unfair and unrealistic to expect the G20 to have solved them. What the G20 can and did do is to provide a platform for the key leaders to come together to discuss the causes and ameliorative solutions and to coordinate their responses to the extent possible. In an important sense its value-added lies in the absence of an alternative in the existing architecture.

Thus no forum can guarantee resolution of clashing interests, but an intimate yet representative group the members of which get to know, understand, and trust one another is likelier to succeed than the G8 or the UN. The G20 should replace the G8 as the grouping that counts, with the UN serving as a universal validating rather than a credible negotiating forum. Forum hopping from the UN and G8 to the G20 will not be particularly useful if the difficulty lies not with the forum but with policy differences that reflect significant variations in interests. As a self-constituted and self-referencing grouping, the G20 has no broader political mandate, no authority to make decisions that are bind-ing on its own members, let alone on others, no formula for sharing costs of jointly approved activities according to an assessed scale of contribu-tions, and no secretariat to provide information and research services before meetings, logistical support during meetings, and implementation and delivery functions after meetings.

Like the UN, the G20, too, will suffer from an exceptionally high "degree of difficulty" rating. Only the most intractable and hard-to-resolve problems make their way to both forums. Unlike the UN, the G20 can be used to leverage top-level political leadership of all the countries that count to break deadlocks between countries and across issues. Even if solutions are not instantly available—they rarely are—the leaders can mandate their officials to work to a solution-oriented agenda. By virtue of its top leaders' representation, the G20 can also serve as the hub of the mandated multilateral organizations. As noted by Berenice Díaz Ceballos, a senior official in Mexico's G20 team, "the G-20 has played a prominent role in enhanced coordination and communication between international organizations."[20]

In surveying the architecture of global governance, the G20 offers the best crossover point between legitimacy (based on inclusiveness and representation), efficiency (which requires a compact executive decision-making body), and effectiveness (where those who make the decisions have the greatest ability to implement or thwart them). The G20 is so composed as to ensure the presence at the top table of the world's steering committee of all countries the size and/or strategic importance of which—whether economic and/or geopolitical—gives them a particularly crucial role in the discussion of global problems, needs, and solutions. When they apply their combined geopolitical weight to press on particularly intractable problems, it becomes a case of will the immovable object give way to the irresistible force?

The core animating purpose of the G20 should be to steer policy consensus and coordination, and mobilize the requisite political will to drive reform and address global challenges while navigating the shifting global currents of power, wealth, and influence. In turn, its impact will be greater if it can combine the personal engagement and informality developed by the G8 summitry, the detailed preparation and follow-up work required to vest summits with successful outcome and delivery, and the unique legitimacy that only the UN can confer as the sole authenticated voice of the collective international community. In other words, the real challenge is how to retain the positive attributes of the existing major nodes of global governance while shedding their pathologies. The answer is to configure and operate the G20 as the hub of a networked global governance.

The last word, appropriately, belongs to Paul Martin: "the time for the G20 to draw the line in the sand is now. What the [leaders] should remember is that they are not there to speak only for themselves, but also for the 173 countries that are not at the G20 table."[21] If the advice is followed, the G20 will survive and consolidate as the world's premier economic steering committee and one of its most important global governance institutions. If the advice is ignored or rejected, the G20 will quickly become a footnote in world history. The G7 was a club of, by, and for the West/North. The G20's destiny is to be the hub of a global network: by the top 20, but of and for all. It is not an incremental institutional reform to mitigate the legitimacy and effectiveness deficits of the G7/8. It is an effort at a transformative reform of the institutional architecture for governing the world by connecting the North to the South, the West to the BRICS, public authorities to the business and civil society sectors, and countries, sectors, and problems to one another across national, bureaucratic, and institutional, borders, compartments, and silos.

Notes

Introduction

1 Thomas G. Weiss and Ramesh Thakur, *Global Governance and the UN: An Unfinished Journey* (Bloomington: Indiana University Press, 2010), 1.

2 Jean-Pierre Lehmann, "Bridging the 21st Century's North–South divide," *theGlobalist* 13 March 2012, www.theglobalist.com/storyid.aspx?StoryId=9525.

3 See Ramesh Thakur, *Towards a Less Imperfect State of the World: The Gulf Between North and South* (Berlin: Friedrich Ebert Stiftung, Dialogue on Globalization Briefing Paper 4, April 2008).

4 Lehmann, "Bridging the 21st Century's North–South divide."

5 Quoted in Johann Hari, "It's Not Just Dominique Strauss-Kahn. The IMF Itself Should Be on Trial," *Independent* (London), 3 June 2011.

6 Ibid.

7 For surveys of these institutions see these and other books in the Routledge Global Institutions series: Edward C. Luck, *The UN Security Council: Practice and Promise* (2006); James Raymond Vreeland, *The International Monetary Fund: Politics of Conditional Lending* (2007); Hugh Dobson, *The Group of 7/8* (2007); Bernard M. Hoekman and Petros C. Mavroidis, *The World Trade Organization* (2007); Samuel M. Makinda and Wafula Okumu, *The African Union: Challenges of Globalization, Security and Governance* (2008); Mark Beeson, *Institutions of Asia-Pacific: ASEAN, APEC and Beyond* (2009); and Kelley Lee, *The World Health Organization* (2009).

8 Remarks by Richard Stanley, Chairman of the Stanley Foundation, at the UN General Assembly President's Thematic Debate on the UN in Global Governance, New York, 28 June 2011, Ramesh Thakur's notes from the event.

9 Rebecca R. Friedman (rapporteur), "Rivalry and Partnership—The Struggle for a New Global Governance Leadership," *Policy Dialogue Brief* (Muscatine, IA: Stanley Foundation, 2011), 8.

10 The last point is made by the creator of the G20 concept; Paul Martin, "The G20: From Global Crisis Responder to Steering Committee," in *The Oxford Handbook of Diplomacy*, ed. Andrew F. Cooper, Jorge Heine and Ramesh Thakur (Oxford: Oxford University Press, forthcoming).

11 Luiz Inácio Lula da Silva, "At Yekaterinburg, the BRICs Come of Age," *The Hindu* (Chennai), 16 June 2009.

12 George Monbiot, "The Best Way to Give the Poor a Real Voice is Through a World Parliament," *The Guardian* (London), 24 April 2007.

13 Paul Martin, "A Global Answer to Global Problems," *Foreign Affairs* 84, no. 3 (2005): 2–4.
14 G. John Ikenberry, *After Victory* (Princeton: Princeton University Press, 2000); Ian Clark, *The Post-Cold War Order: The Spoils of Peace* (Oxford: Oxford University Press, 1991).
15 David Shorr, "Making the G-20 a Reservoir of Global Leadership—A Maximalist Argument," *Policy Analysis Brief* (Muscatine, Iowa: Stanley Foundation, April 2011), 3.
16 See Robert O. Keohane, "Multilateralism: An Agenda for Research," *International Journal* 45, no. 4 (1990): 731–64; John Ruggie, "Multilateralism: The Anatomy of an Institution," *International Organization* 46, no. 3 (1992): 561–98; and Edward Newman, Ramesh Thakur and John Tirman, eds., *Multilateralism Under Challenge?* (Tokyo: United Nations University Press, 2007).
17 See Edward Newman, *A Crisis of Global Institutions? Multilateralism and International Security* (London: Routledge, 2007).
18 Alan Alexandroff and Andrew F. Cooper, eds., *Rising States, Rising Institutions: Challenges for Global Governance* (Washington, DC: Brookings Institution Press, 2010).
19 See Weiss and Thakur, *Global Governance and the UN.*
20 See Ramesh Thakur, *The United Nations, Peace and Security: From Collective Security to the Responsibility to Protect* (Cambridge: Cambridge University Press, 2006).
21 See Thomas G. Weiss, *What's Wrong with the United Nations and How to Fix It* (Cambridge: Polity, 2009).
22 See M.J. Peterson, *The UN General Assembly* (London: Routledge, 2005).
23 See Edward C. Luck, *UN Security Council: Practice and Promise* (London: Routledge, 2006).
24 See Leon Gordenker, *The UN Secretary-General and Secretariat* (London: Routledge, 2010).
25 Ivo Daalder and James Lindsay, "Divided on Being United," *Financial Times Weekend*, 6–7 November 2004.
26 See Ramesh Thakur, ed., *What is Equitable Geographic Representation in the Twenty-first Century?* (Tokyo: United Nations University, 1999).
27 See Ramesh Thakur, "Law, Legitimacy and United Nations," *Melbourne Journal of International Law* 11, no. 1 (2010): 1–26.
28 See Jorge Heine and Ramesh Thakur, eds., *The Dark Side of Globalization* (Tokyo: United Nations University Press, 2011).
29 Warwick Commission, *The Multilateral Trade Regime: Which Way Forward?* Report of the First Warwick Commission (Coventry: University of Warwick, 2007). Andrew Cooper was a member of this commission.
30 Hugo Dobson, *The Group of 7/8* (London: Routledge, 2007), 79.
31 Ibid., 81–93.
32 Timothy Garton Ash, "If Obama Really Wants to Lead us to a Free World, He Should Abolish the G8," *The Guardian*, 26 May 2011.
33 Lula da Silva, "At Yekaterinburg, the BRICs Come of Age."
34 Zhang Yan, "Powering the World," *Indian Express* (Delhi), 28 March 2012.
35 US National Intelligence Council, *Global Trends 2025: A Transformed World* (Washington, DC: US Government Printing Office, November 2008), 7.

36 Lyubov Pronina, Lucian Kim and Alex Nicholson, "BRICs Agree to Boost Global Clout at 'Historic' Russian Summit," Bloomberg, 16 June 2009.
37 Quoted in Pepe Escobar, "The BRIC Post-Washington Consensus," *Asia Times*, 17 April 2010. See also Andrew F. Cooper, "Consolidated Institutional Cooperation and/or Competitive Fragmentation in the Aftermath of the Financial Crisis," *Whitehead Journal of Diplomacy and International Relations* XIII, no. 2 (2011): 19–31.
38 Quoted in Cheng Guangjin and Wu Jiao, "Zuma Praises China's Africa Role," *China Daily*, 26 August 2010.
39 Sunny Verma and Huma Siddiqui, "BRIC Mulls SA, Indonesia & Mexico," *Financial Express* (Delhi), 26 August 2010.
40 Richard Haass, "The Case for Messy Multilateralism," *Financial Times*, 5 January 2010.
41 Colin I. Bradford and Wonhyuk Lim, "Toward the Consolidation of the G20: From Crisis Committee to Global Steering Committee," in *Global Leadership in Transition: Making the G20 More Effective and Responsive*, ed. Colin I. Bradford and Wonhyuk Lim (Washington, DC: Brookings, 2011), 8.
42 See Barry Carin and Ramesh Thakur, "Global Governance for a Global Age: The Role of Leaders in Breaking Global Deadlocks," CIGI Policy Brief No. 7 (November 2008).
43 Gerald F. Seib, "We Get the Global Perils without Global Benefits," *Wall Street Journal*, 13 October 2008.
44 Eric Helleiner, "Make or Break Time for International Financial Regulatory Reform," in *Flashpoints for the Pittsburgh Summit*, ed. Andrew F. Cooper and Daniel Schwanen (Waterloo, Ontario: Centre for International Governance Innovation, CIGI Special G20 Report), 30–35.
45 Anthony Payne, "How Many Gs are There in 'Global Governance' After the Crisis? The Perspectives of the 'Marginal Majority' of the World's States," *International Affairs* 86, no. 3 (2010): 729–40.
46 John Kirton, "The G8-G20 Partnership," *Studia Diplomatica* LXIII, nos. 2–3 (2010): 23–34.
47 James R. Vreeland, *The International Monetary Fund: Politics of Conditional Lending* (New York: Routledge, 2007); Katherine Marshall, *The World Bank: From Reconstruction to Development to Equity* (New York: Routledge, 2008).
48 Although popularized by US President George H. Bush in the aftermath of the invasion of Kuwait by Saddam Hussein's Iraq in 1990, the phrase "new world order" was first used in the context of the dying stages of the Cold War by Soviet President Mikhail Gorbachev in his address to the UN General Assembly on 7 December 1988. Its lineage is even older, having been used by President Woodrow Wilson to describe the emerging post-World War I era that would transcend balance-of-power international politics. For an account that recognized the visionary nature of Gorbachev's speech, see Haynes Johnson, "Vision on the World Stage," *Washington Post*, 9 November 1988. For a skeptical-cum-suspicious contemporary assessment, see John Kohan, "The Gorbachev Challenge," *Time Magazine*, 19 December 1988.
49 Alan Beattie, "The G20: Ad hoc Institution Faces Tough Struggle to Show it has Teeth," *Financial Times*, 10 November 2010.

50 For the classic insider view see Hank Paulson, *On the Brink: Inside the Race to Stop the Collapse of the Global Financial System* (New York: Business Plus, 2010). See also Marc Jarsulic, *Anatomy of a Financial Crisis* (Houndmills: Macmillan, 2010).

51 Dominic Wilson and Roopa Purushothaman, "Dreaming with BRICs: The Path to 2050," Goldman Sachs, *Global Economics Paper* no. 99 (New York: 1 October 2003). See also Leslie E. Armijo, "The BRICs Countries (Brazil, Russia, India, and China) as Analytical Category: Mirage or Insight?" *Asian Perspective* 31, no. 4 (2007): 7–42.

52 Jonas Parello-Plesner, "KIA—Asia's Middle Powers on the Rise?" *East Asia Forum*, 10 August 2008. See also Andrew F. Cooper and Jongryn Mo, "Middle Powers Can Punch Above Their Weight", *Wall Street Journal*, 4 November 2011.

53 Andrew F. Cooper and Agata Antkiewicz, eds., *Emerging Powers in Global Governance: Lessons from the Heiligendamm Process* (Waterloo: Wilfrid Laurier University Press, 2008).

54 See for example, C. Fred Bergsten, "A Partnership of Equals: How Washington Should Respond to China's Economic Challenge," *Foreign Affairs* 87, no. 4 (2008): 57–69; C. Fred Bergsten and C. Koch-Weser, "The G-2: A New Conceptual Basis and Operating Modality for Transatlantic Economic Relations," Paper presented to the TransAtlantic Strategy Group of the Bertelsmann Foundation, Frankfurt, July 2003; and Kishore Mahbubani, "Forget the G8, the US Needs a China-India Summit," *Financial Times*, 18 May 2012.

55 Richard B. Elrod, "The Concert of Europe: A Fresh Look at an International System," *World Politics* 28, no. 2 (1976): 159–74.

56 Geoffrey Garrett, "G2 in G20: China, the United States and the World after the Global Financial Crisis," *Global Policy* 1, no. 1 (2010): 29–39.

57 Andrew F. Cooper, "The G20 as an Improvised Crisis Committee and/or a Contested 'Steering Committee' for the World," *International Affairs* 86 no. 3 (2010): 741–57.

58 A Chatham House and Atlantic Council Report, "New Ideas for the London Summit: Recommendations to the G20 Leaders," March 2009.

1 Rebalancing world order

1 Deepak Nayyar, *Developing Countries in the World Economy: The Future in the Past?* (Helsinki: UN University World Institute for Development Economics Research, WIDER Annual Lecture 12, 2009), 41.

2 Paul Kennedy, *The Rise and Fall of Great Powers* (New York: Vintage, 1989).

3 High-level Panel on Threats, Challenges and Change, *A More Secure World: Our Shared Responsibility* (New York: United Nations, A/59/565, December 2004).

4 Graeme P. Herd, *The Global Puzzle: Order in an Age of Primacy, Power-Shifts and Interdependence* (Geneva: Geneva Center for Security Policy, Geneva Papers, Research Series no. 1, 2011).

5 See Clive Archer, *The European Union* (London: Routledge, 2008).

6 *World Economic Outlook October 2009: Sustaining the Recovery* (Washington, DC: IMF, 2009), www.imf.org/external/pubs/ft/weo/2009/02/pdf/text.

pdf; World Trade Organization, "Time Series on International Trade," Statistics Database (Geneva: WTO), stat.wto.org/StatisticalProgram/WSDB StatProgramHome.aspx?Language = E.

7 *World Economic Outlook September 2011: Slowing Growth, Rising Risks* (Washington, DC: IMF, 2011), xv–xvi, www.imf.org/external/pubs/ft/weo/2011/02/index.htm.

8 Timothy Garton Ash, "One Practical Way to Improve the State of the World: Turn G8 into G14," *The Guardian*, 24 January 2008.

9 See Ramesh Thakur, *The United Nations, Peace and Security: From Collective Security to the Responsibility to Protect* (Cambridge: Cambridge University Press, 2006), chapter 13.

10 See Hugo Dobson, *The Group of 7/8* (London: Routledge, 2007).

11 Michael Zurn, "Introduction: Law and Compliance at Different Levels," in *Law and Governance in Postnational Europe: Compliance Beyond the Nation-state*, ed. Michael Zürn and Christian Joerges (Cambridge: Cambridge University Press, 2005), 37.

12 John English, Ramesh Thakur and Andrew F. Cooper, eds., *Reforming from the Top: A Leaders' 20 Summit* (Tokyo: United Nations University Press, 2005). On the L20 initiative see also Peter C. Heap, *Globalization and Summit Reform: An Experiment in International Governance* (New York and Ottawa: Springer/IDRC, 2008), and Dries Lesage, "Globalisation, Multipolarity and the L20 as an Alternative to the G8," *Global Society* 21, no. 3 (2007): 343–61.

13 Nicholas Bayne, "Promoting Conflict Prevention and Human Security: What Can the G8 Do? Concentrating the Mind: Decision-Making in the G7/G8 System," www.g8.utoronto.ca/conferences/ 2001/rome/bayne-conflict. pdf. See also Sir Nicholas Bayne, "Prospects for the 2005 G8 Gleneagles Summit," presentation to the G8 Research Group, Trinity College, University of Toronto, 22 November 2004.

14 Great Britain, Foreign and Commonwealth Office, "G8 Structure: An Informal Club" (London, 1998), www.ciaonet.org/book/hajnal/hajnal12.html.

15 Andrew F. Cooper, "Stretching the Model of 'Coalitions of the Willing'," in *Global Governance and Diplomacy: Worlds Apart?* ed. Andrew F. Cooper, Brian Hocking and William Maley (Houndmills: Palgrave Macmillan, 2008).

16 Amrita Narlikar and Diana Tussie, "The G20 at the Cancún Ministerial: Developing Countries and Their Evolving Coalitions in the WTO," *The World Economy* 27, no. 7 (2004): 947–66.

17 On legitimacy issues, see Ian Hurd, *After Anarchy: Legitimacy and Power in the United Nations Security Council* (Princeton: Princeton University Press, 2007), and "Legitimacy and Authority in International Politics," *International Organization* 53, no. 2 (1999): 379–408; Michael Zürn "Democratic Governance Beyond the Nation-State: The EU and other International Institutions," *European Journal of International Relations* 6, no. 2 (2000): 183–221.

18 Robert D. Putnam, "Diplomacy and Domestic Politics: The Logic of Two-Level Games," *International Organization* 48, no. 3 (1988): 427–60.

19 "China Leads, BRICS Backs Iran," *Times of India*, 29 March 2012, timeso findia.indiatimes.com/business/india-business/China-leads-BRICS-backs-Iran/articleshow/12449551.cms.

20 *BRICS Summit—Delhi Declaration* (New Delhi: Ministry of External Relations, Government of India, March 29, 2012), para. 21.
21 Ibid., para. 22.
22 In this book we use the "G20" to refer to the actual group of leaders since 2008, the "G20 Finance" to describe its predecessor group of finance ministers, and the "L20" to refer to proposals about a leaders-level group of 20 countries.
23 Barry Carin and Gordon Smith, "Making Change Happen at the Global Level," in *Reforming from the Top*, ed. John English, Ramesh Thakur and Andrew F. Cooper (Tokyo: United Nations University Press, 2005), 26.
24 Paul Martin, "A Global Answer to Global Problems," *Foreign Affairs* 84, no. 3 (2005): 2–6.
25 Klaus Schwab, "Disband G8 Order: WEF Chief," BS Corporate Bureau in New Delhi, 7 February 2004.
26 Adam Harmes, *The Return of the State: Protestors, Power-brokers and the New Global Compromise* (Vancouver: Douglas & McIntyre, 2004), 10–11.
27 The Right Honourable Paul Martin, Speech by the Prime Minister, address on the occasion of his visit to Washington, DC, 29 April 2004.
28 See Richard J. Goldstone and Adam M. Smith, *International Judicial Institutions: The Architecture of International Justice at Home and Abroad* (London: Routledge, 2008).
29 Anne-Marie Slaughter, "Government Networks, World Order, and the L20," in *Reforming from the Top*, ed. John English, Ramesh Thakur and Andrew F. Cooper (Tokyo: United Nations University Press, 2005), 291. See also her "The Real New World Order", *Foreign Affairs* 76, no. 5 (1997): 183–97, and *A New World Order* (Princeton: Princeton University Press, 2004).
30 Ramesh Thakur, "How to Build a Better Brains Trust," *Globe and Mail* (Toronto), 3 June 2004.
31 Andrew F Cooper, *Niche Diplomacy: Middle Powers After the Cold War* (Houndmills: Macmillan, 1997).
32 Colin Bradford and Johannes Linn, "Global Economic Governance at a Crossroads: Replacing the G7 with the G20," The Brookings Institution *Policy Brief* 131 (April 2004).
33 See Peter Willetts, *Non-Governmental Organizations in World Politics: The Construction of Global Governance* (London: Routledge, 2010).

2 G20 Finance as prelude

1 See, for example, Robert Wade, "From 'Miracle' to 'Cronyism': Explaining the Great Asian Slump," *Cambridge Journal of Economics* 22, no. 6 (1998): 693–706.
2 Jeffrey D. Sachs, "IMF Orthodoxy isn't What Southeast Asia Needs," *International Herald Tribune*, 4 November 1997.
3 Martin Khor, "Are Asian Partners to Be Helped or Rivals to Be Hurt?" *International Herald Tribune*, 15 January 1998.
4 Anders Åslund, "The Group of 20 must be stopped," *Financial Times*, 26 November 2009.
5 On these debates see Mark Beeson and Stephen Bell, "The G-20 and International Economic Governance: Hegemony, Collectivism, or Both?

Following the East Asian Crisis of 1997–98," *Global Governance* 15, no. 1 (2009): 67–86; and Andrew Baker, "The G-7 and Architecture Debates: Norms, Authority and Global Financial Governance," in *International Finance Governance Under Stress*, ed. Geoffrey R.D. Underhill and Xiaoke Zhang (Cambridge: Cambridge University Press, 2003): 324–42.

6 On the wider implications of this disciplinary approach see Jakob Vestergaard, *Discipline in the Global Economy? International Finance and the End of Liberalism* (London: Routledge, 2009).

7 John Ibbitson and Tara Perkins, "How Canada Made the G20 Happen," *Globe and Mail*, 18 June 2010.

8 "Malaysia Miffed at Exclusion from G-20," *Euromoney* report, 26 September 1999, at www.euromoney.com. Others interpreted this exclusion as punishment for Malaysia's defiant show of independence from IMF orthodoxy and prescriptions for having briefly implemented controls on the outflow of capital during the Asian crisis. Susanne Soederberg, "The Emperor's New Suit: The New International Financial Architecture as a Reinvention of the Washington Consensus," *Global Governance* 7, no. 4 (2001), 462.

9 The controversy over Argentina's inclusion in the G20 still lingers. For recent commentaries see Andrew Cooper, "Argentina, Bete Noire of the G20," *Huffington Post*, 2 May 2012; Jorge Heine, "Should Argentina Stay in the G20?" *Miami Herald*, 16 May 2012.

10 US Department of Treasury, *Reports on International Financial Architecture: Report of the Working Group on Transparency and Accountability* (October 1998), iii, www.treasury.gov/press-center/press-releases/Documents/report31063.pdf. See also Stephany Griffith-Jones and Amar Bhattacharya, eds., *Developing Countries and the Global Financial System* (London: Commonwealth Secretariat, 2001), 157–58.

11 Quoted in Ibbitson and Perkins, "How Canada Made the G20 Happen."

12 Statement by the Hon. Paul Martin, Minister of Finance of Canada, to the Interim Committee of the IMF, Washington, 26 September 1999, www.imf.org/external/country/can/index.htm?type=9998.

13 Ibbitson and Tara Perkins, "How Canada Made the G20 Happen."

14 Paul Martin, "The International Financial Architecture: The Rule of Law," remarks before the Conference of the Canadian Institute of Advanced Legal Studies, Cambridge, UK, 12 July 1999.

15 Paul Martin, interview conducted by Candida Tamar Paltiel, G8 Research Group, Ottawa, 18 November 2001, www.g8.utoronto.ca/g20/interviews/Martin011118.pdf.

16 Yu Yongding, "China's Evolving Global View," in *Reforming from the Top: A Leaders' 20 Summit*, ed. John English, Ramesh Thakur and Andrew F. Cooper (Tokyo: United Nations University Press, 2005), 196.

17 Gerald Helleiner, "Developing Countries, Global Financial Governance and the Group of Twenty: A Note" (Toronto: University of Toronto, 2001).

18 Quoted in Ibbitson and Perkins, "How Canada Made the G20 Happen."

19 Quoted in ibid.

20 Robert W. Cox, "Gramsci, Hegemony and International Relations: An Essay in Method," in *Gramsci, Historical Materialism and International Relations*, ed. Stephen Gill (Cambridge: Cambridge University Press, 1993), 63.

21 Robert W. Cox, "Democracy in Hard Times: Economic Globalisation and the Limits to Liberal Democracy," in *The Transformation of Democracy?*

Globalisation and Territorial Democracy, ed. Anthony McGrew (Cambridge: Polity, 1997), 59–61.

22 Tony Porter, "The G-7, the Financial Stability Forum, the G-20, and the Politics of International Financial Regulation," Paper prepared for the International Studies Association Annual Meeting, Los Angeles, 15 March 2000.

23 Helleiner, "Developing Countries, Global Financial Governance and the Group of Twenty."

24 Jacqueline Best, "From the Top Down: The New Financial Architecture and the Re-Embedding of Global Finance," *New Political Economy* 8, no. 3 (2003): 363–84.

25 Michael Hodges, "What Future for the Summits?" Concluding Remarks at Conference by London School of Economics, University of Toronto G8 Research Group, and Clifford Chance, 13 May 1998.

26 Beeson and Bell, "The G-20 and International Economic Governance."

27 Leslie Elliott Armijo, ed., *Debating the Global Financial Architecture* (Albany: State University of New York Press, 2002).

28 Roy Culpepper, *Systemic Reform at a Standstill: A Flock of "Gs" in Search of Global Financial Stability*, paper commissioned by the Commonwealth Secretariat (May 2000), www.g8.utoronto.ca/scholar/culpeper2000/index.htm.

29 G-20 Finance Ministers and Central Bank Governors Meeting, 15–16 December 1999, www.fin.gc.ca/g20/news/001-e.html.

30 Culpepper, *Systemic Reform at a Standstill*, 19.

31 "Statement by the Hon. Paul Martin, Minister of Finance for Canada, to the Institute for International Economics," Washington, DC, 14 April 2000 (Ottawa: Finance Canada, 2000).

32 "Speech to the House of Commons Standing Committee on Foreign Affairs and International Trade: The Hon. Paul Martin," Ottawa, 18 May 2000 (Ottawa: Finance Canada, 2000).

33 Peter Hajnal, *The G7/G8 System: Evolution, Role and Documentation* (Aldershot: Ashgate, 2007).

34 The Rt. Hon. Paul Martin, "The Challenge of Global Governance," The Donald Gow Lecture, School of Policy Studies, Queen's University, 27 April 2007. See also Paul Martin, "A Global Answer to Global Problems," *Foreign Affairs* 84, no. 3 (2005): 2–6.

35 Ángel Gurría, "A Leaders' 20 Summit?" in *Reforming from the Top*, ed. John English, Ramesh Thakur and Andrew F. Cooper (Tokyo: United Nations University Press, 2005), 63.

36 Quoted in Barry Carin and Gordon Smith, "Making Change Happen at the Global Level," in *Reforming from the Top*, ed. English *et al.*, 40.

37 Paul Martin, "The G20: From Global Crisis Responder to Steering Committee," in *The Oxford Handbook of Diplomacy*, ed. Andrew F. Cooper, Jorge Heine, and Ramesh Thakur (Oxford: Oxford University Press, forthcoming).

38 Robert D. Putnam, "Diplomacy and Domestic Politics: The Logic of Two-Level Games," *International Organization* 48, no. 3 (1988): 427–60.

39 Andrew F. Cooper, Richard Higgott and Kim Richard Nossal, *Relocating Middle Powers: Australia and Canada in a Changing World Order* (Vancouver: University of British Columbia Press/University of Melbourne Press, 1993).

40 *The Group of 20: A History*, www.g20.org/g20/.

41 Ibid, 50.

42 www.internationalepolitik.de (2004).
43 Ethel Hazelhurst, "Sarkozy's Proposal to Include SA in G8 Meets Mixed Response," *The Star* (Johannesburg), 28 August 2007; and Amit Baruah, "Sarkozy Wants India in Expanded G8," *Hindustan Times* (Delhi), 24 January 2008.
44 Beeson and Bell, "The G-20 and International Economic Governance," 77.
45 G. John Ikenberry, *After Victory: Institutions, Strategic Restraint, and the Building of Order after Major Wars* (Princeton: Princeton University Press, 2001).
46 For more details, see Andrew F. Cooper and Agata Antkiewicz, eds., *Emerging Powers in Global Governance: Lessons from the Heiligendamm Process* (Waterloo: Wilfrid Laurier University Press, 2008).

3 G20 competitors as reform options

1 Anthony Payne, "The G8 in a Changing Global Economic Order," *International Affairs* 84, no. 3 (2008): 519–33; Timothy M. Shaw, Andrew F. Cooper, and Agata Antkiewicz, "Global and/or Regional Development at the Start of the 21st Century: China, India and (South) Africa," *Third World Quarterly* 28, no. 7 (2007): 1255–70.
2 See "Perspectives on Emerging Would-Be Great Powers." Special issue, *International Affairs* 82, no. 1 (2006): 1–94.
3 See Jorge Heine, "Network Diplomacy," in *The Oxford Handbook of Modern Diplomacy*, ed. Andrew F. Cooper, Jorge Heine, and Ramesh Thakur (Oxford: Oxford University Press, forthcoming).
4 See Gregory Chin and Ramesh Thakur, "Will China Change the Rules of Global Order?" *The Washington Quarterly* 33, no. 4 (2010): 119–38.
5 See Ian Taylor, *The Forum on China-Africa Cooperation (FOCAC)* (London: Routledge, 2012).
6 See Richard Woodward, *The Organisation for Economic Co-operation and Development (OECD)* (London: Routledge, 2009).
7 Dominic Wilson and Roopa Purushothaman, "Dreaming with BRICS: The Path to 2050," Goldman Sachs, *Global Economics Paper* no. 99 (New York: 1 October 2003).
8 John Humphrey and Dirk Messner, "The Impact of the Asian and Other Drivers on Global Governance," Paper prepared for the conference on Institutions and Development: At the Nexus of Global Change, 18–19 January 2006, St Petersburg, 2, www.ids.ac.uk/UserFiles/File/globalisation_team/asian_driver_docs/AsianDriversGovernancepaper05.pdf.
9 Jacques Chirac, "Press Briefing by French President Jacques Chirac," 9 June 2004, Sea Island, www.g8.utoronto.ca/summit/2004seaisland/chirac040609.html.
10 J. Brian Atwood, Robert S. Brown, and Princeton Lyman, *Freedom, Prosperity, and Security: The G8 Partnership with Africa, Sea Island 2004 and Beyond* (New York: Council on Foreign Relations, 2004), www.cfr.org/content/publications/attachments/G8Africa.pdf.
11 See Geoffrey Allen Pigman, *The World Economic Forum: A Multi-Stakeholder Approach to Global Governance* (London: Routledge, 2006).
12 International Task Force on Global Public Goods, *Meeting Global Challenges: International Cooperation in the National Interest* (Stockholm:

International Task Force on Global Public Goods, 2006), www.globalpolic
y.org/socecon/gpg/2006/09globalchallenges.pdf.

13 Paul Martin, "Address by Prime Minister Paul Martin on the Occasion of
his Visit to Washington DC," 29 April 2004, Washington, DC, epe.lac-bac.
gc.ca/100/205/301/prime_minister-ef/paul_martin/05-10-06/www.pm.gc.ca/en
g/news.asp@id=192.

14 Nicolas Sarkozy, "Fifteenth Ambassadors' Conference: Speech," 27 August
2007, Paris, www.ambafrance-uk.org/President-Sarkozy-s-speech.html?var_
recherche=Fifteenth%20Ambassadors%20Conference%20Speech.

15 OECD, "Structure of the Heiligendamm l'Aquila Process," www.oecd.org/
document/55/0,3343,en_21571361_40549151_40556654_1_1_1_1,00.
html#working_groups.

16 See Bernd Pfaffenbach, German Sherpa, Interview, *Der Tagesspiegel* (Berlin),
11 December 2006.

17 Thomas Fues and Julia Leininger, "Germany and the Heiligendamm Process," in *Emerging Powers in Global Governance: Lessons from the Heiligendamm Process*, ed. Andrew F. Cooper and Agata Antkiewicz (Waterloo:
Wilfrid Laurier University Press, 2008): 235–62.

18 Quoted in Hugh Williamson, "Great Powers Present and Future Try to
Keep it Casual," *Financial Times*, 4 June 2007.

19 Ibid.

20 Hugh Williamson, "Emerging Powers Flex Muscles to Push for More
Power in the G8," *Financial Times*, 4 July 2007.

21 Quoted in Praful Bidwai, "India's Clumsy Balancing Act," *Asia Times*, 26
June 2007, www.atimes.com/atimes/South_Asia/IF26Df01.html.

22 Tiankai Cui in F. Chen, "G8 Not Platform for Exerting Pressure," Government of the People's Republic of China, Beijing, 4 June 2007, www.gov.
cn/misc/2007-06/04/content_636224.htm.

23 M. Nalapat, "G8 Must Make Way for New System," *China Daily*, 7 July
2010, www.chinadaily.com.cn/think-tank/2010-07/07/content_10073688.htm.

24 Brendan Vickers, "South Africa: Global Reformism, Global Apartheid and
the Heiligendamm Process," in *Emerging Powers in Global Governance:
Lessons from the Heiligendamm Process*, ed. Andrew F. Cooper and Agata
Antkiewicz (Waterloo: Wilfrid Laurier University Press, 2008), 187.

25 Duncan Wood, "A Break with the Past or a Natural Progression: Mexico
and the Heiligendamm Process," in *Emerging Powers in Global Governance*,
ed. Cooper and Antkiewicz, 193–212.

26 See Katherine Marshall, *The World Bank: From Reconstruction to Development
to Equity* (London: Routledge, 2008).

27 See James Raymond Vreeland, *The International Monetary Fund (IMF):
Politics of Conditional Lending* (London: Routledge, 2006).

28 President Lula da Silva quoted in Paul Gillespie, "Brics Highlight Skewed
Nature of Global Power," *Irish Times*, 31 March 2012, www.irishtimes.com/
newspaper/opinion/2012/0331/1224314156764.html.

29 *BRICS Summit—Delhi Declaration* (New Delhi: Ministry of External
Relations, Government of India, 29 March 2012), para. 5.

30 Ibid., para. 6.

31 Ibid., para. 13.

32 Ibid. paras. 8–12.

33 Ibid., para. 18.

34 Charles Grant, *Russia, China and Global Governance* (London: Centre for European Reform, 2012).
35 Guy Faulconbridge, "BRIC Calls off Meeting at G20 as Lula Stays Home," Reuters, 26 June 2010, in.reuters.com/article/2010/06/27/idINIndia-4968092 0100627.
36 Thus the Delhi Declaration merely noted that "China and Russia reiterate the importance they attach to the status of Brazil, India and South Africa in international affairs and support their aspiration to play a greater role in the UN"; "BRICS Summit—Delhi Declaration," para. 26.
37 Gillespie, "Brics Highlight Skewed Nature of Global Power."
38 Meeting summaries can be found at www.l20.org, and in two books chronicling the project: Andrew F. Cooper, John English and Ramesh Thakur, eds., *Reforming from the Top: A Leaders' 20 Summit* (Tokyo: United Nations University Press, 2005); and Peter C. Heap, *Globalization and Summit Reform: An Experiment in International Governance* (Heidelberg: Springer/IDRC, 2008).

4 Financial crisis as catalyst

1 Andrew F. Cooper and Daniel Schwanen, eds., *CIGI Special G20 Report: Flashpoints for the Pittsburgh Summit* (Waterloo, Canada: Centre for International Governance Innovation, 2009); Alan Alexandroff and John Kirton, "The 'Great Recession' and the Emergence of the G20 Leaders' Summit," in *Rising States, Rising Institutions: The Challenge of Global Governance*, ed. Alan Alexandroff and Andrew F. Cooper (Washington, DC: Brookings Institution Press, 2010).
2 Steve LeVine and Theo Francis, "Obama Team Lays Groundwork for G20 Success," *Business Week*, 28 March 2009, www.businessweek.com/blogs/money_politics/archives/2009/03/obama_team_lays.html.
3 Martin Wolf, "Why the G20 Leaders Will Fail to Deal with the Big Challenge," *Financial Times*, 1 April 2009.
4 Brian Knowlton and Michael M. Grynbaum, "Greenspan 'Shocked' That Free Markets are Flawed," *The New York Times*, 23 October 2008.
5 For a discussion of the UN as a site and an actor, see Ramesh Thakur, "Multilateral Diplomacy and the United Nations: Global Governance Venue or Actor?" in *The New Dynamics of Multilateralism: Diplomacy, International Organizations, and Global Governance*, ed. James P. Muldoon, JoAnn Fagot Aviel, Richard Reitano, and Earl Sullivan (Boulder, Colo.: Westview, 2011): 249–65.
6 Quoted in Harvey Morris, "Sarkozy Presses for Capitalism Summit," *Financial Times*, 24 September 2008.
7 Ibid.
8 John Kirton, "The G20 Takes Centre Stage," in *G20: Growth, Innovation, Inclusion: The G20 at Ten* (Toronto: G20 Research Group, November 2008), 17, www.g7.utoronto.ca/newsdesk/G20at10.pdf.
9 Henry M. Paulson, *On the Brink: Inside the Race to Stop the Collapse of the Global Financial System* (New York: Business Plus, 2010), 373.
10 "EU Chiefs Confront Markets Crisis," BBC News, 12 October 2008.
11 Peter Mandelson, *The Third Man: Life at the Heart of New Labour* (London: Harper Press, 2010), 459.

12 Matthew Franklin, "PM Kevin Rudd's Role in International Crisis Summit," *Australian*, 25 October 2008. These reports in the Australian media were circulated widely but not in the US media. Rudd confirmed the veracity of the accounts in a conversation with Ramesh Thakur in Brisbane in July 2010.

13 John Kirton, "The Performance of the Meeting of the G20 Finance Ministers and Central Bank Governors," G20 Information Centre, University of Toronto, 9 November 2008.

14 Stephanie Hell, "The Response of the United Nations to the Global Financial Crisis," *FES Fact Sheet* (New York: Friedrich Ebert Stiftung, December 2008), www.library.fes.de/pdf-files/iez/global/05953.pdf.

15 Transcript of press conference by Secretary-General Ban Ki-moon at United Nations Headquarters, 11 November 2008 (New York: Department of Public Information, United Nations, 11 November 2008), www.un.org/News/Press/docs/2008/sgsm11916.doc.htm.

16 "Latest Trends in Negotiations and Processes: The United Nations System and the G20," The Secretary-General's Retreat 2010, Alpbach, Austria, 5–6 September 2010.

17 Roger C. Altman, "Globalization in Retreat," *Foreign Affairs* 88, no. 4 (2009): 2–9.

18 Gu Jing, John Humphrey, and Dirk Messner, "Global Governance and Developing Countries: The Implications of the Rise of China," *World Development* 36, no. 2 (2008): 274–92. For a skeptical note on the G2, however, see Gregory Chin and Ramesh Thakur, "Will China Change the Rules of Global Order?" *Washington Quarterly* 33, no. 4 (2010): 119–38.

19 William H. Overholt, "China in the Global Financial Crisis: Rising Influence, Rising Challenges," *Washington Quarterly* 33, no. 1 (2010): 21–34.

20 "After the Fall: The Global Economic Summit," *The Economist*, 15 November 2008.

21 Kirton, "The G20 Takes Centre Stage."

22 Transcript of a Press Briefing by Guido Mantega, Finance Minister of Brazil and Chairman of the G20, Washington, 11 October 2008, www.imf.org/external/np/tr/2008/tr081011.htm.

23 Emily Kaiser, "World Looks for New Leaders as Crisis Outgrows G7," Reuters, 12 October 2008, www.reuters.com/article/reutersEdge/idUSTRE49B3H220081012.

24 Gordon Brown, "Out of the Ashes," *Washington Post*, 17 October 2008.

25 Doug Saunders, "The Man Who Saved the World Banking System," *Globe and Mail* (Toronto), 15 October 2008.

26 George Parker and Alex Barker, "Vacuum in US Stymies Planning for G20," *The Guardian*, 11 March 2009.

27 Patrick Wintour, Nicholas Watt and Julian Borger, "G20 Summit: Late Night Hotel Peace Talks That Rescued Deal," *The Guardian*, 3 April 2009.

28 Andrew F. Cooper and Andrew Schrumm, "One Year On: The G20 and Economic Leadership," *e-International Relations*, 21 October 2009, www.cigionline.org/articles/2009/10/one-year-g20-and-economic-leadership.

29 C. Fred Bergsten, "A New Steering Committee for the World Economy?" in *Reforming the IMF for the 21st Century*, ed. Edwin M. Truman, Special Report no. 19 (Washington, DC: Peterson Institute for International Economics, 2006): 279–92.

30 Barry Eichengreen, "The G20 and the Crisis," VoxEU.org, 2 March 2009, www.voxeu.org/index.php?q=node/3160.
31 Brown, quoted in Sumeet Desai, Darren Ennis and David Ljunggren, "Old World Fault Lines Evident at G20 Chiefs Meet," Reuters, 25 September 2009, www.reuters.com/article/idUSTRE58N5SJ20090925.
32 Bergsten, quoted in Richard Wolf, "Obama G20 Unite on Recovery Package" *USA Today*, 3 April 2009, www.usatoday.com/news/world/2009-04-02-g20-summit_N.htm.
33 Stewart Patrick, "G20: Present at the Creation of a New Economic Order," Council on Foreign Relations, First Take, 25 September 2009, www.cfr.org/publication/20296/g20.html?breadcrumb.
34 Quoted in Dennis B. Roddy, "G20 Objectors Promoting Varied Agendas," *Pittsburgh Post-Gazette*, 23 August 2009.
35 See Cesare Merlini, "The G-7 and the Need for Reform," *International Spectator* 29, no. 2 (1994): 5–25.
36 See Alan Alexandroff and Andrew F. Cooper, eds., *Rising States, Rising Institutions: The Challenge of Global Governance* (Washington, DC: Brookings Institution Press, 2010).
37 Daniel W. Drezner, "The New New World Order," *Foreign Affairs* 86, no. 4 (2007): 34–46.
38 See Chin and Thakur, "Will China Change the Rules of Global Order?"; and Andrew F. Cooper and Thomas Fues, "Do the Asian Drivers Pull their Diplomatic Weight? China, India and the United Nations," *World Development* 36, no. 2 (2008): 293–307.
39 Quoted in Gabriel Elizondo, "Rising Power of the G20," *Al Jazeera*, 15 November 2008.
40 "Eurozone Bid for G20 Seat 'Unrealistic'," *EU Business*, 19 January 2010.

5 Consolidating or fragmenting the G20

1 Geoffrey Garrett and Barry R. Weingast, "Ideas, Interests and Institutions," in *Ideas & Foreign Policy: Beliefs, Institutions and Political Change*, ed. Judith Goldstein and Robert O. Keohane (Ithaca, NY: Cornell University Press, 1993).
2 Anders Åslund, "The Group of 20 Must be Stopped," *Financial Times*, 26 November 2009.
3 Ignazio Angeloni and Jean Pisani-Ferry, "The G20: Characters in Search of an Author," Bruegel Working Paper 2012/04; Alan S. Alexandroff, "Stuck in Transition: Conflicting Ambitions for the G-20's Future," *Global Asia* 5, no. 2 (2010), www.globalasia.org/V5N3_Fall_2010/Alan_S_Alexandroff.html.
4 Quoted in "Global Crisis Battle a Success Says G20," *Gulf Daily News*, 26 September 2009. See also Colin I. Bradford and Johannes Linn, "The April 2009 London G-20 Summit in Retrospect," *Brookings Commentary*, 5 April 2010, www.brookings.edu/opinions/2010/0405_g20_summit_linn.aspx.
5 "Lula da Silva Skips G20 Because of Floods and Presidential Election," MercoPress, 26 June 2010.
6 On the FSB's role see Stephany Griffith-Jones, Eric Helleiner and Ngaire Woods, "The Financial Stability Board: An Effective Fourth Pillar of Global Economic Governance?" CIGI Special Report (Waterloo, Ontario: Centre for International Governance Innovation, 2010), www.cigionline.

org/publications/2010/6/financial-stability-board-effective-fourth-pillar-global-economic-governance.

7 "Global Plan for Recovery and Reform," G20 Final Communiqué, 2 April 2009, www.g20.org/Documents/final-communique.pdf.

8 Julian Beltrame, "Harper's Korean visit focuses on economic issues," Canadian Press, 6 December 2009.

9 Rebecca M. Nelson, *The G-20 and International Economic Cooperation: Background and Implications for Congress* (Washington, DC: Congressional Research Service, 10 August 2010), 10.

10 Paul Martin, "Making Globalization Work," in *G8-G20: The 2010 Canadian Summits*, ed. John Kirton and Madeline Koch (London: Newsdesk Media, 2010), 69.

11 Statement of Mario Draghi, Chairman of the Financial Stability Board to the International Monetary and Financial Committee Washington, 25 April 2009, www.financialstabilityboard.org/press/st_090425.pdf.

12 Steve Slater, "US Reform Plan Hurts Global Effort—Barclays CEO," Reuters, 9 February 2010, in.reuters.com/article/2010/02/09/idINIndia-4602 2820100209.

13 Huw Jones, "G7 Under Pressure to Keep Regulation on Track," Reuters, 4 February 2010, in.reuters.com/article/2010/02/04/idINIndia-45918120100204.

14 Tony Chang, "S. Korea, Canada Renewing Ties to Lead World Out of 'Fragile' Recovery: Harper," Organisation of Asia-Pacific News Agencies, 7 December 2009, www.oananews.org/node/93591.

15 Kwak Soo-jong, economist, Samsung Economic Research Institute, quoted in "Korea Gears Up for G20 Seoul Summit," *Korea Times*, 9 December 2009.

16 ASEAN Secretariat, "Views of ASEAN Sought for G-20 Agenda: ASEAN Secretariat," 10 February 2010, www.aseansec.org/24319.htm.

17 "G20 Statement on the Situation in Haiti," Mexico City, 14 January 2010, www.mofa.go.jp/mofaj/press/release/22/1/PDF/011501.pdf.

18 Lesley Wroughton, "IMF Shifts Gears, Moves into Post-crisis Mode," Reuters, 3 December 2009, www.reuters.com/article/2009/12/03/imf-idUSN0 39700820091203.

19 "IMF Aims at Building Stronger Post-crisis Global Economy and International Monetary System," IMF Press Release 09/441, 3 December 2009, www.imf.org/external/np/sec/pr/2009/pr09441.htm.

20 Tom Barkley, "IMF, G-20 Start Work on Creating More Balanced Global Economy," Dow Jones Newswire, 15 January 2010.

21 Kumiharu Shigehara, "For More Effective Multilateral Surveillance," *Japan Times*, 23 May 2011.

22 Robert Wielaard, "European Union to Pursue Climate Deal Through G-20," AP Newswires, 8 January 2010, articles.boston.com/2010-01-09/news/29284 819_1_climate-deal-van-rompuy-climate-change.

23 Colin I. Bradford and Wonhyuk Lim, "Toward the Consolidation of the G20: From Crisis Committee to Global Steering Committee," in *Global Leadership in Transition: Making the G20 More Effective and Responsive*, ed. Colin I. Bradford and Wonhyuk Lim (Washington, DC: Brookings, 2011), 8.

24 Althia Raj, "G20 Achievements 'Historic,' Harper says," *Edmonton Sun* online, 26 September 2009, www.edmontonsun.com/news/world/2009/09/26/ 11130411-sun.html.

25 Sheldon Alberts, "Eight No Longer Enough: G20 to be Main Forum," *National Post* (Toronto), 26 September 2009.
26 Sheldon Alberts, "Transition to G20 will Broaden 2010 Summit in Canada," *Financial Post* (Toronto), 26 September 2009.
27 John Kirton, "The G8: Legacy, Limitations and Lessons," in *Global Leadership in Transition: Making the G20 More Effective and Responsive*, ed. Colin I. Bradford and Wonhyuk Lim (Washington, DC: Brookings, 2011), 16–34.
28 Julian Beltrame, "Canada Looks for Ways to Keep G7 Alive, Sees Loss of Stature in New G20," Canadian Press, 14 January 2010, www.cigionline. org/articles/2010/01/canada-looks-ways-keep-g7-alive-sees-loss-stature-new-g20.
29 See Rorden Wilkinson and David Hulme, eds., *The Millennium Development Goals and Beyond: Global Development After 2015* (London: Routledge, 2012).
30 Sewell Chan, "G-20 Split on the Need for a Global Tax on Banks," *The New York Times*, 23 April 2010.
31 Gideon Rachman, "Will Berlusconi Finish Off the G8?" *Financial Times*, 24 November 2008.
32 Andrew F. Cooper, "The G20 and its Regional Critics: The Search for Inclusion," *Global Policy Journal* 2 (May 2011): 203–9.
33 Brunei, Malaysia, New Zealand, Philippines, Singapore, and Vietnam from Asia-Pacific; Bahrain, Qatar and United Arab Emirates from the Middle East; Botswana, Rwanda, and Senegal from Africa; Belgium, Ireland, Liechtenstein, Luxembourg, Monaco, San Marino, Sweden, and Switzerland from Europe; and Bahamas, Barbados, Chile, Costa Rica, Guatemala, Jamaica, Panama, and Uruguay from Latin America and the Caribbean. See also Andrew F. Cooper, "The G20 and Regional Dynamics," in *Global Leadership in Transition: Making the G20 More Effective and Responsive*, ed. Colin I. Bradford and Wonhyuk Lim (Washington, DC: Brookings, 2011), 275–84.
34 Barry Carin, Paul Heinbecker, Gordon Smith, and Ramesh Thakur, "The Future of Summits," Issues for 2010 Summits Background Paper (Waterloo: Centre for International Governance Innovation, 3–5 May 2010), 8.
35 Ibid., 9.
36 Quoted in Ravi Kanth, "S'pore to Host 3G Group During WEF Informal Coalition to Discuss how it can Strengthen, Support Global Governance," *Business Times* (Singapore), 3 February 2010.
37 Cho Jin-seo, "Five Non-G20 Nations Invited to Seoul Summit," *The Korean Times*, 24 September 24 2010, www.koreatimes.co.kr/www/news/biz/2010/09/301_73469.html.
38 Jean Pisani-Ferry and Agnes Benassy-Quere, "Managing a new North-South Asymmetry is the New Challenge for G20," 19 September 2010, www.cepii.fr/francgraph/presse/2010/a_ABQJPFbusinessstd180910.pdf.
39 Stephen Grenville and Mark Thirlwell, "A G-20 Caucus for East Asia," www.lowyinstitute.org/Publication.asp?pid=1153.
40 Robert B. Zoellick, "Whither China: From Membership to Responsibility," Remarks to National Committee on US-China Relations, 21 September 2005, 3, www.ncuscr.org/files/2.%20notes_06wsp.pdf.
41 See Ramesh Thakur, *Towards a Less Imperfect State of the World: The Gulf Between North and South* (Berlin: Friedrich Ebert Stiftung, Dialogue on Globalization Briefing Paper 4, April 2008).

42 See Lai-Ha Chan, Pak K. Lee, and Gerald Chan, "Rethinking Global Governance: A China Model in the Making?" *Contemporary Politics* 14, no. 1 (2008): 3–19.
43 See Yuli Ismartono, "Lone Voice from Southeast Asia," *Courier* (Stanley Foundation), 72 (Fall 2011): 6–7.
44 Chris Landsberg, "A Need for Leadership on Africa," *Courier* 72 (Fall 2011): 8–9.
45 Paul Martin, "The G20: From Global Crisis Responder to Steering Committee," in *The Oxford Handbook of Diplomacy*, ed. Andrew F. Cooper, Jorge Heine, and Ramesh Thakur (Oxford: Oxford University Press, forthcoming).

6 The G20 between the dynamics of innovation and constraint

1 Philip Stephens, "Only By Reshaping the Postwar Settlement Can it be Preserved," *Financial Times*, 24 February 2006.
2 See Stewart Patrick, *The G20 and the United States: Opportunities for More Effective Multilateralism* (New York: Century Foundation Report, October 2010).
3 Paul Martin, "Address by Prime Minister Paul Martin on the Occasion of his Visit to Washington, DC," 29 April 2004.
4 Ngaire Woods, "Global Governance after the Financial Crisis: A New Multilateralism or the Last Gasp of the Great Powers?" *Global Policy* 1, no. 1 (2010): 51–63; and Mathias Koenig-Archibugi, "Understanding the Global Dimensions of Policy," *Global Policy* 1, no. 1 (2010): 16–28.
5 David Held, *Cosmopolitanism: Ideals, Realities and Deficiencies* (Cambridge: Polity, 2010), 204.
6 Peter Wilson, "'Rigid' G20 is Too Big and Slow, Says Founder," *Australian*, 15 March 2012.
7 "G20 Show How Not to Run the World," *Financial Times*, 12 November 2010.
8 Chris Giles, "Meetings Yet to Reach Their Peak of Achievement," *Financial Times*, 3 November 2011.
9 Stephen Krasner, *The G20 and Global Governance Reform* (Seoul: Yonsei University, Asian Institute for Policy Studies, 2010).
10 Ian Bremmer and Nouriel Roubini, "A G-Zero World: The New Economic Club Will Produce Conflict, Not Cooperation," *Foreign Affairs* 90, no. 2 (2011): 2–7. See also Edwin M. Truman, "The G-20 is Failing," *Foreign Policy* (12 April 2012), www.foreignpolicy.com/articles/2012/04/12/the_g_20_is_failing?
11 Andrew F. Cooper and Eric Helleiner, "Advances in Global Economic Governance Amid the Obstacles at the Seoul G20 Summit," *Social Europe Journal* 5, no. 2 (2011): 10–14.
12 Colin Bradford, "Contrasting Visions of Fiscal Stimulus," in *Flashpoints for the Pittsburgh Summit*, ed. Andrew F. Cooper and Daniel Schwanen (Waterloo, Ontario: Centre for International Governance Innovation, CIGI Special G20 Report), 37.
13 Quoted in Alan S. Alexandroff, "The Challenge to Global Trade in the Financial Crisis," in *Flashpoints for the Pittsburgh Summit*, ed. Cooper and Schwanen, 45.
14 UK Prime Minister David Cameron, quoted in Alan Beattie and Christian Oliver, "US Defensive on Dollar at G20," *Financial Times*, 12 November

2010. See also David Cameron, *Governance for Growth: Building Consensus for the Future* (London: Prime Minister's Office, 2011).

15 Two years after the event, the Office of the Independent Police Review Director, Ontario's independent police watchdog, found that police violated civil rights, detained people illegally and used excessive force; Colin Perkel, "G20 Report Blasts Police for 'Unlawful' Arrests, Civil Rights Violations," *Globe and Mail*, 16 May 2012. As one prominent Toronto columnist wrote, "for one miserable weekend in June 2010, Toronto was transformed into an unrecognizable city, an urban gulag where much of the lawlessness was perpetrated by law enforcement"; Rosie DiManno, "Why Won't Chief Bill Blair Say Sorry for Police Actions During G20?" *Toronto Star*, 18 May 2012.

16 See David Hulme, *Global Poverty: How Global Governance is Failing the Poor* (London: Routledge, 2010).

17 Justin Yifu Lin and Doerte Doemeland, *Beyond Keynesianism: Global Infrastructure Investments in Times of Crisis*, World Bank Policy Research Working Paper no. WPS 5940 (Washington, DC: World Bank, 10 January 2012), go.worldbank.org/5GZ6GNMO20.

18 World Bank, *Postcrisis Growth and Development: A Development Agenda for the G-20* (Washington, DC: World Bank, 17 November 2010), issuu.com/world.bank.publications/docs/9780821385180.

19 IMF, *World Economic Outlook* (Washington, DC: IMF, September 2011), xv.

20 Jacob Kierkegaard, "The European Crisis and the G20 Summit," *East Asia Forum*, 29 November 2011, www.eastasiaforum.org/2011/11/29/the-european-crisis-and-the-g20-summit.

21 Doug Saunders, "Canada's Tough Love to Europe: Don't Look to Us for a Bailout," *Globe and Mail*, 7 November 2011.

22 Stephen Harper, "It's Time for Europe and the G20 to Act Decisively," *Globe and Mail*, 13 October 2011.

23 Wolfgang Münchau, "Summitry Again Proves its Own Irrelevance," *Financial Times*, 6 November 2011.

24 Chris Giles and Alan Beattie, "Forum's High Ambitions Deliver Meagre Results," *Financial Times*, 5 November 2011.

25 Len Edwards, "Missing in Action, the G2 Must Step up at Cannes," *Globe and Mail*, 3 November 2011.

26 Lourdes Aranda, "G20's Chance to Steady the Ship in Choppy Waters," *Australian*, 12 March 2012. See also G2012 México, "Discussion Paper: Mexico's Presidency of the G20" (January 2012) www.g20.org/images/pdfs/disceng.pdf.

27 On the role of think tanks generally, see James McGann and Richard Sabatini, eds., *Global Think Tanks: Policy Networks and Governance* (London: Routledge, 2010).

28 Andrew Elek, "How Can Asia Help Fix the Global Economy?" *East Asia Forum*, 2 October 2011.

29 "Declaration of the Summit on Financial Markets and the World Economy," Washington, 15 November 2008, para. 15, www.g20.utoronto.ca/2008/2008declaration1115.html. All the G20 summit communiqués, as well as other helpful official documentation, are accessible at www.g20.utoronto.ca, courtesy of the University of Toronto G20 Research Group.

30 Bruce Jones, "Beyond Blocs: The West, Rising Powers and Interest-Based International Cooperation," *Policy Analysis Brief* (Muscatine, Iowa: Stanley Foundation, October 2011), 10.

31 See Rorden Wilkinson and David Hulme, eds., *The Millennium Development Goals and Beyond: Global Development After 2015* (London: Routledge, 2012).

32 Gunnar Myrdal, *Asian Drama: An Inquiry into the Poverty of Nations* (New York: Twentieth Century Fund, 1968).

33 Razeen Sally, "Liberty Outside the West," Lecture for the Hayek Tage, Freiburg, 10 June 2011.

34 Zhongying Pang, "China's Soft Power Dilemma: The Beijing Consensus Revisited," in *Soft Power: China's Emerging Strategy in International Politics*, ed. Mingjiang Li (Lanham, Md.: Lexington Books, 2009): 125–42; and Stefan Halper, *The Beijing Consensus: How China's Authoritarian Model Will Dominate the Twenty-first Century* (New York: Basic Books, 2010).

35 For elaboration, see Gregory Chin and Ramesh Thakur, "Will China Change the Rules of Global Order?" *Washington Quarterly* 33 no. 4 (2010): 119–38.

36 See Gregory Chin, *China's Automotive Modernization: The Party-State and Multinational Corporations* (Basingtoke: Palgrave Macmillan, 2010).

37 The dichotomy may well be exaggerated. Ha-Joon Chang argues that all major developed economies used interventionist policies—tariffs, capital controls, protection of infant industries—when ascending the ladder to prosperity, and then decided to kick away the ladder, rewrote the rules of international trade and commerce to forbid the remaining poor countries from following in their paths, and used international institutions like the World Bank, the IMF and the WTO as global enforcers of these tough new rules. Ha-Joon Chang, *Kicking Away the Ladder: Development Strategy in Historical Perspective* (London: Anthem Press, 2002), and *23 Things They Don't Tell You About Capitalism* (New York: Bloomsbury Press, 2010).

38 *Achieving Food Security in the Face of Climate Change* (Copenhagen: Commission on Sustainable Agriculture and Climate Change, November 2011).

39 See D. John Shaw, *Global Food and Agricultural Institutions* (London: Routledge, 2008).

40 Jennifer Clapp, "G20 Must Take Broader Approach to Food Security," *The G20 Agenda and Process*, CIGI, 2011.

41 See Sophie Harman, *Global Health Governance* (London: Routledge, 2011); and Kelley Lee, *The World Health Organization (WHO)* (London: Routledge, 2008).

42 Mark W. Zacher and Tania J. Keefe, *The Politics of Global Health Governance: United by Contagion* (New York: Palgrave Macmillan, 2008).

43 See Jorge Heine and Ramesh Thakur, eds., *The Dark Side of Globalization* (Tokyo: United Nations University Press, 2011).

44 See Franklyn Lisk, *Global Institutions and the HIV/AIDS Epidemic: Responding to an International Crisis* (London: Routledge, 2009).

45 See Ilona Kickbusch, "Advancing the Global Health Agenda," *UN Chronicle* 48, no. 4 (2011): 37–40.

46 D.E. Bloom, *et al.*, *The Global Economic Burden of Noncommunicable Diseases* (Geneva: World Economic Forum, September 2011), 5, www.weforum.org/EconomicsOfNCD.

47 See Harriet Bulkeley and Peter Newell, *Governing Climate Change* (London: Routledge, 2010).

7 The G20 as the answer to the crisis of global governance

1 Thomas S. Kuhn, *The Structure of Scientific Revolutions*, second edn (Chicago: University of Chicago Press, 1970).
2 See Thomas G. Weiss and Ramesh Thakur, *Global Governance and the UN: An Unfinished Journey* (Bloomington: Indian University Press, 2010), chapter 9.
3 See Barry Carin and Ramesh Thakur, "Global Governance for a Global Age: The Role of Leaders in Breaking Global Deadlocks," *CIGI Policy Brief* No. 7 (Waterloo: Centre for International Governance Innovation, November 2008).
4 Robert B. Zoellick, President of the World Bank, "The End of the Third World?" in *G8-G20: The 2010 Canadian Summits*, ed. John Kirton and Madeline Koch (London: Newsdesk Media, 2010), 99.
5 Paul Martin, "The G20: From Global Crisis Responder to Steering Committee," in *The Oxford Handbook of Diplomacy*, ed. Andrew F. Cooper, Jorge Heine, and Ramesh Thakur (Oxford: Oxford University Press, forthcoming).
6 Bruce Jones, "Making Multilateralism Work: How the G-20 Can Help the United Nations," *Policy Analysis Brief* (Muscatine, Iowa: Stanley Foundation, April 2010), 6.
7 Juan Somavia, "The Global Jobs Crisis: The G-20 Must Act Now to Avoid a Lost Decade," *The Hindu*, 3 November 2011.
8 Stewart Patrick, *The G20 and the United States: Opportunities for More Effective Multilateralism* (New York: Century Foundation Report, 2010), 19–20.
9 Jin-seo Cho, "5 Non-G20 Nations Invited to Seoul Summit," *Korea Times*, 24 October 2010.
10 For elaboration, see Diana Tussie, "Process Drivers in Trade Negotiations: The Role of Research in the Path to Grounding and Contextualizing," *Global Governance* 15, no. 3 (2009): 335–42.
11 Barry Carin, "A G20 'Non-Secretariat'," in *The New Dynamics of Summitry: Institutional Innovations for G20 Summits, Issue and Essays*, ed. C. Bradford and W. Lim (Seoul: Korea Development Institute, 2010): 383–91.
12 Colin I. Bradford and Wonhyuk Lim, "Toward the Consolidation of the G20: From Crisis Committee to Global Steering Committee," in *Global Leadership in Transition: Making the G20 More Effective and Responsive*, ed. Colin I. Bradford and Wonhyuk Lim (Washington, DC: Brookings, 2011): 1–10.
13 Paul Martin, "Making Globalization Work," in *G8-G20: The 2010 Canadian Summits*, ed. John Kirton and Madeline Koch (London: Newsdesk Media, 2010), 68.
14 This argument is hardly new, having been made, for example, by the late Susan Strange more than a decade ago: Susan Strange, "The Westfailure System," *Review of International Studies* 25, no. 3 (1999): 345–54.
15 Charles A. Kupchan, *No One's World: The West, the Rising Rest, and the Coming Global Turn* (New York: Oxford University Press, 2012).
16 Ian Bremmer and Nouriel Roubini "A G-Zero World: the New Economic Club will Produce conflict not cooperation." *Foreign Affairs*, 2011. See also Stefan A. Schirm, "Global politics are domestic politics: How societal interests and ideas shape ad hoc groupings in the G20 which supersede international alliances," Paper prepared for International Studies Association, 2011, www.sowi.rub.de/mam/content/lsip/schirmg20isa2011.pdf

17 Charles Grant, *Russia, China and Global Governance* (London: Centre for European Reform, 2012).
18 David P. Fidler, "Health Diplomacy," in *The Oxford Handbook of Diplomacy*, ed. Andrew F. Cooper, Jorge Heine, and Ramesh Thakur (Oxford: Oxford University Press, forthcoming).
19 David Shorr, "Making the G-20 a Reservoir of Global Leadership—A Maximalist Argument," *Policy Analysis Brief* (Muscatine, Iowa: Stanley Foundation, April 2011), 5.
20 Quoted in "The Apex of Influence—How Summit Meetings Build Multi-lateral Cooperation," Policy Memo (Muscatine, Iowa: Stanley Foundation), 18 May 2012.
21 Martin, "Making Globalization Work," 68.

Select bibliography

As the G20 is a brand new institution, the literature on it is as yet very thin and still in the making. The following list includes some of the seminal newspaper columns and material on other, complementary institutions of global governance as well as a few books and articles about the G20 itself.

Alan Alexandroff and Andrew F. Cooper, eds., *Rising States, Rising Institutions: Challenges for Global Governance* (Washington, DC: Brookings Institution Press, 2010). An edited collection that puts the "rise" of the G20 into the context of wider trends in global governance. A particular highlight is the number of analytical chapters from leading US academic experts.

Ignazio Angeloni and Jean Pisani-Ferry, "The G20: Characters in Search of an Author." Bruegel Working Paper 2012/04. This paper, written between the Cannes and Los Cabos G20s, is a more balanced assessment than its title might suggest. The work points to past success in the "high-noon" moment of 2008–09 and the extended timeline needed for technical work. At the same time, though, it highlights the disappointments in terms of delivery and the need for improvements in terms of efficiency if the G20 is going to retain its pivotal role.

Timothy Garton Ash, "One Practical Way to Improve the State of the World: Turn G8 into G14," *The Guardian*, 24 January 2008. A call in January 2008 from an eminent commentator that the G8 be expanded to a G14, with the addition of China, India, Brazil, Mexico, South Africa, and Indonesia. Among the issue-specific rationales that Ash points to with respect to the need for a more representative forum was the "the fragile state of globalised capitalism."

Anders Åslund, "The Group of 20 Must be Stopped," *Financial Times*, 26 November 2009. This article provides a blunt critique of the perceived "command and control" G20 style in the aftermath of the first meeting at the leaders' level in Washington, DC. Åslund expresses concern about the G20 declaring itself the supreme world economic institution with power over all the countries of the world. The focus is on the legitimacy gaps of a G20 as a "self-selected" entity.

Nicholas Bayne, *Staying Together: The G8 Summit Confronts the 21st Century* (Aldershot: Ashgate, 2005). An inside look at the G7/G8 summits to 2005 by an author with personal experience of the summit process.

Alan Beattie, "The G20: Ad hoc Institution Faces Tough Struggle to Show it Has Teeth," *Financial Times,* 10 November 2010. This is an insightful and sober commentary on the prospects of the G20 written at the time of the Seoul summit. The main theme of the piece is that while divisions among the G20 membership were hidden during the crisis of 2008–09, key national differences have since emerged.

Mark Beeson and Stephen Bell, "The G-20 and International Economic Governance: Hegemony, Collectivism, or Both? Following the East Asian Crisis of 1997–98," *Global Governance* 15, no. 1 (2009): 67–86. This scholarly article is a valuable source that combines conceptual insight with the context in the evolution of the G20 from its original creation as a forum for finance ministers and central bankers. Although extensive use is made of theories of hegemony, the authors conclude that the G20 allows some scope for other nations to influence outcomes.

Colin I. Bradford and Wonhyuk Lim, eds., *Global Leadership in Transition: Making the G20 More Effective and Responsive* (Washington, DC: Brookings, 2011). This book supplies extensive coverage from diverse authors on the range of actual and possible innovations through the institutionalization of the G20. Special attention is devoted to the G20's role on the development agenda highlighted at the Seoul November 2010 summit.

Barry Carin, Paul Heinbecker, Gordon Smith, and Ramesh Thakur, "The Future of Summits," Issues for 2010 Summits Background Paper (Waterloo: Centre for International Governance Innovation, 3–5 May 2010). Written by three former senior Canadian diplomats and a former senior UN official, this paper examines the role and prospects of summits just before the Toronto G20 summit.

Barry Carin and Ramesh Thakur, "Global Governance for a Global Age: The Role of Leaders in Breaking Global Deadlocks," CIGI Policy Brief No. 7, November 2008. Argues the case for a new global leaders-level summit for addressing the accumulating global deadlocks on a range of substantive issues.

Chatham House and Atlantic Council, "New Ideas for the London Summit: Recommendations to the G20 Leaders," March 2009. This report focuses on the crucial April 2009 London G20 in the midst of the collapsing world economy. A major recommendation is that rather than a "one size fits all," the G20 must provide a clear plan about burden sharing in terms of a fiscal stimulus plan.

Gregory Chin and Ramesh Thakur, "Will China Change the Rules of Global Order?" *The Washington Quarterly* 33, no. 4 (2010): 119–38. A sympathetic account of the implications of the rise of China for the normative architecture of global order.

Andrew F. Cooper and Agata Antkiewicz, eds., *Emerging Powers in Global Governance: Lessons from the Heiligendamm Process* (Waterloo: Wilfrid Laurier University Press, 2008; Chinese translation: Shanghai People's Publications,

158   *Select bibliography*

2009). This edited volume offers the most complete look at the G8 Heiligendamm Process, with an in-depth look at the opportunities and constraints presented by a dynamic that allowed a focused but asymmetrical interaction between established and rising states. A number of comparative perspectives are included in chapters by different experts.

Andrew F. Cooper and Daniel Schwanen, eds., "Flashpoints for the Pittsburgh Summit," CIGI Special G20 Report, 8 September 2009. This is a specialized publication by a mix of analysts from academic and practitioner backgrounds with recommendations for the September 2009 Pittsburgh G20. Topics dealt with include international financial regulatory reform, central banking, and macro-imbalances.

Andrew F. Cooper and Paola Subacchi, eds., "Global Economic Governance in Transition," *International Affairs* 86, no. 4 (2010). A special issue of a leading UK journal that explores the implications of the financial crisis for global economic governance from historical, ideational, and issue-specific perspectives.

Hugo Dobson, *The Group of 7/8* (London: Routledge, 2007). This accessible book serves as a very useful counterpoint to the G20 in Routledge's Global Institutions series. The book addresses the history and development of the G7/8 summit process, perspectives of member states, and achievements as well as criticisms and challenges.

John English, Ramesh Thakur and Andrew F. Cooper, eds., *Reforming from the Top: A Leaders' 20 Summit* (Tokyo: United Nations University Press, 2005). This edited collection, with a number of distinguished contributors, points to the logic of creating a new forum for dealing with global problems—the Leaders' 20 (or L20).

Geoffrey Garrett, "G2 in G20: China, the United States and the World after the Global Financial Crisis," *Global Policy* 1, no. 1 (2010): 29–39. This article examines the critical China–US relationship generally but with some specific attention to G20 dynamics.

Peter I. Hajnal, *The G8 System and the G20: Evolution, Role and Documentation* (Aldershot: Ashgate, 2007). This book discusses the origins, characteristics, evolution, role, and agenda of the G7 and G8 system, and looks at proposals to reform the G8-G20.

Peter C. Heap, *Globalization and Summit Reform: An Experiment in International Governance* (New York: Springer, 2009). This book describes the collaborative, multi-year L20 project between the Centre for Global Studies at the University of Victoria and the Centre for International Governance Innovation in Waterloo, Ontario.

John Ibbitson and Tara Perkins, "How Canada Made the G20 Happen," *Globe and Mail*, 18 June 2010. A well-researched journalistic account of the origins of the G20—both at the finance and leaders' level—that pays particular attention to the influential role of Paul Martin. The article was written just before the Toronto summit.

Bruce Jones, "Making Multilateralism Work: How the G-20 Can Help the United Nations," *Policy Analysis Brief* (Muscatine, Iowa: Stanley Foundation,

April 2010). Discusses the complementarity and synergy between the G20 and the United Nations.

John Kirton, *G20 Governance for a Globalized World* (Aldershot: Ashgate, forthcoming). This work when published will yield a detailed examination by a close observer of summitry both with respect to the G7/8 and the G20.

Paul Martin, "A Global Answer to Global Problems," *Foreign Affairs* 84, no. 3 (2005): 2–6. This seminal article by the former Canadian prime minister advocates the formation of the L20, grounded in a forceful argument that the "right countries" must be "sitting down around the same table at the same time" on an issue-specific basis. The need was to get political leaders to do "what they alone can do—making tough choices among competing interests and priorities."

Rebecca M. Nelson, *The G-20 and International Economic Cooperation: Background and Implications for Congress* (Washington, DC: Congressional Research Service, 10 August 2010). Traces the background to the G20 and assesses the implications of its establishment from an explicitly American perspective.

Stewart Patrick, *The G20 and the United States: Opportunities for More Effective Multilateralism* (New York: Century Foundation Report, October 2010). A concise and insightful report that points to the opportunity provided by the G20 to enhance the effectiveness of multilateral global governance.

David Shorr, "Making the G-20 a Reservoir of Global Leadership—A Maximalist Argument," *Policy Analysis Brief* (Muscatine, Iowa: Stanley Foundation, April 2011). Argues the case for broadening the G20 agenda from financial to other pressing global issues.

Ramesh Thakur, *The United Nations, Peace and Security: From Collective Security to the Responsibility to Protect* (Cambridge: Cambridge University Press, 2006). The book maps the changing peace and security agenda of the United Nations from 1945 to 2005.

Thomas G. Weiss, *What's Wrong with the United Nations and How to Fix It*, second edn (Oxford: Polity Press, 2012). A robust argument that the United Nations as it exists is ill-equipped to deal with contemporary challenges to world order. The book also offers tips on how to mitigate the problems.

Thomas G. Weiss and Ramesh Thakur, *Global Governance and the UN: An Unfinished Journey* (Bloomington: Indiana University Press, 2010). This book traces the advance of UN-centered global governance through filling five analytical gaps: knowledge, normative, policy, institutional, and compliance.

Ngaire Woods, "Global Governance after the Financial Crisis: A New Multilateralism or the Last Gasp of the Great Powers?" *Global Policy* 1, no. 1 (2010): 51–63. Discusses the changing nature of multilateral governance as a consequence of the global financial crisis.

Index

164   *Index*

Routledge Global Institutions Series

Books currently under contract include:

The Regional Development Banks
Lending with a regional flavor
by Jonathan R. Strand (University of Nevada)

Millennium Development Goals (MDGs)
For a people-centered development agenda?
by Sakiko Fukada-Parr (The New School)

UNICEF
by Richard Jolly (University of Sussex)

The Bank for International Settlements
The politics of global financial supervision in the age of high finance
by Kevin Ozgercin (SUNY College at Old Westbury)

International Migration
by Khalid Koser (Geneva Centre for Security Policy)

Human Development
by Richard Ponzio

Religious Institutions and Global Politics
by Katherine Marshall (Georgetown University)

The International Monetary Fund (2nd edition)
Politics of conditional lending
by James Raymond Vreeland (Georgetown University)

The UN Global Compact
by Catia Gregoratti (Lund University)

Institutions for Women's Rights
by Charlotte Patton (York College, CUNY) and Carolyn Stephenson (University of Hawaii)

International Aid
by Paul Mosley (University of Sheffield)

Global Consumer Policy
by Karsten Ronit (University of Copenhagen)

The Changing Political Map of Global Governance
by Anthony Payne (University of Sheffield) and Stephen Robert Buzdugan (Manchester Metropolitan University)

Coping with Nuclear Weapons
by W. Pal Sidhu

Crisis of Global Sustainability
by Tapio Kanninen

Private Foundations and Development Partnerships
by Michael Moran (Swinburne University of Technology)

The International Politics of Human Rights
edited by Monica Serrano (Colegio de Mexico) and Thomas G. Weiss (The CUNY Graduate Center)

For further information regarding the series, please contact:
Craig Fowlie, Publisher, Politics & International Studies
Taylor & Francis
2 Park Square, Milton Park, Abingdon
Oxford OX14 4RN, UK
+44 (0)207 842 2057 Tel
+44 (0)207 842 2302 Fax
Craig.Fowlie@tandf.co.uk
www.routledge.com